The History Curr~
for Teacher

The History Curriculum for Teachers

Edited by
Christopher Portal

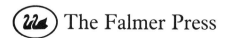 The Falmer Press

(A Member of the Taylor & Francis Group)
London, New York and Philadelphia

UK   The Falmer Press, Falmer House, Barcombe, Lewes, East Sussex, BN8 5DL

USA   The Falmer Press, Taylor & Francis Inc., 242 Cherry Street, Philadelphia, PA 19106-1906

First published 1987

Library of Congress Cataloging in Publication Data

Portal, Christopher.
  The history curriculum for teachers.

  1. History—Study and teaching (Secondary)—Great Britain. I. Title.
  D16.4.G7P67   1987   907′.1241   86-29305
  ISBN 1-85000-165-0
  ISBN 1-85000-166-9 (pbk.)

Jacket design by Caroline Archer

Typeset in 10.5/12 Plantin by
Imago Publishing Ltd, Thame, Oxon

Printed in Great Britain by Taylor & Francis (Printers) Ltd, Basingstoke

Contents

Contents

Preface

Starting from the issue of history's value as a secondary school subject (chapter 1), this volume turns to the problem of what criteria to apply in building a history course at various levels in the school.

Theoretical considerations and experimental investigation may be of use in guiding the choices that have to be made, and chapter 2–5 involve attempts to distill practical conclusions from the legacy of Piaget (chapter 2), from theories of explanation (chapters 3 and 4) and of empathy (chapters 4 and 5). Chapters 2, 3 and 4 also include substantial accounts of pupils' methods of work in history and their responses when questioned about the subject. Such investigation is an essential means to clarify what children can and cannot be expected to achieve intellectually at various ages or stages of development. Note, for example, the suggestion that imaginative approaches to teaching may allow pupils to transcend the conventional stage-limits derived from Piaget (chapter 2) and the question whether source material can be used as evidence with pupils whose thinking has not developed beyond the concrete (chapter 3). Although the contributors in this section are not in complete agreement about some issues, such as the significance of Piaget's 'stages' or the definition of empathy, there is unanimity about the implications of the nature of history as a discipline. History teaching should be about issues of some importance, presented coherently and in depth and taught so as to encourage pupil participation. Such qualities are seen as more important than content or coverage as a starting point for curriculum planning.

The chapters in section B address questions governing the actual shape of a school history course in an age of grade-criteria and specific teaching objectives. Chapter 6 lays down some important principles for planning such a course—principles transcending the neat pigeon-holes which may be essential to justify one's work but not necessarily inspiring for the consumers. The next three chapters (7, 8 and 9) apply mainly to different age-levels in the secondary school and may be seen as interesting reactions to the challenge that 'History 13–16' has left with all history teachers. Evidently, if the 'new history' is worth having for GCSE, it is not satisfactory to retain an old-fashioned or inferior version of the subject for junior classes or in the sixth form. Here, it must be essential for others to know what is being done, and the principles employed, by those who are trying to meet this challenge.

Good assessment is a part of good teaching. Chapter 10 makes public the experience of one examining board in testing skills rather than information or literacy. Again the message comes through that good practice (choice of topic and the type of questions set) transcends the change from one historical emphasis to another. However, the discussion of the issues involved in setting 'unseen' or 'method' questions in history should be invaluable for those planning to use this type of assessment internally. The final chapter on computing as an exciting way of learning history lays stress on how programmes may increase pupil participation and initiative rather than simply replacing typescript reference material. This could certainly be one field where the application of 'new history' principles more generally might increase the appreciation of history as a useful and interesting school subject.

Since 1972, 'History 13–16' has exerted a powerful influence that has extended more widely than to the examination classes taking the new syllabus. The time has now come to build on this foundation, recognizing and developing what is good in the new approach and translating it into practice throughout the curriculum. It is hoped that this book will support and encourage those responsible for taking the next steps.

Section A

1   *History — the Past as a Frame of Reference*

Peter Rogers

Synopsis

This chapter is concerned with presenting a case for history as a compulsory subject in the school curriculum. It is argued that a 'capital benefit' is likely to accrue from its study which cannot be expected to be achieved by any other means. This 'capital benefit' is identified as a 'frame of reference', a set of working assumptions, in terms of which *present* experience may be rightly understood. This argument has crucial implications for the content to be studied and some attempt is made to suggest criteria for content choice.

The argument proceeds in terms of an analysis of two key aspects of historical knowledge—its *explanatory* nature, and its use of *analogy*. It is argued that these are of fundamental importance in building the 'frame of reference' which it is suggested is the main reason for school pupils to study history at all.

If the pupils' experience of history is to be genuine (and, hence, useful) the 'patch' approach is shown to be inevitable for practical reasons and acceptable for epistemological ones. Taken together with the explanatory nature of history this provides a necessary corrective to the *exclusive* stress laid upon enquiry by *uncritical* advocates of the 'new history'. Nevertheless, the new history, rightly understood, is shown to be the only viable approach because no other is epistemologically valid.

History

Introduction

Much has been written in recent years about the place of history in schools and the related questions concerning how it should be taught. It is unfor-

tunate that much of the impctus for this has come less from the consideration of history as a form of knowledge than from a slightly desperate
attempt to provide a defence for its place in the curriculum. The main
form which the defence has taken—and this is perhaps the main feature of
the 'new' history—is a marked shift away from mere mastery of factual
material towards a stress upon enquiry skills and problem-solving. It
would be a caricature of traditional history teaching to suggest that it
always consisted of the dreary conning and regurgitation of dictated notes
and dates from which enquiry, discussion and even thought were absent;
but like most caricatures, this one contains enough truth to make stress
upon the importance of enquiry thoroughly justified. Not only were many
pupils bored by history, and many adults highly sceptical as to the point of
their studying it, but all too often the teaching seriously misrepresented the
nature of history itself. In philosophical terms 'know how' was grossly
neglected in the interests of 'know that'. The present writer has elsewhere
argued that this neglect is not only psychologically damaging but logically
absurd, since if the pupils acquire no acquaintance with the sort of ground
and procedure upon which valid knowledge claims may rest, they are
devoid of any means of appraising the truth of what they learn and, so far
from being able to establish further knowledge, they lack 'the right to be
sure' about even the information they have been given.[1]

The neglect of 'know how', then, is destructive of the subject, and
renders it educationally sterile. But the contrary danger must also be
guarded against—namely the tendency for the 'new' history to put *all*
stress upon enquiry skills ('detective work') which can colloquially be
summed up in the slogan 'content doesn't matter'; provided only that the
children are 'interested' in what is chosen for study, and that something
which may be described as 'enquiry' is promoted by it, all, apparently, is
well. Again epistemology exposes the error. Just as there can be no 'know
that' except as the outcome of 'know how', so there is no material upon
which historical 'know how' can be exercised or developed except that of
genuinely historical questions. One is not teaching *history* when one asks
children to speculate on what God may have thought of 'Bloody' Mary's
actions[2] and the same is unfortunately true of many other enquiries.

And there is a second danger. If 'content doesn't matter', then attention may be concentrated upon questions which, while genuinely historical
in that they are concerned with justly establishing true propositions about
the past, are intrinsically trivial and are chosen because they happen
(allegedly) to be interesting, ('What did the Romans wear underneath their
togas'?).[3] No matter how sophisticated and ingenious the enquiry procedures the children are inducted into may be, history will neither command
nor deserve respect if the outcome of its enquiries is never more than
mildly interesting triviality.

These seem to be the main weaknesses of the 'new' history as it is
often practised—that *undue* stress upon enquiry, and the wider epistemolo-

gical ignorance of which it is part and consequence, may result in a failure to discriminate enquiries which are genuinely historical, or may concentrate upon those which, while perhaps genuinely historical, are of little account because of indifference to content. All these dangers must be guarded against if history is to be taken seriously in the curriculum. This chapter is an attempt to offer some solution to the last by suggesting criteria to distinguish serious from trivial enquiries.

Before attempting this, however, two preliminary points must be clarified. It was said above that trivial questions are often chosen for investigation because they are, or are thought to be, interesting. Obviously, this must not be taken to imply that if a thing is interesting it is therefore trivial. On the contrary, we must seek by all means within the limits of appropriate presentation—that is, means consistent with the nature of history—to make the questions studied interesting if learning is to occur. Nor is there any objection in principle to the study of 'trivial' content by the younger pupils, since procedures and deeper concepts have both to be mastered by degrees; though it should not be supposed that such studies are necessarily the best way of doing this. Moreover, history can provide, *inter alia*, a range of hobbies which some people find fascinating and there is no reason whatever why optional time should not be spent in commencing their pursuit—always provided, of course, that the conditions of genuine historical study are satisfied.

But this chapter is not concerned with history as an option. It presupposes a core curriculum, compulsory for every pupil and occupying perhaps two-thirds of school time, in which history has a prominent place. There can be no justification for devoting compulsory core time to enquiries whose outcome is trivial, and it is self-contradictory to *compel* pupils to study something because it is interesting—especially when 'interesting' may be exactly what they do not find it to be! The central place for history as a compulsory subject for all pupils must rest upon altogether less exiguous grounds—namely that its study may be expected to result in some capital benefit, not otherwise, or equally well, to be attained. This must now be explained.

Theme and Context

The attempt starts by examining the way in which historical accounts are given, and their cardinal feature, it is suggested, is that they are *selective* in order to be *explanatory*.[4] This character of a historical account can be brought out by contrasting history with chronicle. The main difference between the two is that, while the latter is typically a mere listing of events, the former seeks, analyzes and exposes connections among events, so as to give an explanation of development, and the desire to give such explanation is what guides and determines the selection of facts. It is the absence of this explanatory purpose rather than selectivity *per se* which, fundamentally makes history and chronicle different. For chronicles, too, select. When the monkish writers of the Annals of Ulster (1481) tell us

> Brian, son of Phelim O'Reilly, died this year: to wit, protecting head of bardic bands and mendicants and the one who had the greatest knowledge and hospitality and guest-house that was in his own time.

> Turlough Maguire was slain this year in treachery in his own castle by Donagh Maguire: he was the son of a sub-king that was best in hospitality and leadership and that had best knowledge of every science and was best in intelligence and most sought of bardic composition that was in Ireland in his own time was that Turlough.

they are not (of course) giving us a comprehensive account of all, or nearly all, the events which they must have known to have occurred in that year. Their report represents a heavy selection of those happenings which seemed important to them but the criterion of importance is not, as would be the case with an historical account, the utility of the selected facts for an explanatory purpose: facts are merely stated as ends in themselves.

For the historian the matter is different. His selection of particulars is made in order to explain why events turned out as they did. Constructing an historical narrative thus involves a process of winnowing, of differentiation between the various members of a mass of crude facts and of showing their significance in relation to some theme or development. In a word, historical narrative involves 'explaining an event by tracing its intrinsic relations with other events and locating it in its historical context'.[5]

Consider a phrase such as 'Napoleon's foreign policy'. Now literally this is a mere abstraction. It consisted of thoughts and purposes 'floating in the mind' of a man long since dead—indeed, even that goes beyond what we know directly. We assume certain thoughts and purposes to have existed in the mind of Napoleon because of actions which he performed or attempted to perform and events which followed—in short we infer purpose from action. But it is of the nature of purpose that it is frequently, or even usually, wider in scope than any specific action—that its realization requires a plurality of actions. If Napoleon's foreign policy could be summed up as 'French hegemony in Europe' we could hardly deduce this from any one action: we can and do deduce it from a whole panoply of actions. It follows, surely, that no one of them can be fully explained in isolation from at least some of the others. Some—the treaty of Lunéville, for example, which by finally securing for France her 'natural' frontiers, achieved the aim of French governments since the Allied invasions of 1791—are more nearly self-contained than others because they show and sum up what has long been at stake: but none would be fully explicable alone.

Historical narrative, then, is constructed by means of tracing themes of development which link related events in explanatory and causal chains. However, it must not be thought that this process assumes, and relies on revealing, the plan of a master-mind, or even the unravelling of a previously formulated programme. Consider, for instance, the rise of monopoly capitalism. Clearly, no one planned it. But it by no means follows that it will not fit the thematic model. For the nature and features of the capitalist system were such that capitalists were faced with the need to rationalize production, to reduce ruinous competition in some industries and reap the benefits of very large-scale production in others. The changes grew out of the bleak facts of the situation.

It is important that the thematic pattern be thoroughly followed. Events typically, if not always, have connections with more than one explanatory chain. The convenient division between foreign and domestic affairs, for example, does not alter the fact of their interpenetration. How far were internal political considerations important for British foreign policy in the Suez crisis or, more recently, in the Falklands campaign? The same multiple role within many chains will be found for almost any event. Thematic treatment will require that *all* connections an event possesses with other events shall be explored and mapped, so that a rich and complex network of connections will be the result of an adequate historical narrative.[6]

The point is that valid historical accounts fundamentally involve *reconstruction*—reconstruction of a past which really happened but which has now vanished save for traces of it which fortuitously remain, and which can now be known only from appropriate handling of these traces. Now there was a degree of over-simplification in the dichotomy between history and chronicle asserted above. The chronicler's record is one of the most important of these traces, providing a prime source of information for the historian to build his explanation. But this 'raw data' role, while valuable, is not the main point. The selective nature of its record—the fact that the chronicler regards *some*, but only some, facts as worth recording—means that, while not overtly or intentionally explanatory, as is the historian's narrative, a chronicle is so *de facto* in the sense of revealing unawares the assumptions and values of the society it records.

To penetrate those assumptions and values is, of course, fundamental to reconstruction, but because the chronicler reveals them unawares they are only to be grasped by inference and imagination. One must read not only on, but between, the lines of a record to achieve reconstruction. But this usually cannot be done, without an underpinning of enabling knowledge. The function of historical imagination (and inference) is to recreate as nearly as can be a past reality which actually did exist, not to invent a purely fanciful one which did not, and to operate significantly, imagination and inference must be constrained within a framework of fact. If, for example, one is to 'recreate' the course of the Anglo-Irish treaty negotiations then one's 'imaginings' and 'inferences' must be limited, shaped and guided by facts known to the participants. One cannot usefully imagine the negotiators thinking, or infer that they meant, things they could not possibly have thought or meant given such facts as the Easter Rising and its aftermath, the General Election result of 1918, Lloyd George's relations with the Conservatives and the looming Party conference, the attitude of Craig and so on, none of the negotiators could possibly have imagined that the third Home Rule Bill was now a possible basis for a settlement, for example.

In theory, all facts relevant for an historical reconstruction *could*, of course, be ascertained from sources—that, after all, is where scholars ultimately obtain them! But there are overwhelming reasons for not attempting to do so even with the most mature pupils. Shortage of time and limited availability of sources alone renders any such ambition quite unrealistic. But there is a more compelling reason. What is a 'fact'? Consider and compare the undoubted (overwhelmingly well-attested) fact that Luther nailed his ninety-five theses on the church door at Wittenberg on 31 October 1517, with the conventional 'fact' that this event marks the commencement of the Reformation. A moment's reflection shows that the latter is not a 'fact' in the same way as the former. It can only be stated after a considerable lapse of time and is in reality an assessment—not the only possible one—of the significance of Luther's action. Yet nine people out of ten (who know enough of the matter to reply at all) if asked to state the date of the Reformation would unthinkingly answer '1517', and would believe that they had stated a 'fact'. This well illustrates, albeit at a very elementary level, how hard it is to disentangle facts and their interpretations. Skill in handling facts, and experience in assessing their significance and the connections among them—that is, their interpretation—makes up much of historical scholarship and is what historical narratives largely are. It is also a skill that pupils, by definition, have not got, and largely what it is the purpose of historical education to cause them, in some measure, to learn. This cannot be done without a fairly extensive study of historical narratives in which the pupils are led to observe and examine the structure of the process, to notice documentation and—crucially—to study what *constitutes* an argument.

The point at issue could be summarized by stating that historical enquiry cannot be carried on without *context* while, at the same time context is what one's previous study of history has largely provided. Historical knowledge is cumulative. Within quite wide limits, the more one knows the more one is in a position to learn, for the outcome of previous learning provides the context within which fresh learning may occur.

Why Teach History?

The Ubiquitous Past: Tyrant or Handmaiden?

Building context is, then, fundamental to history and, hence, to its rightful teaching and learning and it requires a judicious blend of source-based enquiry and the study of scholarly work. But how does it contribute—indeed how is it relevant—to justifying the place of history as a compulsory study for all pupils? The answer is that there is no way to escape the past. *Some* version of it, however scrappy or unbalanced, has necessarily been internalized in the process of growing up and of socialization, and whatever it is—accurate, informed, shallow, ignorant, prejudiced—it powerfully colours how the present is viewed, and powerfully affects present behaviour. Orwell in *1984* makes the point starkly. 'Who controls the past controls the future: who controls the present controls the past'. He was, of course, presenting a fictional nightmare; but is his nightmare entirely the stuff that dreams are made of? If both the past and the external world exist (or, at least, can be known) only in the mind, it is not only deliberate intent by a Big Brotherly Central Authority that can programme society with bigotry, hatred and fear. The ordinary process of socialization may do so almost as effectively—largely because it, too, controls and defines the only version of the past which most of its members ever encounter.

It is important to realize that these 'versions of the past' do not consist of coherent and articulated accounts. Dr. Kitson Clark has well described what happens.

> From a haphazard mass of misty knowledge, scraps of information, fiction in fancy dress and hardly conscious historical memories is woven a network of historical association which stretches over the whole field of human consciousness. Thus words are converted into spells, symbols are endowed with emotional force and stereotypes emerge which pretend to describe whole groups of people, and predict from their past their probable conduct in the future. Here in fact are some of the most powerful forces which control the human mind. They are of much use to those who wish to invoke irrational loyalties, they are also of great value to those who wish to use and to direct the emotion of hatred.[7]

They are the more pernicious for this because, being fragmentary and largely unconscious, they are hard to confront or question. It is this that makes education so important. Given that the social group itself is the source of these unquestioned and, indeed, largely unconscious assumptions, it is vain to look there for any criticism or corrective of them. On the contrary, they are constantly reinforced by the fact of group membership. If some critical review is not experienced in school it will not, by the vast majority of children, be experienced at all: and to the extent that the framework of assumption represents and grows from a version of the past, the need for history in education is obvious.

Or is it? On what grounds can we be sure that the version of the past experienced in historical education is preferable to those acquired in the ordinary process of growing up? Does 'preferable' mean more than a different version deliberately biased to off-set the prejudices of the existing one? Could it lack even *that* justification and be no more than an alternative prejudice? How can we know that it is not?

The Historical Past: Fact, Analogy and Frame of Reference

First, it is of the nature of history that it is contentious because it deals, at least in part, with essentially contested matters. Any idea of there being 'a right answer' to be dispensed to the masses through education (or to anyone else by any other means) involves a total misunderstanding of what history is, and what anything validly claiming to be a course in it could possibly be. What history includes, and what (in scaled down form a school course in history should offer) is the range (for school purposes, *a* range) of versions of the past which may reasonably be held; and 'reasonably' means two things. First, accounts must respect and be consistent with the facts. It *was* Luther who nailed the theses to the church door, and it *was* in 1517 that he did so: he *was* excommunicated: he *did* translate the Bible into German: he *did* take a certain position on the Peasants' War (which *did* take place): he *did* take part in the Colloquy of Marburg with Zwingli, and the two men *did* take different and identifiable positions on '*hoc est corpus meum*'. The framework of fact is sacrosanct and while, as was shown above, fact and interpretation may be hard to separate, no interpretation which *violates* that framework is admissible.

But interpretation needs more than facts, and to understand what, another element of historical knowledge must be considered, namely its use of analogy.

The commonplace claim that 'history repeats itself' may be untenable, but if there were nothing in the idea, it is hard to see how it could have crystallized at all. Obviously, in a literal sense the same thing never happens twice. On no two occasions of apparent similarity are circumstances or actors identical. But this is just the point. Why, despite manifold discrepancies, can and do we speak of 'similarity' at all? What is it—what can it be—that strikes us as similar? To take an actual example, consider Professor Nove's account of Lenin's decision to abandon War Communism and substitute NEP.

> In his notes he (Lenin) has left us some interesting insights into his thought-processes. One such note reads: '1794 versus 1921'. The Jacobins, in the French revolution, had found that the terror and

economic centralization had lost their raison d'etre with the victory of 1794. The beneficiaries of the revolution especially the more prosperous peasants, had pressed for relaxation and freedom to make money. This had swept away Robespierre, and the whole revolution moved to the right after 'Thermidor' (the month of Robespierre's downfall). All Russian revolutionaries had the example of France vividly before them. Lenin's notes show that he intended to carry out the economic retreat to avoid a head-on clash with the forces that broke Robespierre. Robespierre, in his view, failed to take into account the class nature of his enemies, had struck out against individuals and had been swept away in the end. He, Lenin, would avoid such political consequences by keeping the levers of political power firmly in the hands of a disciplined party. So it was not a coincidence that the beginnings of NEP were accompanied not only by the final ban on all political parties other than the Bolsheviks, but also—at the tenth party congress in March 1921—by a ban on factional organization within the Bolshevik party itself.[8]

The main point is not whether Lenin's analogy is entirely just but that it was natural to him, as to all of us, to think *in terms* of analogies because of how the nervous system functions. We see the world in terms of our picture of it, and that picture is not a mere agglomeration of random sensory chaos but the outcome of a classificatory process which has grouped and separated experiences according to a sense of like/unlike— which process is itself developed and matured by its own operation.[9] Essentially the process is innate, but the *course* of its development is overwhelmingly shaped by the nature of the experiences undergone. It is, in other words, *learned*. If Lenin had never studied the French Revolution he could not have thought in terms of the analogy with Robespierre: but in that case, memory of some other event which was perceived as analogous to his present situation might well have filled the gap. And that analogy would have been produced by the image of reality resulting from whatever learning experience he *had* had.

But this indicates why the study of history is so important. *Which* analogies we draw matters exactly because they determine our perceptions of, and behaviour in, the present. *All* versions of the past are likely to use analogies, the polemical and propagandist just as much as the scholarly. What is superior about those drawn by historians, and the perceptions and behaviour based upon them, is that they are drawn between events whose identities have been established by the most stringent processes available [10] for investigating the past. The historian's analogies are thus fully committed to, and by far the best representations of, the *truth* of the matter, with all that this entails for their aptness and delimitation. It is thus a matter of definition that nothing could be more deserving of confidence than their accounts. We have no way to think without comparisons, and these are the most reliable comparisons available. To suggest, therefore, that *historical* versions of the past are merely alternative *prejudices* to those of folklore is to empty the term 'prejudice' of meaning: while to refuse to prefer the historical accounts almost questions the concept of rationality itself by implying indifference to truth.

But the process of classification into like/unlike is not confined to one-to-one analogies between pairs of events such as the French and Russian revolutions. As study continues, analogies multiply and an adequate study of history builds, over time, a whole explanatory framework of the kinds of event which make up public experience in which the world may appropriately be viewed. To see what this means consider this passage, chosen at random, from a recent scholarly work. The author, Dr Richard Shannon, is discussing the significance of the first Moroccan crisis (1906) for British foreign policy. He writes

> The crucial implication was that what the Germans were trying to do in Europe was even more vital from the point of view of British interests than what they were trying to do in the way of 'world policy'. The implication of 'world policy' centred on relative naval strength. This became, from Grey's point of view, increasingly a side issue. It did not cease to be important because it touched Britain and British public opinion very directly, and it imposed on the government increasing and unwelcome financial burdens. But Britain could, if necessary, keep the required margin of superiority against Germany comfortably enough by jettisoning finally the old Two Power Standard of 1889. Britain, in other words, would not go to war with Germany over the issue of naval programmes.
>
> The question that Grey had to face was: would, or should, Britain go to war with Germany for the sake of the 'balance of power' in Europe, which in practice meant the preservation of France as a Great Power and, as a necessary corollary, the preservation of the Franco-Russian alliance? And if the answer to this question was Yes, could Britain make the necessary contribution in the application of power by essentially naval means, as the admirals argued, using military force in a diversionary strategy—say, against Schleswig-Holstein—or by essentially military means, as the generals argued, by sending over to operate with the French Army such a proportion of the British Army as would make a decisive contribution to an ultimately successful result? And what would, in that case, constitute such a proportion of the British Army?'[11]

To understand this passage what does the reader need to know? Clearly, many particular facts. Who was Grey? What was the Two Power Standard? What was the Franco-Russian alliance?—and so on. But far more important than these readily-ascertained particulars is the whole conceptual frame presupposed by the writer without which the particulars are meaningless—the nature and hence significance of the 'balance of power' and the whole concept of vital national interest, of what sorts of thing make it up or constitute a threat to it, and what sort of action the latter is likely to provoke. Without such a frame of reference such passages are virtually unintelligible because their significance cannot be grasped.

But (it might be objected) perhaps it is in terms of frames of reference built from analogies that historical events are explained and understood but what has this to do with understanding our present world? The point is that Morocco was contemporary once. That crisis was to be understood in terms of a frame of reference built from previous learning. But analogies for Morocco do not now exist only among its antecedents. Study of that event has itself contributed to the further articulation of the frame of reference, and thus to the classification and understanding of *subsequent* similar events—in this case, occasions of international crisis and tension. We learn *about* Morocco; but we also learn *through* Morocco.[12]

It might well be that half of the foregoing argument might be readily allowed. One might agree that the world is rightly to be understood in terms of appropriate frames of reference—but might doubt whether the study of history is mainly responsible for their acquisition. Where, then, could such frames come from? It seems most unlikely that they can be just acquired automatically in the process of growing up because it is hard to see what there could be in the tacit processes of socialization which could prompt the acquisition of such concepts. As a variant, it might be argued that such acquisition is a part (or rather an outcome) of the *general* process of education. Certainly there is some truth in this. One study, for example, reports fundamental differences in attainment of the concept of conservation of liquid between schooled and unschooled children—far greater than the difference between urban and rural. In fact, a related study showed that adults who had no schooling as children did not progress in the mastery of this concept beyond the level reached by 9-year-old school pupils.[13]

Yet it is a fact of experience that schooling does not always produce such effects and there seems no doubt that a high level of general education does not of itself produce all the frames of reference which a person needs to understand the world—such as those relevant to the sort of issues in international affairs raised by Shannon's analysis. An experiment has been reported elsewhere which indicated that a large group (176) of honours graduates, representing among them a very wide spread of subjects, proved to have virtually no insight into the rationale of the Russian intervention in Czechoslovakia in 1968 because they lacked any frame of reference in which a Great Power's behaviour under perceptions of threat (and of what is likely to constitute such a threat) might appropriately be viewed. One quarter of the sample could make no response at all although the questions were put in the immediate aftermath of the event when information and understanding were presumably at their height.[14]

The subjects in this experiment belong, by definition, to the most highly educated and, probably, the most intelligent, group in society. If *their* maturation and education has done so little to give them an appropriate frame of reference in important areas of experience outside their own specialism then it is difficult to believe that such frames are to be acquired at all by the mere course of growing up, or as an outcome of *general* education. It seems that they have to be specifically *learned*, and it is claimed that education in history is at least an important source. Consider an attempt to understand the occupation of Czechoslovakia—or, better still, an attempt to anticipate before the event whether it was likely to occur. No such anticipation could rationally be held, and no explanation *ex post facto* could really be followed, without a sense of how states in fact behave and why; and where could this sense come from but from learned experience? Its grasp grows from a multiplicity of analogous cases, each of which modifies or deepens the conceptual frame by the different chain of particulars it brings within it. And such a multiplicity of cases is to be found only in history, not only because the great bulk of analogous events lies in the past, but because the historian's knowledge of the outcome of past events, his hindsight,[15] makes his account of them much more reliable than those of contemporaries, distorted by unavoidable ignorance and confused by direct involvement. (It is noteworthy that historians in the graduate group performed significantly better than any other specialist group.)

In a word, the study of history provides us, *inter alia*, with a stock or repertoire, so to speak, of analogies which together constitute a framework of reference, a 'way of looking' in terms of which alone many contemporary events may be *appropriately* classified and understood. And to fail to understand them is not only in some sense to fail as an educated person; it is always unfortunate, and may be disastrous, because of the practical misjudgments it may produce.

While this chapter was being written the hijack of the American airliner from Beirut occurred. As I write, the problem is still unresolved. It offers a sad but excellent example of the fundamental need for historical knowledge and understanding in following, and intelligently responding to, contemporary events. Of what would enlightening and enabling knowledge consist? It *must*, centrally, involve the historical record of the Shia's experience which shapes their perceptions and determines their behaviour. To ignore, or wilfully to remain ignorant of, those facts is simply to refuse to listen to the Shia case at all and—this is important—irresponsibly and fatally to foreclose by default the possibility of a relevant response— relevant in the sense of 'likely to promote the desired objective rather than to be counterproductive to it'.

In this connection a very interesting opinion (if interesting is the word) was expressed in a discussion of the problem. One speaker urged that the terrorists should be 'played at their own dirty game'. The Shia prisoners in Israel should themselves be used as hostages. An ultimatum should be issued: release the American hostages unharmed within one day or 'five of yours will be shot for every one of ours'. It is highly significant that the speaker, on his own admission was totally ignorant of the Shia case (that is, of the historical facts that largely make it up) and that, when partially informed, he most radically changed his view agreeing that, apart from the ethics of the matter, such a step would almost surely produce disastrous consequences for Western interests. It is not suggested that the enlightenment provided by the historical record always produces more sensible behaviour; but only such knowledge can we start to *think*, not just react, because we can understand the motives moving our opponents. And the knowledge must include not only particular facts but a realistic way of looking at the problem. It may not have been the initial intention of the radical hijackers to provoke a violent American response but it would be extraordinarily convenient for them if it were to follow. (Surely helpful analogies exist here, for such provocations are commonplace in history.)[16] The moderate Shia leadership would have failed (or would be perceived as having done so) and the position of the radicals would be strengthened, perhaps to the point of take-over. And what stands behind them, ultimately, but the Iranian revolution? It is no more possible to strike an exact balance of relative importance in foreign policy between perceived national interest and the export, or support, of ideological belief in the case of contemporary Iran than it is in any of the historical analogies which might be drawn—English foreign policy under Cromwell, for instance. What is important is that by the proper study of history, such analogies are found to exist, are understood, and are therefore built into the wider frame of reference which defines, in general terms, what sort of things count as 'interests' and, specifically here, the sort of means by which they may be served. It is in terms of this historically-derived awareness that a *present* situation may be understood, its potential development anticipated, and its dangers (perhaps) avoided or minimized, by intelligent action.

The degree of linkage between Iran's regional objectives and the domestic Lebanese problem—linkage which could not possibly be to the West's advantage—will thus be powerfully influenced by the degree of informed insight shown in the Western response to the hijack. Such informed insight must involve the relevant historical facts, and the really frightening thing is than an enraged American public opinion, almost entirely devoid of such knowledge, might force its government into some rash act inimical to Western interests without saving the hostages.[17]

But not only such facts are needed: what makes the phrase 'Iran's regional objectives' (for example) an intelligible expression? To be meaningful, it must be set in a frame of reference which embodies and explains what sort(s) of things count as a state's 'interests' and, in particular, what objectives characterize Iranian policy. The first is derived from the study of history: the second is the historical record of what objectives Iran has shown interest in attaining, and why.

Implications

The first section of this chapter was concerned with some of the characteristics of historical knowledge—with what it is to study history and, hence, with what is entailed if *history* is to be studied at all. The second section was concerned with explaining why history is important, and why it should figure prominently within the curriculum. This final section attempts to make quite explicit the implications of all this for teaching. It is assumed, as stated in the first section, that history is a core subject compulsory for all pupils: that, except in providing the younger pupils with their initial experience of studying history, core time is not spent on enquiries whose content and outcome are trivial, no matter how sophisticated and scholarly they may be: but that nothing must be deemed trivial just because it is interesting.

What is needed, of course, is a criterion for 'trivial' or, rather, for 'non-trivial'. Now the argument of this chapter suggests an answer. It is concerned neither with history as a minority-time option nor with the initial training of specialist historians, but with 'programming' *all* pupils, as citizens-to-be, with frames of reference appropriate for the intelligent handling of particular and important areas of experience. This is why 'content doesn't matter', and the near-exclusive concentration upon enquiry skills found among the less critical practitioners of the 'new' history, is so mistaken. It probably would be a complex matter to discover what the Romans *did* wear under their togas, for example. Supposing it were to be conclusively shown, what would it contribute to one's understanding of the world? Specifically, how would the outcome of such enquiries contribute to the growth of analogy and frames of reference which has been made the main justification for making history a compulsory subject? Taken literally, therefore 'content doesn't matter' is near-nonsense. Epistemologically it is the mirror image of the arid formal teaching which its advocates rightly attacked. Whereas traditional teaching seemed oblivious to 'know how', *unreflective* practitioners of the 'new' history trivialize 'know that' by making *what* is studied little more than a matter of idiosyncratic preference and chance whim.

Yet 'content doesn't matter' has a spurious plausibility over and above its value as a slogan for combating 'good old grinding'. For it is of the nature of things that the expression 'history of...' can be put in front of almost anything. A decision about what history should be studied is therefore not fundamentally a question about *history* at all; it concerns what *things* are important, and which 'histories' are therefore most important to study. While it would be vain to expect unanimity on this matter there would, surely, be a broad consensus that the (related) big social, political and economic questions are the stuff and fundament of our collective existence, understanding of which is, on any democratic assumption, a prerequisite for effective and intelligent living. To argue, for example, that the contest for the European Cup is more important than (or anything like comparable in importance with) the course of events in, say, the Middle East, comes near to emptying the concept 'important' of all meaning. Why, exactly, apart from the instinctive feeling that it is so? Without attempting a comprehensive answer, a key point is surely that the latter is fraught with dire possibilities potentially ominous for huge numbers of people, whereas the former is devoid of anything of the kind. And if it is replied that many people, including almost certainly a large majority of our pupils, find the first more *interesting*, that simply indicates the utter inadequacy of 'interest' as the main criterion for curriculum decisions.

Content for history in the core, compulsory curriculum, then, must consist of political, social and economic affairs. For reasons shown in the second section it is in these areas of experience that the articulation of analogies into a frame of reference is most important for our citizens-to-be and this cannot be done without history. But within these limits there is a sense in which content *doesn't* matter: no particular period is picked out by the criterion. Provided the experience undergone by the pupils is appropriate and adequate for building the frame of reference needed to view the world intelligently, any period(s) will do: and there seems no reason, *a priori*, to suppose any particular one to be better than any other for this purpose.

Here two apparently conflicting further criteria must be introduced. To 'view the world intelligently', not only analogies are needed, but particular *facts*. To appraise the Lebanon, for example, we need not only a general sense of 'how states behave in what sort of circumstances' which may enable us to follow, say, Israeli-Syrian rivalry for influence within a statelet which both view (for reasons we can comprehend) as strategically important to them: we need a very considerable knowledge of the *particulars* concerning Lebanon itself. In so far as 'understanding the world' is the reason for making history compulsory, it would seem to follow that *modern* history must be the chosen content. And this argument is perhaps strengthened by the self-evident need for a knowledge of economics if the world is to be understood; it is scarcely an exaggeration to say that the more modern the period studied the more economics is required to understand the course of events, and the more its acquisition is part and parcel of historical education. The bitter controversy over the Corn Laws cannot be comprehended above a misleadingly superficial level without a good working knowledge of economics. A sixth former who cannot understand the seeming paradox 'free trade is the mercantilism of the strong' (whether or nor those actual terms are used) will not achieve a *full* understanding of international relations and rivalries before the First World War and, in particular, of the conduct of British foreign policy. Such a pupil will be unable fully to assess the claim that imperial rivalries were the root cause of war. In later periods similar considerations hold. *Why* all the fuss (and agony) over the gold standard? Why was the international depression so prolonged? These and similar questions form a large part of what constitutes study of the period, but they are not really accessible to the economically innocent. And what of 'dollar diplomacy', America's informal empire, and many other crucially important and economically rooted issues in the contemporary world?

These examples are chosen almost at random but they all illustrate not only the *contemporary* relevance of history but the essential role of economic literacy for giving, or following, a significant historical narrative. And the more modern the period studied, the heavier does the 'weighting' of economics become.[18]

But as against this modernist 'tilt' it must be remembered that an important objective of studying history is to give pupils the experience of *contrast*. It has already been strongly urged that the assumptions of our own society need critical review, and this cannot but be facilitated by the study of other societies where the assumptions were significantly different. Things do not have to be just as we know them. So far from cutting across the prime aim of building a frame of reference, the study of contrast aids its achievement. For, amid the manifold and manifest differences between other societies and our own world, run strands of familiarity which make it possible to take those differences seriously, as relevant to our own experience and action. A touch of nature makes the whole world kin. We see the actions of Israel in Lebanon, or read of (say) British punitive expeditions against the Afghans. 'Let them hate, as long as they fear' said the Romans of the 'tribes' on *their* frontiers.[19] To have penetrated the rationale of 'If you want peace, prepare for war' through the record of many conflicts between societies more or less different from our own is to have grasped not only the structural similarity of state conflicts, which preserves the cogency of the analogy, but the differences, and reasons *for* the differences, among them, which force relevant modifications of it to be made. In our own day, for example, the hideously increased risk factor, and changes in the distribution of power, must profoundly modify former notions of war as an instrument of policy or of the classical balance of power. Yet no one, surely, questions the continuing relevance of such concepts in themselves. To grasp their continuing root relevance while understanding the modifications, more or less radical, which changing circumstances have produced up to and including the present time, is just what it is to build a frame of reference and just what the rightful study of history is calculated to produce.

Two things are strongly implied in all this. First, while the need for particulars directly concerned with events in the modern world may cause modern history to be emphasized, the need for *contrast*, both to promote a critical attitude to present assumptions and to promote the adequate articulation of analogies, means that substantial attention must be paid to earlier periods also.

The second implication is that history must be studied for a long time—in fact throughout the pupil's school life—if the desired cardinal benefits are to be secured. Apart from the sheer time required for the number of patches which must be studied, the concepts to be mastered and frames of reference to be built require mature pupils for their full accomplishment—though it is quite mistaken to suppose that this cannot be *begun* with children.[20]

It also follows that pressure of time alone will force any proper teaching of history into a 'patch' approach; but it can now be seen how this approach well suits the kind of course depicted as desirable by the foregoing argument. Given that study is to include all (or, being realistic, a substantial number of) the themes needed for an adequate explanation of a period, given that a range of periods have to be studied in order to have available a wide enough range of parallels with which to interpret contemporary events, and given that in order to achieve this each period must be studied in depth and detail, including considerable amounts of source-based work, the 'patch' approach is not so much being recommended as prescribed. But a possible danger in this whole process must be anticipated. Although no particular 'patches' are prescribed for study by the argument, yet it is true that, whichever are chosen, the criterion for choice is to study them not just for themselves but for their usefulness in helping to explain subsequent states of affairs—namely, the present. But is this not the 'practical' history against which Professor Oakenshott[21] warns us, where the choice of subject and the selection and use of evidence are determined by the desire to produce a version of the past which will butress a *desired* view of the present—a version which may degenerate into mere propaganda?

This is a real danger: but forewarned is forearmed. It is crucial to distinguish the motive for studying something from the nature of what is studied. The motive for the core and compulsory role allotted to history in the curriculum is, admittedly, to help equip citizens-to-be to live effectively in a world subsequent to the events studied. But history can only fulfil this role if the versions of the past it provides, the analogies it draws, and, thus the frame of reference it builds are *true*. It follows that the only history which can be *useful* in the relevant sense is true history—that produced by the full rigour of genuine historical enquiry. Our motive for studying it is not 'for its own sake', but our *manner* of studying it must be *as if* for its own sake. This does not mean that, in teaching, the pupils will not be trained to draw analogies; it does mean that every analogy suggested will be subjected to the most rigorous scrutiny. In comparing the French and Russian revolutions, for example, the differences will be fully stressed and evaluated. To test Lenin's comparison cited above would be an excellent example; so would the assertion that 'France made war because she had had a revolution: Russia had a revolution because she was engaged in unsuccessful war'. How important and significant is this difference for any analogy which may be attempted between the two events?

Perhaps enough has been said to reassure the reader that genuine historical study is being insisted upon. Professor Oakeshott's 'practical' history is a real and dangerous reef, but ample navigational aids are provided to avoid it.

Summary

It is hoped that this chapter may have thrown some light on what is involved in teaching history and that the claim for its central place in the curriculum may have been made clear in terms of the 'capital benefit' which its study is likely to provide for our pupils.

Notes

1   For a more extended discussion of this crucial point see ROGERS, P.J. (1979a), chapter 1.
2   See HALLAM, R. (1972).
3   See MOORE, R. (1982).
4   For a much fuller account of historical explanation, including its selective nature, see ROGERS, P.J. (1973 and 1979a).
5   WALSH, W.H. (1967) p. 59. Professor Walsh discusses the process thoroughly under the term 'colligation'.
6   The last four paragraphs closely follow my discussion of the subject in ROGERS, P.J. (1973). I wish to acknowledge permission from Pergamon Press to make use of the material here.
7   KITSON CLARK, G. (1967) p. 7.
8   NOVE, A. (1972), pp. 81–2.
9   For a parallel discussion of this point in terms of Piaget's assimilation/accommodation model see ROGERS, P.J. (1984) p. 28.
10 *Ibid*, pp. 22–3.
11 SHANNON, R. (1974) p. 414.
12 International crisis and foreign policy have been used as an example of the process involved. In no way is it meant that only political events are concerned. On the contrary, analogy affects every area of life of which we have significant understanding for this is, in important part, an outgrowth of experience and is essentially backwards-referencing.
13 GREENFIELD, P.M. (1967).
14 For a full account see ROGERS, P.J. (1979b). For a brief analysis see ROGERS, P.J. (1984) pp. 34–5.
15 For this crucial aspect of historical work see DANTO, A. (1965) p. 149. For a brief discussion see ROGERS, P.J. (1984) pp. 22, 25 and 27.
16 Consider, for example, the role of Bismarck's Ems telegram in provoking war with France in 1870.
17 Happily, a violent American response was avoided and the immediate crisis was

resolved. The passage is left unchanged because its argument seems as valid as ever. Similar crises with similar temptations and dangers are latent within the Middle East situation.

18 Further important practical questions are '*how much* economics is needed' and 'are formal courses in it required?'. It is hoped to deal with these questions on a subsequent occasion. In the meantime, what has been said connects closely with the role of history in *integrating* the curriculum. See ROGERS, P.J. (1973) section 1 and ROGERS, P.J. (1982) pp. 1–10.

19 *The Economist*, 11 May 1985, p. 11.

20 For an attempt to introduce 10–13 year olds to 'high politics' using Bruner's spiral curriculum see ROGERS, P.J. (1979a) pp. 39–48 and chapter 5. This present chapter (as the examples and discussion show) is concerned with older pupils.

21 OAKESHOTT, M. (1962) pp. 147–54. For a short discussion see ROGERS, P.J. (1973) pp. 108–10.

References

DANTO, A.C. (1965) *Analytical Philosophy of History* Cambridge University Press.

GREENFIELD, P.M. (1966) On culture and conservation in BRUNER, J.S., OWER, R.R. and GREENFIELD, P.M. *Studies in Cognitive Growth.* JOHN WILEY, chapter 11.

HALLAM, R. (1972) 'Thinking and learning in history', *Teaching History*, II, 8, pp. 337–50.

KITSON CLARK, G. (1967) *The Critical Historian*, London, Heinemann.

MOORE, R. (1982) 'History abandoned', *Teaching History*, 32, February, pp. 26–8.

NOVE, A. (1972) *An Economic History of the USSR*, London, Penguin.

OAKESHOTT, M. (1962) *Rationalism in Politics*, London, Methuen.

ROGERS, P.J. (1973) 'History', in DIXON, K., (Ed.) *Philosophy of Education and the Curriculum*, Pergamon, pp. 75–134.

ROGERS, P.J. (1979a) 'The New History—Theory into Practice', Historical Association.

ROGERS, P.J. (1979b) 'History and political education', *Teaching Politics* 8, 2, pp. 153–69.

ROGERS, P.J. (1982) 'Epistemology and history in the teaching of school science', *European Journal of Science Education*, 4, 1, pp. 1–10.

ROGERS, P.J. (1984) 'Why teach history?' in DICKINSON, A.K., LEE, P.J., and ROGERS, P.J., (Eds) *Learning History*, Heinemann, pp. 20–38.

WALSH, W.H. (1967) *An Introduction to the Philosophy of History*, Hutchinson's University Library.

2 Ages and Concepts: A Critique of the Piagetian Approach to History Teaching

Martin Booth

Synopsis

Until recently research into children's thinking and learning has been dominated by the theories of Jean Piaget. This chapter argues that this has had a restricting effect on the history curriculum and our ideas about the development of children's historical understanding. It outlines recent research which gives a more optimistic view; and it advances a theory of learning and indicates teaching strategies which can help to raise our expectations of children's potential in history.

In 1984 the Secondary Examinations Council set up a Grade Related Criteria Working Party in History. Its brief was to determine the major elements or domains (up to six) which go to make up the discipline of history and then to establish four levels of mastery or competence which pupils ranging from low to high ability should be able to show at the age of 16. Criterion referencing had come to history. No longer would we be able to get away with vague statements about what our pupils should be able to do at the end of the history course. We would have to show the extent to which pupils had mastered the historical concepts, historical skills or techniques of historical enquiry which the working party had established as essential assessment elements for pupils of all abilities.

The draft *Grade Criteria* were published in September 1985; they are intended to replace the grade descriptions which form part of the *National Criteria for History*, published in January 1985. Together they provide both a structure for history and a series of bench marks against which we can measure a pupil's level of attainment in history. They are, I think, a significant contribution to the teaching and learning of the subject, not only for those who will take the General Certificate of Secondary Education (GCSE) at 16+ but for pupils of all ages. For criterion referencing will extend down into the middle and primary school; it will be adopted for the 16–19 age group; and we will have eventually mapped out a structure of progress which will indicate the levels of thinking and conceptualization for which we should be aiming during the span of compulsory schooling and beyond.

Now there are those whose immediate reaction may be: the demands are too high. The grade related criteria are concerned with difficult concepts such as cause and effect and change and continuity, and with empathetic understanding; they require pupils to engage in the comprehension, analysis and evaluation of historical source material; they demand that historical enquiry is undertaken. Surely most 16-year-olds are unable to think in history in these ways—let alone the younger pupils. All that most of them can do is to learn some information which they can then reproduce in simple form.

This was a view which was reinforced by many of the former Mode I CSE examinations in history. Questions relied heavily on recalled information and rarely demanded more than a narrative or description; and where source material was used it was often no more than a stimulus for the regurgitation of more information. Such papers, designed as they were for a majority of examination youngsters, were a reflection of the belief that memorization and recall of knowledge were all that most 16-year-olds could cope with; they simply had not the mental capacity for engaging in historical thinking of a higher order. Research in the 1960s and 1970s seemed to lend some support to this view.

Now much of this work took as its starting point the developmental psychology of Jean Piaget. Many teachers, of course, will be familiar with the main principles of this but at the risk of misrepresenting a theory which is both extensive and complex it is perhaps worth emphasizing some of its main elements. First, Piagetian pyschology is concerned with the development of logical, interrelated systems or thinking patterns known as 'operations'. That is, it focusses on the creation of logical, deductive thinking in people and the ways in which they develop the capacity to think in abstract terms, to pose hypotheses and to reach conclusions—their ability, that is, to 'problem solve'. The development of this ability is the result of the interaction of the child with its environment. New experiences are assimilated into existing thought patterns. Where, however, no immediate fit is possible—where, that is, the experience does not 'click' with the schemes already possessed—then the child either abandons them or alters or extends the schemes to accommodate them.

To a certain extent, therefore, the child's actions and the environment in which it operates are of fundamental importance in its emotional and intellectual development; but Piaget makes it clear that there are distinct limits to the extent to which a child's thinking can be accelerated, limits which are determined by the child's neural and physiological make up. Hence Piaget's emphasis on the four-part stage-development structure, in which each stage is distinct, deals with a particular structure or kind of thinking and is tied to a particular age range. The first two stages—from birth to about the age of 2 and from 2 to about 7—are 'preoperational', in that the child's thought processes often seem to be illogical. The very young child develops from a situation in which the world and the self are the same and where actions are little more than conditioned reflexes to one in which actions are organized in relation to the immediate environment— the child begins to see itself as one object among many that occupy the world. The illogicalities of this understanding emerge with the development of language. The child feels no need to prove an argument and has no capacity for generalizing. It will often leap from one point to another or make wild assumptions on the basis of limited evidence. It is only with the appearance of 'concrete operations' from the age of 7 onwards than the beginnings of logical and deductive reasoning can be seen. But Piaget uses the word 'concrete' to emphasize that the child can deal only with the immediate, the observable, the tangible; it is not as yet able to suggest possibilities—to deal with what could exist or what might be—or to arrive at general covering laws. This capacity appears only at the 'formal' operational stage from the age of 11 or 12. This is the realm of 'pure thought' where the child shows the ability to take the results of concrete operational thought, to shape them into propositions or hypotheses and then deduce further information from them. Piaget (1958) summarizes his work on formal operational thinking and gives details of the sixteen experiments used to test the child's capacity to think 'operationally'.[1] All the tests concern problems in the field of the natural sciences; there are metal rods of varying lengths and thicknesses and the child has to deduce the laws determining the flexibility of the rods; there is a pendulum and the child has to determine the factor governing the amplitude; it has to consider the specific gravity of objects in water. On the basis of the children's reactions to these tests, Piaget elaborated the structure of formal operational thought and arrived at a concept of an elaborate 'mental scaffolding held up by a number of girders . . . so that the agile subject can move from one point to another without ever reaching impasse'.[2]

Piaget therefore has drawn up a framework which directs our attention to the development of rational, deductive thought and gives us a series of grade descriptions which will allow us to analyze the child's thinking and to chart its gradual refinement. As such, its potential for creating greater understanding of the ways in which children's logical thinking develops is enormous; but unfortunately the Piagetian framework has only too often had a limiting or even stultifying effect. The reasons I think are two-fold. In the first place, the framework has often been used in what might be called an insensitive, possibly over-simplistic manner.

In history, for example, there have been at least twenty-four theses and dissertations completed in the UK since 1955 reporting Piagetian-based projects. All of them come to the conclusion that when using historical information children find it harder to think hypothetically and deductively than in other subjects. Roy Hallam, for example, suggests that the stage of formal operations which Piaget shows appearing from about the age of 11 begins in history at the mental age of 16.5. Dismayed by this he went on to see if he could do anything to accelerate the progress from concrete to formal operational thought. Certainly the lively and challenging teaching he adopted had some effect on the thinking levels of the 9 and 10-year-old children in his research sample; but the 13 and 14-year-olds remained remarkably unaffected and showed no significant improvement towards formal operational thinking in comparison with the control groups who were being taught in a traditional 'chalk and talk' manner.[3]

Hallam's conclusions show clearly the constrictions the Piagetian framework can place both on expectations and the curriculum.[4] 'The material must be so selected that it "matches" the pupils' schemata or thinking skills' (p. 169); 'history...for nearly all the pupils under 14 years of age should not be over abstract in form, nor should it contain too many variables' (p. 168); 'a great deal of ancient history can be taught as a concrete subject: the homes, daily life, industries, agriculture and trade of the prehistoric period' (p. 169). History then, during the years when it is a compulsory part of the curriculum (over 50 per cent give it up at the end of the third year of the secondary school), must not deal with ideas, attitudes or concepts such as change and continuity, cause and consequence; it cannot be speculative or imaginative; pupils cannot be expected to evaluate source material. They simply have not reached the stage of formal thought which would enable them to operate in this manner. Our history must be didactic, uncontroversial and concerned as far as possible with objects rather than ideas, things rather than thoughts.

There are a number of reasons for challenging this position. First, I would take issue with the tests used by the research workers. Hallam, for example, used short 'textbook' passages dealing with events widely separated in time; they may well have had no connection with the history the pupils were studying or had recently studied. More than this, the passages they were asked to study were too brief for the pupils, unfamiliar with the period, to attempt meaningful answers to the questions posed, particularly as some of the questions are literally unanswerable. For example, after a short passage on Mary Tudor, the pupils were asked: 'Mary Tudor thought that God wanted her to take England back to the Catholic church. (a) What would God have thought of her methods? (b) Can you think of any reasons why Mary Tudor should use such methods to make people follow her religion?'. Indeed, it is quite clear that throughout the tests the aim has been to ask questions the answers to which could be then be assigned to the appropriate Piagetian level rather than probe issues or understandings which are central to the study of history.

A second reason for the way in which Piagetian psychology has only too often lowered our sights and restricted our expectations of children's potential must focus on the theory itself. Criticism of Piaget's developmental psychology is not new but the last few years have seen an increase in the numbers of books and articles which have taken issue with his theories. Some have tended to question the direction and emphasis of his research, arguing for example that Piaget gives excessive weight to physical activity and the manipulation of objects and that he has dismissed as unimportant the child's observation. Others go much further than this and have attacked the whole theory with its emphasis on a child's intellectual development passing through a rigid sequence of stages with the successful negotiation of one stage being an essential prerequisite of the next. Research, they claim, has shown that Piaget's stages really have little meaning as there seems to be such a huge variation in the ages at which they are attained. How can one talk of a 'stage' unless it is clearly defined by reference to an age group? More pertinent to the historian is the argument that formal operations are not thinking skills which can be applied to any problem and any subject; different materials, different contexts and situations will demand different thinking approaches. As one author puts it, 'rather than looking for content-independent and universal structures of thought, we need to assess the specific thinking within the content of the task given'[5]

Kieran Egan also questions the value of using the theory as a general framework.[6] He points out that Piaget's theory deals mainly with the development of formal logico-mathematical thinking which in fact represents only a small part of the intellectual equipment which children bring to making sense of the world and their experiences. They enact situations or use pictures to create understanding; attitudes, feelings and senses as much as logic play their part. Hunches or intuition, sheer chance and vivid imagination are often resorted to rather than deductive thinking. Yet the constraints which Piaget emphasizes on young children's formal logical ability are read very frequently as constraints on the totality of their thinking; and a curriculum which is based on his theory will impose a limiting, rigid and uniform pattern on pupils whose capacity for understanding may well be through a diversity of routes.

My argument is therefore that not only is the research based on Piagetian theories flawed but that the very view the theory gives us of children's capacity to think historically is limited and restricting and that it focusses our attention on a small part only of what it means to think historically. Piagetian psychology directs us to the logical and requires us, to quote Peter Lee, to see history 'as a kind of abstract pattern or calculus in which terms are manipulated for mysterious academic purposes or for examinations'.[7] Of course there is a place for such rigorous, logical thinking but to concern ourselves with this alone is to rule out a range of imaginative and empathetic elements which bring the dry bones of the past to life and turn historical knowledge into historical understanding. Perhaps therefore the first requirement of anyone concerned with the development of pupils' historical thinking is to determine the particular nature of the discipline and the learning and teaching it requires (to establish, that is, what Jerome Bruner would call the 'structure' of the subject); only then can one begin to establish how far and by what methods pupils can actually engage in such activity.

At the start, I would assert that historical thinking is not primarily about hypothesis, induction and deduction or the testing or creation of new laws. We are indeed in a different ball game from that of the natural scientist. We deal with the activities of people in a vanished past. Our sources of evidence are the traces they have left—usually incomplete—traces which can include anything from oral evidence to air photography, artefacts to account books, landscape to letters. To interpret this, to extract the meaning or significance which it may contain, the historian has to ask questions; and to do this he has to reply far more on 'common sense judgments', to use Jack Hexter's phrase, than on 'strict logical entailments'. Indeed, the prime task of the historian is not to solve problems (though of course his researches will involve detective work), still less to verify laws or produce new ones. Rather his task is to put forward the most convincing account of the past; and the sort of thinking that can produce this is best 'described as a form of speculation, directed imagination or vicarious living'.[8] It demands a combination of imagination, feeling and historical knowledge which may well be shaped by the operation of some guiding idea or concept. Thus the historian has much of the creative artist in him. He aims to recreate (usually in words though it could be in other forms) a credible understanding of the world we have lost. He is concerned with drawing together related events to some common centre, to construct an imaginative web which is the hallmark of Collingwood's historical thinking. Such thinking does not of course take place in a mind which is *tabula rasa*. No historian approaches his evidence without any preconceptions and inevitably a range of concepts, attitudes and understandings will be brought into play as evidence is analyzed, facts established and the overall picture of the past event or topic created.

Clearly then Piaget's framework of cognition is far too limited and restricting an instrument to use for analyzing the complex strands which go to make up pupils' thinking and understanding in history. What is needed is a more open-ended analysis based on an understanding of history's particular structure or knowledge form. More recent research has adopted just this approach and has presented us with a view of pupils' thinking in history which is at once optimistic, liberating and suggestive of new approaches. In the second part of this chapter I want to discuss two such research projects with which I have been involved and a series of classroom approaches.

The first of these projects was prompted by my view of historical knowledge and my misgivings about research based on a narrow understanding of Piaget's theories. It was a longitudinal study of the development of fourth and fifth year pupil's thinking in history. The pupils were at a secondary comprehensive school (11–16 age range) in the South of England and were following a two-year modern world history syllabus which covered such areas as Europe, America, the Far East and new nations in the twentieth century. The sample covered a wide range of ability as measured by the AH4 test of General Ability. The emphasis of the course was on pupil participation and discussion, the use of a variety of sources (especially film) and project work. The aim of the research was to measure the improvement over a seventeen-month period of the pupils' ability to reason historically using primary documentary evidence, to deduce from written cues key concepts covered by the course (for example, communism, cold war, slump/depression) and to assess the pupils' change in attitude to history as a subject and to national or racial groups and situations with which the syllabus dealt. I was also very much concerned with the pupils' capacity for thinking in abstract and speculative ways when presented with pictorial and written evidence from the period. How far could they see patterns and connections? How far could they speculate or derive meanings which were inferred? A full discussion of the results of the research is given elsewhere[9] but let me indicate here the main features.

The written testing showed that the pupils had made marked and significant gains on both the documentary skills test and the concepts test during the seventeen months which had elapsed between the first and second testing, both in comparison with the scores established on the first occasion and with those of a group of pupils of similar age and intelligence who were not studying history. The history pupils also made significant gains on the three sections of the attitude questionnaire; that is, by the end of the course they showed a reduction in the incidence of facile generalizations about national or racial groups or historical situations. What was particularly interesting in all this was that the analysis of the data indicated that the major factor behind the increased scores was not general intelligence or greater maturity but a syllabus and teaching method which was specifically geared to the development of conceptual understanding and the skills of historical reasoning.

The capacity of these pupils to engage in genuine historical thinking emerged clearly during the oral testing using the pictures and written evidence. A little more explanation of this is required to indicate the significance of their achievement. Each history pupil was seen on two separate occasions. On the first occasion the pupil was shown twelve uncaptioned photographs and pictures of important people and events in late nineteenth and twentieth century history—colonial situations in Africa, Gandhi and disciples, a Hitler youth rally and so on. On the second occasion they were given twelve very short quotations from famous speeches and documents of the same period. For example, there was the key sentence from the Truman Doctrine speech, a short extract from Carnegie's essay on *wealth* and the comment from Alfred Mahan that 'whether they will or not, Americans must now begin to look outward'.

The pupil was instructed to group the pictures or quotations together into sets and explain why it was that he had put particular pictures or quotations together. It was emphasized that there is no 'correct' answer and that the evidence can be grouped logically in a number of different ways. The pupil was placed, therefore, in an open-ended situation in which he was not asked to prove anything, or, initially, to answer any questions; the evidence was there to be worked upon and provide the basis for divergent yet constructive thinking.

It quickly became apparent that the history pupils formed sets in one of two ways. The first was where the sets were based on the immediate content of the material. The pupil made no effort to go beyond what was obvious and apparent and the 'surface' impression of the evidence provided the clue for the formation of the set. The reasons for the grouping were given in descriptive terms. For simplicity, such sets were categorized 'concrete'. For example, a girl linked pictures of white tax gatherers, Africa, late nineteenth century, with one showing a conference between the Swazi and the British c. 1870, because they show 'black and white peace talks'. This is a logical reason for forming the set but it rests solely on what is immediately apparent in the pictures. A boy grouped four pictures showing blacks and whites in Africa saying they show 'the training of the Africans'. Another boy put two African pictures together because the country 'looks the same'.

With the quotations the most common form of concrete grouping was to form a set on the basis of a key word in the text. Thus a girl put two quotations together because the word 'independence' appears in both, another because of the word 'communist', a third because of the name 'Truman'. A number of pupils made sets on the basis of the dates of the quotations. There were somewhat more ambiguous sets than with the pictures but a careful analysis of the comments made by the pupil (every interview was tape recorded) usually left little doubt as to which category the set belonged. For example, a girl put the quotation from the Churchill speech in 1940 ('victory at all costs. . .') with a description of the bombing of Hiroshima in 1945, and called the set 'war'. Her comments showed that her thinking went no further than the obvious fact that both passages were dealing with warfare. By contrast, a boy had linked the same quotations but had used the phrase 'total war' to describe the set. He contrasted the Second World War with the First ('It was more total than the First World War') and his comments showed that he was thinking about the nature of the fighting and the extent of civilian involvement. It was clearly a case of thinking that belonged to a different category, for it went beyond the immediate content of the evidence and was both deeper and more comprehensive.

The other form of grouping was where the pupil gave evidence of thinking that was more adventurous, creative and accurately imaginative, the hallmarks of genuine historical thought. Pupils who formed sets in this category showed the ability to comprehend and analyze the material and then to group the evidence into sets. But the essence of this grouping was that it was not based on the immediately observable features of the picture or the key word of the quotation, but rather on inferred qualities or ideas. The picture or quotation was seen not from the outside, so to speak, but from the inside; its potential or immanent meaning was perceived. The reasons for the grouping were given in explanatory terms. For simplicity, such sets were categorized 'abstract'. Thus a boy, having talked perceptively and accurately about the pictures, put a photograph of Gandhi with one of independence day in Upper Volta, because they were to do with 'independence'. Four pictures showing scenes from Africa in the late nineteenth century he grouped together because they show events in the last century and concern 'white power over the blacks—whites controlling the blacks. Racialism, perhaps'. The phrase he used to describe the set was 'British empire'. A girl identified two sets of pictures which can be termed abstract. She put three pictures together commenting 'They're all to do with the colonies in Africa'. Here she has gone beyond the immediately observable data to the ideas which the pictures express on control, submission, inferior and superior races. Her second abstract set consisted of British officials and soldiers of the West African Frontier Force in the 1890s and the Punch cartoon of Rhodes the Colossus standing astride the African continent. She commented: 'They're both to do with perhaps the joining of two different parts of Africa'. Here the ideas of conquest and expansion have been extracted and an abstract concept adduced.

With the quotations, the same grading criteria were applied. A set was graded abstract if the pupil could logically group the quotations on the basis of information or ideas inferred from the passages. Thus a girl put together quotations from Nyerere talking about independence, Ian Smith proclaiming UDI and Bourgiba of Tunisia on the problem of newly independent countries because 'they are to do with racial problems in Africa'; quotations from the Truman doctrine and Mahan on the interest of late nineteenth-century America in sea power were linked by a boy under the concept of American imperialism; while another boy put the quotation from the Truman doctrine with the extract from Carnegie's justification of wealth because they are 'anti-communist'.

Now 71 per cent of the pupils were able to draw two or more pieces of pictorial evidence together into a connected, imaginative synthesis. They found it more difficult to operate in this way with the written evidence (the quotations). Even so, 58 per cent were able to form sets of two or more pieces of evidence. Further analysis of the data indicated the complexity of this thinking. First, it is dependent on accurate, relevant knowledge. It is generated by analytical ability and shaped by appropriate conceptual understanding. Attitudes to the subject, personal experience and verbal ability all play their part. Intelligence (as measured by the AH4 test of general intelligence) is of less importance. Clearly, then, though the majority of pupils were capable of thinking in this manner, there was a wide variation in the ease with which it was achieved. One or two of the pupils had the ability to relate imaginatively all twelve pieces of evidence, some only two; it depended on the extent to which those factors which made up the complex of this thinking had been developed and brought into play. But it is equally clear that an attempt to assess these thought processes in terms of Piagetian stages is both inappropriate and restricting, for logical structures and hypothetico-deductive thinking have only a very limited connection with the imaginative, inferential thinking which was being displayed by pupils in these circumstances.

My research therefore took as its starting point the nature of history and the teaching methods and syllabus which tried to realize this. It attempted then to probe the extent to which the pupils were able to operate and think historically; and my conclusion was quite simply that provided you look for the diversity of historical thinking and are not constrained by notions of clinical, calculating deductive thinking, and given an emphasis on pupil enquiry, discussion and the use of a range of source materials, it is remarkable what pupils aged 14–16 of a wide range of ability can actually achieve in history.

My second piece of research was concerned with 11-year-olds—the first year, in fact, of a large comprehensive school in the South East of England. The four classes a colleague and I investigated were in mixed ability groupings and were following a humanities course which involved elements of RE, sociology, history and geography. Our research focussed on the history within the course and was concerned amongst other things with the pupils' understanding of key concepts, their skill in handling written evidence and their language and understanding when placed in situations which would give them the opportunity to talk. For example, small groups handled and discussed a pile of Roman shards; they listened to the story of Theseus and the minator and considered how far it might be true in the light of three pieces of evidence we showed them; we set up drama and role play events.

The results once again indicated the potential of the pupils. For example, all four classes made marked and significant gains on the objectively scored concepts test, scores which reflect the interest and challenge of the course, the commitment to it of the teachers concerned, and in particular their constant invitation to the children to think: to consider not only how things arose, but how we can know; to speculate about the nature of evidence, change and development. Another important element would seem to be the stress on types of knowledge and the connections between them.

With the questionnaires measuring their attitudes to people and problems in history, there was a clear indication of more critical thinking by the end of the year, a consequence no doubt of a course which was challenging the pupils' easy assumptions and emphasized open-ended discussion, the exchanging of views and the exploitation of new ideas.

Interestingly, the pupils' performance on the written test which involved a series of graded questions on a story about cave man paintings was disappointing. Scores were not particularly high at the beginning of the year and there was virtually no increase in the total group score by the second testing in July. With two of the forms the mean scores had actually decreased. We were hesitant in suggesting reasons for this but an analysis of the data suggested certain factors. First, though there was little overall change in the size of the score being made on the skills test, there was some change in rank order; the skills test scores by the end of the school year were more closely correlated with intelligence. To put it another way, the less able had tended to score the lower marks, the more able the higher. Intelligence, therefore, rather than teaching technique or syllabus content seemed to have had more effect in determining these scores; the less able had tended to regress during the course of the year and the more able had not increased their scores in line with their intelligence.

We are hestitant in suggesting factors which may help to explain these results, for the research was limited both in methods and contact with the school. What follows are some tentative hypotheses based on flimsy evidence.

The first point concerns the teaching styles and emphases. It is significant that in the lists of attributes for success in humanities which the teachers drew up and against which they rated their pupils, all put emphasis on such qualities as 'enthusiasm', 'self confidence', 'alertness', 'interest'; but only one mentioned specifically the attribute of the 'ability to communicate ideas orally/on paper'. It could be argued that whereas the humanities department placed strong emphasis on questioning and class discussion, it seemed less concerned with the development of reading and writing skills. It was also significant that the Head of Humanities stressed that written work was generally left for homework. We saw no examples of pupils' written homework but the results of a questionnaire designed to assess the home background did seem to indicate that the pupils came from homes that were not very supportive, certainly as far as the school's humanities course was concerned. There were few books and little discussion of school work; in particular, nearly 40 per cent of the sample claimed that they had no room or special place at which to work at home. Is it unreasonable to suggest that homework aimed at developing writing skills was often being undertaken at home in conditions that were not conducive to academic attainment? Would the course and the pupils have been better served had more time been devoted to these matters in class?

I emphasize these points and highlight the contrast between the conceptual and wider understanding of these pupils and their written analytical skills because they substantiate the argument I have been making: pupils of a wide range of ability and ages can engage in proper history; teaching for particular skills and understandings can, and does, make a difference. But we must consciously determine our objectives and teaching methods in the light of our understanding of what history is. Failure to achieve a particular objective will almost certainly be a result of lack of care over these matters and not a function of the Piagetian level at which the pupil is supposed to be.

Further work I have undertaken with pupils has helped to support this view; it suggests that it is often through the imaginative and empathetic approaches that pupils first become involved in history and so are enabled to develop high level conceptual understanding. Take, for example, a field expedition with second year pupils from a Cambridge city comprehensive.

The expedition was to Burwell village some eight miles from the city. It lies on the edge of the Fens and its interest for us was in the deserted village which is to the west of the present buildings. In 1143, Geoffrey de Mandeville, one of the great lords of England, fell from power and rebelled against King Stephen. Establishing himself on the Isle of Ely, he attacked the surrounding country. In an attempt to contain him, Stephen ordered a chain of castles to be built along the edge of the Fens. The castle at Burwell, whose remains are clearly visible, was never completed. In the process of its construction, a number of the villagers' huts had to be pulled down and built over. Why was the castle sited in this position? What were the reactions of the villagers? And why was it that the building was so abruptly stopped?

We spent the morning closely examining the site. We traced the foundations of the huts that were spared, measuring the size of the rooms and the crofts. We walked along what was once the main street and inspected the fish ponds. Then with the help of an aerial photograph and a site plan we tried to identify various parts of the castle—the moat dug, the mound for the keep and ramparts raised but little else done. In the afternoon we learned the truth: even while the castle was being built, Geoffrey de Mandeville had been killed in battle. The need for a castle at Burwell died with him. But what of the villagers? How had they reacted to the affair? Did their loyalties lie with Stephen or de Mandeville? And what of the building of the castle with the destruction of huts that it caused? Using the site we attempted to recreate some of the tensions and drama of the time. The pupils were divided into family groups with names and occupations. They established their identities and homes on the sites of the old village. The authority figures of reeve, priest and lord of the manor intervened with demands, not least that of building the castle for the king. Geoffrey de Mandeville also appeared with attempts to curry support. The day ended with a fierce encounter between the king's and de Mandeville's troops on the ramparts of the half-finished castle.

I daresay the balmy weather and the attractiveness of the site, poised as it is on the edge of the vast 'nothing' landscape with the stump of Ely's octogan tower in the distance, helped to make the day a success. But the combination of evidence—both pictorial, map and site—and active pupil participation through site work, analysis of documents and role play combined to produce some genuine, speculative historical thinking. These processes were not of a kind which could be classified in neat Piagetian terms. In a way, they were too chaotic and uneven—the sudden flash of understanding, the reversion to anachronism, the more carefully reasoned response. But the situation was open-ended enough for all of these; it helped to produce in the pupils both an understanding of the continuity of the past with the present and the common bond of humanity, as well as a realization of the fragmentary, uncertain nature of the evidence on which our understanding of the past is based.

The other example I want to mention is work done with some third year pupils at the same city comprehensive. The pupils had been studying the French Revolution; we decided to focus our attention on the reaction of the silk manufacturing town of Lyons to the execution of the king and the rule of the Jacobins. The class was divided into five groups—priests, silk merchants, poor, shopkeepers and nobles. Each group was given a briefing sheet. For example, the priests were told: 'The new republic has shut down the monasteries, taken control of the appointment of bishops and demanded an oath of allegiance from every priest. The Pope, the head of your church, has condemned all this. Some of you sympathize with the revolution. After all, many of you are poor and downtrodden, too. Can you convince the Jacobin officers of your loyalty; or, if you are against the Revolution, have you the courage to speak out and go to a martyr's death? Choose your names from the list below: Père Jean Chinon, Père Nicholas de Mandeville (son of a nobleman)...'. But each pupil had received and studied a general briefing sheet which gave key dates and set the task:

Key dates	**LYONS IN THE FRENCH REVOLUTION**
April 1792	France declares war on Austria and Prussia. France becomes a republic.
August 1792	Prussian army crosses into France. Checked at Valmy. Retreat of Prussians.
September 1792	September massacres—murder of prisoners in Paris by sans-culottes.
January 1793	Execution of Louis XVI.
February 1793	France declares war on England.
June 1793	Jacobins take over complete control of the country. The Terror begins.

August 1793   Levée en Masse.

September 1793   Law of Suspects.

June 1794   French victory at Fleurus: danger from invading
                     armies now over.
                     Fall of Robespierre: end of Terror.

Your task

It is November 1793. You are living in Lyons, in the South of France. Your occupation or class is given on a separate sheet. Your city is the second most important city in France. It produces silk. Many people in the city, especially the wealthy, have refused to obey the Jacobin Committee of Public Safety. The city raised an army. Troops were sent by the Jacobins from the capital to bring Lyons under the control of Paris. In October 1793 Lyons was conquered. The Committee of Public Safety is now determined to get rid of all trouble makers. COUTHON and COLLOT D'HERBOIS, officers of the Committee of Public Safety, arrive from Paris on 4 November 1793. They have ordered a guillotine. On 25 November their troops arrive. Couthon and Collot D'Herbois will be questioning all suspects. They will want to know what your feelings are about the Jacobin Committee of Public Safety, the Levée en Masse, the Law of Suspects and the invasion of France by Austrian, Prussian and British armies. They know little about your background but they will be anxious to guillotine you on the smallest excuse. They are not merciful men. Read the sources below. Using these, and the key dates above, prepare your case...

The eight sources were a map showing France and her enemies without and within; an extract from a Paris Jacobin letter to local branches, 1793 ('Friends, we are betrayed! To arms!...'); extracts from the Levée en Masse, August 1793 and the Law of Suspects, September 1793; a portrait of Maximilien Robespierre (1758–1794); a declaration of the Convention, made by demand of the Committee of Public Safety ('The city of Lyons shall be destroyed. Every habitation of the rich shall be demolished: there shall remain only the houses of the poor...'); a description of the entry of the Paris troops into Lyons, 25 November 1793, by the commander ('Terror was painted on every face. The deep silence that I took care to recommend to our brave troops made their march even more menacing and terrible...'); and finally a table showing the price rise during the period June 1790–September 1793.

The learning therefore centred on two interrelated activities: the careful study of the sources and the role play in which Couthon and Collot D'Herbois questioned the inhabitants of the city. Speculative thinking with a nice regard to such evidence as there was, was thus the main ingredient of the understanding that took place during the lively cross examination. The whole exercise was summed up in written work. Some wrote a description of the trial; others followed a more structured form.

LYONS IN THE FRENCH REVOLUTION
Answer all these questions from the point of view of the person whose role you played on Monday 25 June.

1 What role did you play? Give your name and occupation or class.

2 Give a brief (one paragraph) description of your character and where you live.

3 List FIVE words which best describe your feelings about events in Lyons, November 1793. Choose the most important of the five words and in a sentence or two explain why it is the most important word for you.

4 Look at source 1, the map. Now study sources 2, 3 and 4. From the point of view of the role you play, say how justified these attitudes and measures are. Mention each of the sources in your answer which should be about a paragraph in length.

5 Look at source 5. From the point of view of the role you play, in a paragraph indicate your feelings about Robespierre. Will he make a good leader?

6 Using all the sources, write FIVE questions which you, in role, would like to put to Robespierre. Choose the question you think most important and in a sentence or two explain why you consider it to be so.

Sarah's answer is as follows (spelling and syntax retained):

1 I played the part of Madam Beauchamp and was a shopkeeper.
2 I live in the middle of Lyons and own a grocery shop. I favoured the early part of the revolution but these policies of the Committee of Public Safety scare me as they want to get rid of the wealthy people and I do have quite a bit of money. However, armies do need to be clothed and fed and this might make me even wealthier.
3 My five words which best describe the events in Lyons are: unjustly, horrifying, violent, heartless. The most suitable word of the four is unjustly as the Jacobins have no right to kill all those who have money. The wealthy should be allowed a defence and not so hastily sent to the gillotine.
4 *Source 2.* This Paris Jacobin club letter to local branches is very unfair. It is leading people to kill others and threatens that if we do not kill the conspirators we shall be killed. It is a very unjustly letter as those who are conspirators should not be killed. I do not

agree with the Jacobins methods but see myself as no threat to a powerful army.

Source 3, article I. People should not be made to fight in the armies. A woman's job is to look after the children and a man's is to earn an honest living for them. I cannot be expected to make tents and clothing. I have to look after my shop. Certainly no children of mine would be forced to make lint from old linen.

Article II If public buildings are converted into barracks this means that are city would no longer have a church and we would not be able to walk down the street in fear of being arrested. It would make the city into a war zone.

Article IV This is indeed unfair as people like me need our horses to carry the food we sell. People have paid good money for horses and should not be forced to give them away. Many children have become attached to them.

Article V If Lyons is made into a factory of arms we are bound to be a set target for attacks and violence.

Source 4 These reasons for death are far too strong. Some of the reasons, for example, those who are unable to justify their means of existance are absolutely ridiculous.

5 Maximilien Robespierre frightens me very much. He is a very heartless man who has very strong opinions. If anyone disagrees with him they will be gillotined. He will make a very bad leader and everyone will fear him. He is far too cruel and merciless.

6 I would like to put this questions to Robespierre:
For what reasons do you feel so strongly for the poor?
Why are you prepared to take such drastic measures to make everyone equal?
What are your plans for Lyon in the future?
How will you make it into a once more pleasant community?
What will happen to the 1st and 2nd Estates?
I feel that question 3 is the most important that I would like to put to Robespierre because the future of Lyon is a very sensitive thing. Many of us are very anxious about how our lives are going to be changed in the future.

This shows, I feel, a real ability to weld sources together to show insight and understanding of the situation. She is, for example, clear that the Levée en Masse will upset the 'natural' order; families will be torn apart, churches desecrated, sources of livelihood taken away.

It would be naive to claim that the use of source material, site work, role play and speculative discussion will guarantee that pupils will engage in genuine historical reasoning; but they are the basic ingredients which will allow the teacher to set up situations in which pupils can operate in a variety of ways, unconstrained by notions of levels of thinking or formal operations. Time and again those of us who have embarked on these exploratory, open-ended exercises have been amazed at what has been achieved in terms of the pupils' understanding and their ability to get to grips with complex, abstract ideas such as imperialism, medieval economy, authority, power and class loyalty. By sloughing off the constraints of the Piagetian framework, we are immediately released into a world where virtually anything is possible with pupils, *provided that a way can be found of addressing the problem or issue*. We are, I am glad to say, being richly blessed with guidance in this matter. The pages of the Historical Association's journal *Teaching History* are full of descriptions of successful class teaching; the Schools Council Project 'History 13–16' and the Southern Regional Examination Board's admirable *Explorations* has much practical advice about teaching and assessing historical understanding. We are now in a position to say firmly: the national criteria for history are attainable by pupils of a wide range of age and ability. We have the materials, we have the teaching methods, we have the pupils; let us grasp the opportunity to make history a worthwhile and rewarding subject for all children.

Notes

1 INHELDER, B. and PIAGET, J. (1958) *The Growth of Logical Thinking from Childhood to Adolescence*. (English edition), Routledge and Kegan Paul.
2 *Ibid.* p. xx.
3 HALLAM, R.N. (1975) 'Study of the effect of teaching method on the growth of logical thought with special reference to the teaching of History'. PhD thesis, University of Leeds.
4 HALLAM, R.N. (1970) 'Piaget and thinking in history', in BALLARD, M. (Ed.) *New Movements in the Study and Teaching of History*. Temple Smith.
5 DRIVER, R. (1978) 'When is a stage not a stage?' *Educational Research* 21, pp. 54–61.
6 EGAN, K. (1983) *Education and Psychology* Methuen.
7 LEE, P.J. (1984) 'Historical Imagination' in DICKINSON A.K., LEE, P.J. and ROGERS P.J. *Learning History*. Heinemann. pp. 85–116.
8 WATTS, D.G. (1972) *The Learning of History* Routledge and Kegan Paul. p. 33.
9 BOOTH, M.B. (1980) 'A modern world history course and the thinking of adolescent pupils'. *Educational Review* 32, 3. pp. 245–257.

3 Adolescent Ideas About Evidence and Methodology in History

Denis Shemilt

Synopsis

Adolescent ideas about the nature and uses of historical evidence are investigated using samples of pupils following Schools Council Project 'History 13–16' and more traditional examination courses. A phenomenological methodology that directs attention away from issues of historical knowledge and linguistic competence and towards the conceptual apparatus that adolescents use to make sense of historical material is employed. The resultant model of adolescent conceptualization is close to that advanced *a priori* by Dickinson, Gard and Lee (1978)[1] and differs significantly from the model of attainment implicit in the proposals of the S.E.C. Grade Related Criteria (GRC) Working Party (1985).[2] Results from the present study suggest, first, that the distinction between 'historical reasoning' and 'historical enquiry' might prove unnecessary and perhaps ill-founded; and second, that GRC domains might be dimensioned in ways which emphasize the registration of increments in recalled knowledge and linguistic competence at the expense of increments in historical understanding. It must be stressed however, that findings of the present study are susceptible to more than one interpretation, and that the implied criticism of GRC domains is one of degree and not an absolute condemnation.

The Evaluation Strategy of British Schools Council Project History 13–16

The evaluation of the Schools Council Project 'History 13–16' involved the collection of two sorts of data relating to pupil performance. One group of data derives from a formal experimental design employing control groups, partialling out the influence of relevant independent variables and testing for pupil ability to transfer ideas and skills from taught to untaught contexts. Analyses of these data appertain both to the appraisal of teaching resources and methods, and to the identification of significant attainment correlates. A second group of data derives from more limited investigations into the ways in which adolescents make sense of what they are taught. The objects of enquiry in this instance are not *conceptual attainments* as such but the *constructs adolescents use to render the conceptual apparatus of the historian personally accessible and intelligible*. These data are used to suggest reasons as to why some teaching methods appear more successful than others, and why some concepts and tasks are relatively difficult to acquire and accomplish. The present chapter focusses solely upon this second strand in the evaluation of the Schools Council History Project.

The principal evaluation technique used to investigate adolescent conceptions of historical method was the interview. One hundred and sixty-seven 15-year-olds from twenty-four schools were interviewed over a five-month period. Interviews lasted between 60 and 90 minutes and were conducted individually. Interviewees were selected from a larger sample of around 1200 in order to facilitate matched pairs comparisons. Control and project pupils were matched for sex, IQ and social background. Interviews with 170 children grouped into eighty-five matched pairs being projected. Attrition of various kinds reduced the usable sample to seventy-three matched pairs for the investigation into pupils' methodological constructs.

In order to make interviews as fair as possible to both control and experimental subjects, a phenomenological interview technique was employed. Interviews were phenomenological in that:

(i) Pupils' own ideas about history rather than anything supplied by the interviewer were the objects of discussion. These 'ideas' were obtained in response to a pencil-and-paper elicited construct test inspired by the construct theory of George Kelly. The construct elicitation form invited respondents to construe paired statements as more or less sensible and to give their reasons for so doing. Ideally, supplied propositions should reference hypothetical events in order to minimize interference from substantive belief, but it was felt that this could confuse the concrete thinker and propositions relating to the origins of World War II, an event taught to none but known to all, were used instead.

The form succeeded in eliciting many curious and intriguing ideas, although few were cast in the neat bipolar form predicted by personal construct theory, for example,

Statement A is more sensible than B because...if there's only one event there can only be one cause.

Statement B is less sensible than A because...same reason.

Again:

> Statement A is more sensible than B because...A big effect needs a lot of causes to make it happen—the bigger the effect the more causes are needed.
>
> Statement B is less sensible than A because...It makes less sense.

The ECT was a failure insofar as results could not support the close construct analysis originally intended, but successful in that it proved an adequate platform on which to stage the phenomenological interview.

(ii)   The interviewer employed no fixed schedule but played the idiot-boy, refusing to accept anything as unequivocal or understood. In essence, his role consisted in declining to invent sense or meaning for the subject's constructions of history, in suspending the canons of intersubjectivity and of a shared 'form of life' upon which such interrogations normally rely. In practice, each subject was asked to clarify and amplify his ideas, to state the implications which could and could not be drawn, and to explicate the logic of his arguments—what made him think something, how he knew something, on what basis he would determine something and so on. The process continued until the respondent either came full circle to self-sustaining tautology, or until the questions ceased to make sense and provoke response. At this point, it was assumed, the interview had reached the limit of the subject's construction of reality—the point at which he perceived no question to be answered, no meaning to construe.

An iterative process of categorization, cluster analysis and recategorization was employed in an attempt to refine the model (or map) of adolescent thinking about history. This process was stopped after the third cycle because time did not allow for a more prolonged analysis.

This chapter concentrates upon two substantive clusters, dealing with *ideas about evidence* and *ideas about what historians do*. Transects through the ideational topography of these linked clusters are cut at four points. Although it is assumed that these transects correspond to arbitrarily fixed but genuine developmental stages, it should be noted that this is no more than an assumption, albeit one tested against measures of mental age, and that the developmental stages posited refer to the natural history of adolescent *ideas* not to *invariant* stages in the growth of *operational intelligence*. These four stages are discussed below.

Stage I: Knowledge of the Past is Taken-for-Granted

In terms of adolescent ideas about sources and about what historians do, this stage might be designated 'Evidence equals knowledge' and 'The historian as memory man' respectively. While pupils in receipt of the SCP 'History 13–16' course yield rather different ideas than those following traditional courses, the structural and developmental equivalence of ostensibly dissimilar constructs is worth noting.

Ideas about Historical Sources

For some adolescents the methodological problem of *how* we know does not appear to exist. Pupils *know* that what the teacher says is true because the truth is there to be known, just as they know that the teacher is talking because he is there to be seen and heard. Historical facts are construed as inviolate and pre-existent entities which might prove awkward to remember but are no more difficult to know than to read and write about. Although no adolescent would think of 'knowledge as being justified by authority' they frequently fall back upon the authority of teacher and text-book in order to explain why knowledge need not be questioned, for example:

> ...I just don't know. I've never thought about it...Teacher always tells us...

Despite being introduced to primary sources, other pupils see no sense in the question 'How do we know?' because the 'how' is given by the 'what': the past speaks for itself. For these students, people in the past left behind *knowledge* rather than *evidence* about their lives and activities. The following extract contains what is in one respect an extreme instance of this view:

INT: How do you know (that Hitler started World War II)?
SUB: I've read it.
INT: How did (sic) the author (of the book) know?
SUB: He might've been in the war or have been alive and knew what happened.
INT: How do people who write books know about cave men?
SUB: The same...only they've to copy the books out again and translate some of 'em.
INT: Are you saying that cave men wrote history books?
SUB: No, they'd carve it on the rocks.

One problem with many teaching materials based upon primary sources is a failure to allow for stage I thinking. Even if knowledge about evidence-based methods is not demanded, understanding of the question 'How do we know?' is usually presupposed. In practice, many adolescents required to use primary sources are given the means to answer questions they have not yet learned to ask. These pupils cannot distinguish the concepts *evidence* and *information*, and dismay their teachers by using primary sources exactly as they would text-book narratives.

Other problems arise when teachers make too abrupt a transition from 'read-and-copy' methods to enquiry-based approaches based on primary source materials and, in particular, when pupils use source materials with a minimum of teacher intervention. The enquiry based approach to learning can appear nonsensical to students unable to perceive a methodological problem and lacking a rudimentary concept of evidence. One 14-year-old delivered the following verdict upon the Schools Council 'What is history?' pack: 'There is too many questions and yet these questions don't learn you anything...You just learn bits and pieces about certain things...in some cases we didn't even find out what happened'.

Methodological questions specifically designed to focus attention upon evidence *qua* evidence can irritate pupils for whom the only sensible questions are those of fact, for example:

> ...some of the questions are pointless like 'what evidence does *The Times* put forward!?' Well what do we want to know that for?

Again:

> I would consider the project not historical knowledge but method of using logic.

And even when level I pupils adjust to enquiry-based learning, they do so by transforming it into a species of *search-and-record mission*:

> ...all the information is written down, you've just got to find the answers in the book.

With the difference that she now plays hide-and-seek with facts, this girl is engaged in exactly the same activity as when paraphrasing traditional text-books. Looking for 'answers' in the book, moreover, occasions difficulty when faced with sources tending to the same conclusion, for example:

> In this kind of history it gives you different opinions on things that you already know are true (because you've read them elsewhere).

Supportive evidence is here construed as crass redundancy. Likewise, contradictory sources make little sense, for example:

> ...as most evident in the Richard III booklet, most of the witnesses were lying and so, as far as I'm concerned, it was a total waste of time having most of them in.

Even 'detective' simulations fail when students conceive detective work as unearthing clues that, quite literally, *say* what happened, as though the Truth, wholly formed and readily identifiable, awaits discovery. Such pupils may consider themselves 'sensible' detectives when they resort to reference books for 'the answer'. This is not, however, to argue against the early introduction of pupils to original source materials, but merely to suggest that the evidence-information distinction cannot be taken-for-granted but must, in most cases, be painstakingly taught to children. This, of course, is difficult to do without reference to sources—which, however, may be relics rather than records in the first instance.

Three problems remain with the portrayal of stage I thinking about historical sources offered herein. The first problem is that the 'evidence-information' distinction ignores the logically primitive distinction between 'information' and 'knowledge'. This is perfectly true but does not signify inasmuch as the latter distinction is far from being developmentally primitive, even able adolescents finding it difficult to grasp the fact that secure and unequivocal knowledge does not automatically follow from full and reliable information, ie. that there is information that tells us such-and-such about x may be 'known' beyond a peradventure, but knowledge about x is bounded by the questions we ask as much as by the information we use and its status and security are determined to a large extent by the processes of inference and generalization employed to interrogate evidence and by the conclusions we are disposed to find reasonable and coherent.

For all practical purposes, therefore, the critical distinction must be that between 'evidence' and 'information/knowledge'.

The second problem follows from the fact that many pupils take knowledge about the past for granted because they have done little or no work with sources and have rarely, if ever, been asked 'How do we know?' Such pupils are rather different from those who construe sources as fragments of knowledge surviving from the past into the present, as pages from an original text book written as it was that tells it as it is. Both groups of pupils take knowledge of the past for granted, but do so for different reasons. This difference may be ignored to the extent that *all* GCSE candidates will henceforth have the opportunity to work with sources and address basic questions of epistemology and methodology.

The third and least tractable problem is whether or not stage I ideas, the disposition to see sources as offering text-book-like accounts of the past, can be remedied by teaching or whether they are manifestations of concrete operational thinking and remain, in consequence, incorrigible to teaching. This question is significant for assessment as well as for teaching given the overriding necessity for domain levels to reflect learnt attainments not the ability to learn.

There is no clear answer to this question. Stage I ideas certainly seem to exhibit many of the characteristics of concrete operational thinking. The failure to make sense of the abstract question 'How do I know?' other than as the concrete query 'How is this knowledge presented to me?' is consistent with explanations in terms of operational intelligence. Equally typical is the failure to grasp that a source may be taken to mean more than one thing. For these pupils there is no difference between source interpretation and source comprehension, hence their frustration with teachers who attempt to exploit uncertainty or ambiguity in the meaning of sources; for them, ambiguity is close to meaninglessness and a source either means something or it doesn't. Privately they may suspect that the teacher is covering up and doesn't really know the answer! The most interesting feature of stage I thinking is the inability to make sense of negative information (and hence of negative evidence), information as to what is not or cannot be the case. Knowing that x is *not the case*, knowing ~ x, is construed as ignorance not knowledge. Thus, for example, pupils at stage I are disposed to ignore evidence about who *could not* have been buried at Sutton Hoo on the grounds that this is not knowledge or, at the least, on the grounds that this is not anything worth knowing. As one boy wrote, 'I could say that my Grandad isn't buried there, but where does that get you?' It is easy to claim that the ability to appreciate and make proper use of negative information and evidence presuppose at least the readiness to move onto class logic and lattice operations, but is this in fact the case? Is it possible that the problem is conceptual not operational, that it follows from the premises given to pupils rather than from the logic they employ? The concept of *the known* is superordinate to those of the *known to be the case* and the *known not to be the case* as below:

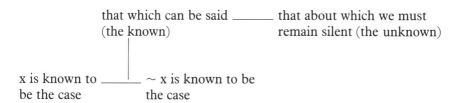

In class, however, pupils are routinely asked to give true and positive statements about what is the case and are censured for telling the teacher what s/he knows not to be the case. This latter is called 'false' or 'wrong'. The consequence is that the hidden curriculum of the classroom establishes and reinforces the following set and structure of constructs about knowledge:

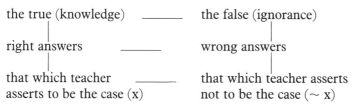

The implications of the learned construct, the right and true v the wrong and false, extend beyond the ability to use negative as well as positive information/evidence inasmuch as the crucial distinction between 'that which can be asserted or denied (the known)' and 'that about which we must remain silent (the unknown)' is not admitted at all. When knowledge about the past is construed solely in terms of 'known to be right' and 'known to be wrong' no allowance can be made for uncertainty in history. (It would be interesting to know how such pupils make sense of irrational numbers in mathematics!)

More sophisticated stage I pupils equate 'uncertainty' with incomplete information. The past still speaks for itself but the narrative has been torn to shreds and must be re-assembled, much like a jigsaw, from the surviving remnants—the proper name for which is 'primary sources'. Unfortunately, some pieces of jigsaw are lost and this means that the historian cannot always be sure what happened. What is 'known', however, is known with the same certainty as the *facts* of science and the solutions to algebraic equations.

As previously noted, this conceptual explanation of at least some features of stage I thinking is conjectural. Evidence now emerging from Peter Lee's video recordings of group work with low attainers promises to support the basic contention that the problem is largely ideational and not, or not entirely, one of operational intelligence, and that pupils of very modest abilities can be taught to operate at far higher levels than is usually assumed. (This is not to suggest, however, that Lee's current researches will verify the model of adolescent ideas and attainments advanced herein). There is thus every reason to suppose that all GCSE candidates can be taught to progress beyond stage I in their use of sources.

Teaching that asks children to suggest *possible answers* and then proceeds to discuss ways of determining *the* answer, or the *best* answer, can help ground necessary conceptual distinctions in *a live classroom regimen*. Equally, a teacher may ask pupils to suggest possible consequences instead of merely requiring them to memorize the contents of past lessons. The basic hypothesis here is that since the pupil's role as a history student is the only *experience* of what history is and how it is conducted, his construction of the subject must, to some extent, be generalized from this experience.

Ideas About What Historians Do

Adolescents accustomed to working with sources construe the historian's job as that of memory man who reads all the sources and remembers what they say. The historian knows all about the past, and he knows because he has read the sources—almost invariably termed 'the evidence'. In other words, the historian is just like one of themselves excepting that he could write for days and days and always get 10 out of 10, or 10,000 out of 10,000. And his knowledge is justified in the same way as their own—it comes from reading the sources and it's right because it's right.

Pupils unused to working with original sources typically offer bizarre and inappropriate answers to the question 'How do we know?' Some, for instance, assume that the historian 'finds out' in the same way as the scientist, although none interviewed were able to illustrate how this might be done.

> *INT:* Yes! ...Have you ever tried to solve problems in history in this way—I mean, have you ever tried this method to see if it works?
>
> *SUB:* ...Not really, no. But that's how we do it in chemistry, so I know it works OK.

Other adolescents view the historian as a used-ideas salesman, a purveyor of propaganda:

> *SUB:* ...you can't do an experiment (in history). You just have to guess.
>
> *INT:* How can the historian distinguish a good guess from a bad guess? (This is a leading question but the respondent copes with it.)
>
> *SUB:* A good guess would be based on the facts you've got and not assuming anything. (She almost invents the concept of 'evidence').
>
> *INT:* Explain 'not assuming anything'.
>
> *SUB:* If you're not sure whether something happened or not, you might assume it did and make up an idea based on that.
>
> *INT:* Good. But how would you distinguish between two guesses which could (...transcript garbled...) known facts?
>
> *SUB:* You pick which one you like best...which is most interesting—or the one that's for your (social) class.

The confusion here is between opinion and *justifiable assertion*, and the student fails to realize that when no one account can be given rational preference over alternative possibilities, no account can be offered. The teacher has encouraged class discussion, encouraging pupils to propound their own ideas, but in allowing them to consider these ideas uncritically— or even as valid by existential fiat—he has led them to accept 'what they think' as naïvely as other students accept the printed word. The impression is very strong, however, that had this girl (and many other stage I subjects) been introduced to source-based history, they would quickly leave stage I ideas a long way behind.

Stage II: Evidence = Privileged Information About the Past

Stage II thinking is characterized by the realization that historical truth is negotiable; by the acceptance of 'How do we know?' as a sensible question; by a dawning apprehension of what evidence is; and by the acquisition of a specific methodological vocabulary. In the following extract, for example, the respondent uses words like 'bias' and accepts that there may be more than one possible answer to questions of fact and interpretation:

SUB: It depends on which way the historian looks at it which conclusion he comes to.
INT: Are all these conclusions as good as each other?
SUB: Not really...(..)...it just depends on how biased the historian is—like with a newspaper.
INT: Can we say which is the best conclusion—the best answer?
SUB: No because this depends on the people alive at the time and even they'd disagree.

This argument is flawed: differences of interpretation are rarely reducible to the bias of professional historians, nor should contemporary *witnesses* be accorded the degree of authority bestowed by this boy. In this he is a typical stage II thinker, however. Evidence is frequently identified with the *reports* of *eyewitnesses*, and these reports are typically construed as problematic for the historian only insofar as some contain second-hand material, others are written long after the occurrences in question when memory is failing, and still others record the testimony of biased and otherwise unreliable witnesses. The past is still seen as speaking for itself, but it is no longer thought to speak with a single authoritative voice, nor are its utterances accepted without question.

Ideas About Historical Sources

Although stage II pupils hold tight to the notion of evidence, conceptual understanding is deficient in two crucial respects. First, pupils fail to distinguish records from relics, sources claiming to *report* events or document situations (archives, registers, directories, diaries, autobiographies and so on) from sources making no conscious commentary or catalogue but standing as a constituent element within the events or situations evidenced (Acts of Parliament, popular ballads, advertisements, indentures, ditches, dykes, scrimshaws, etc). The borderline between 'records' and 'relics' is as blurred as that between 'primary' and 'secondary' sources; archives, for example, are records of practical use to the people for whom they are kept and may play a very practical role in institutional life. Depending upon the historian's purposes, certain categories of source may be treated as either record or as relic evidence.

Adolescents err in two ways. First, by treating all relics as though they were records and scanning them for information they fail to recognize inferences as inferences. A 1923 London-Edinburgh train ticket is evidence that tickets were used on British railways and may give some indication of the cost of rail travel, but it makes no general statements about anything at all. Tickets may have been exceptional. The charge recorded may have been unusually high or low for any one of a number of reasons.

Second, adolescents typically interrogate all sources for reliability. Properly speaking, this can only be asked of 'records' not of 'relics'. If a 'relic' is authentic it is reliable—simply because it is a piece of the past and not testimony about the past. Of course, even authentic relics can mislead the historian, but the problem here is one of inference and inductive generalization not of reliability. The 1923 railway ticket was a record testifying to an LMS guard that *the person holding it* had paid his fare (not proof positive against fraud but proof beyond peradventure). An abandoned ticket on a station platform signified nothing in 1923 and asserts nothing to the historian in 1980. Once abandoned it ceased to serve as a record. A relic is a piece of the action which may help the historian reconstruct what happened—actually or typically. It no more describes the action than the exchange of a banknote describes the transfer of goods or the movement of gold in bank vaults.

Of course, *relics* that are also *records* may contain inaccurate information—designed to mislead contemporaries, for instance! An assertion about the accuracy or honesty of the evidence necessarily involves collateral assertions about the facts of the case evidenced, if only because the evidence *is* one of the facts in the situation evidenced. In the case of all relics, therefore, whether they are also records or not, the concept of reliability is redundant. What has to be established, in lieu of source reliability, is the nature of its relation to the situation evidenced, is exactly what it is, and this may not be what it appears or pretends to be. Stage II students persist in treating 'relic' sources as though produced by witnesses for the benefit and possible deception of small boys engaged in Schools Council projects; instance the examination candidate who deemed King John's household expenses 'biast so you'd think King John was very clean taking baths everywhere he traveled. Its not reliable neither because I don't think King John would spend so much money he just wanted to make you think he wasn't so mean as he was' (1976 unseen methods paper 16+). The problem for the teacher is that most documentary and pictorial evidence actually *says* something, in words or pictures, susceptible to misconstruction as the account of a witness producing testimony for posterity. Artefactual and site evidence, which just 'is' and 'says' nothing about anything, is eminently suited to pupils at this stage of conceptual development.

The second deficiency in stage II thinking subsumes the first. It is the failure to fully differentiate the concepts *evidence* and *information*. Two ideas are involved here:

(i) The historian *evaluates* evidence; that is, he does not necessarily accept what a source purports to say or show.

(ii) The historian *goes beyond the information given:* that is, he may use a source as evidence to support propositions that the source *does not* purport to assert.

At stage II, pupils have realized the need for evaluation but not for inference. (They may, in fact, make inferences without being conscious of doing more than 'clever' comprehension). The failure to *reflexively* go beyond the information given reinforces the disposition to approach all sources as though listening to testimony which may be accepted or rejected but under no circumstances added to. For such pupils, the historian's picture of the past is *reconstituted or reassembled* from evidence rather than *reconstructed upon the basis of* evidence. If at stage I the historian may be compared to a rich gallery owner collecting pictures of the past, at stage II he is seen as something close to a restorer of old masters.

A secondary feature of stage II conceptualization is the tendency to accept and to use technical vocabulary without fully comprehending the substantive concepts to which these terms refer. The adolescent grasps something of the importance of 'bias', for example, and can identify it with reasonable precision, but his *picture concept* of the source-reality nexus means that a *biased account* is indistinguishable from *an account revealing prejudice*. An account of J.S. Mill addressing a proletarian audience and inveighing against the inveterate mendacity of the English working-class is considered biased. Students who legitimately if unconsciously *infer* bourgeois liberal prejudice against the nineteenth century proletariat conclude that they have *evaluated* the source and demonstrated its *bias* and unreliability.

A tendency to equate *authenticity* and *reliability* derives from the same epistemological error. Reliability is thought to relate to that which a source directly avers; and the notion of a source being reliable evidence of something it does not purport to say (Bismarck's motives, Henry II's conscience or whatever) makes little sense to the stage II student. Similarly, the concept of *authenticity* becomes redundant when every source is treated as though it were an eye witness *report* (even if known not to be) and 'accuracy' thought the only issue of consequence.

Because the stage II student only construes evidence as something to be criticized and not as a basis for inference, he can only link the concept of reliability to what a source directly says or shows. He sees the historian as no more than a good listener and sagacious critic and cannot, in consequence, relate the notion of reliability to the historian's questions and purposes. It follows, therefore, that the reliable source is seen to *inherit the authority divested from the text book narrative*, and the question of exactly *how* this reliable evidence is to be used does not arise: the answer is self-evident, for example:

INT: How would you find out?
SUB: Study the evidence.
INT: How would that help?
SUB: ...The evidence would help...because you'd have to find the connection.
INT: How would you find 'the connection'?
SUB: ...By studying the evidence.

This girl knows that evidence is important but can see no difficulties attaching to its use.

One manifestation of the transfer of *authority* from text-book to evidence is the precedence accorded primary over secondary sources. Adolescents readily see the wisdom in basing their own essays upon a careful and (to them) exhaustive evaluation of available sources, but fail to realize that they are producing secondary accounts. (They are doing homework which is something very different). The secondary accounts of other people are, in consequence, often regarded as akin to fiction—'the writer didn't see what happened, so how can he know?'—rather than as critical syntheses of primary evidence. When secondary and primary accounts differ, stage II pupils almost invariably prefer the latter, rarely stopping to consider that the primary source may have been weighed and found wanting.

Ideas About What Historians Do

The role of the historian is thought to involve the identification of true and accurate pictures of the past.

Stage II students understand that knowledge of history is not self-guaranteeing but rests upon evidence that may itself mislead, for example:

...it is showing how difficult it is to establish what happened...I think they are trying to show how difficult it is to establish facts because of differences in evidence. And they are trying to show that history is detective work, because of the need to sift through evidence to get to the core.

Typically, this boy sees the historian's job as winnowing the true from the false, but he has clearly distinguished 'facts' and 'evidence', source and narrative, and has progressed some way towards stage III thinking.

Pupils are also beginning to apprehend the uncertainty attaching to the essence, and not merely to the completeness, of historical narrative, for example:

It (the Schools Council Project) also showed me that everything we read in a history book is not necessarily true and that a number of points can be argued and different conclusions found.

The point at which the student begins to think of ways of reducing this uncertainty marks the transition to stage III.

Stage III: Evidence is a Basis for Inference About the Past

In the student's mind, the concepts *evidence* and *information* are now fully differentiated and, as inference from evidence becomes self-conscious, the stage III thinker begins to look for a method to guide his use of source materials. This would seem to demand the exercise of elementary logic, but in history pure deduction rarely yields usable and, in particular, very interesting conclusions. Ideally, therefore, the adolescent should be forced back upon contextual knowledge and what Hexter calls the 'second record'[3] to suggest propositions worth testing against evidence. He should then use evidence in a way that is logical without being analytical, a method Martin Booth has characterized as 'adductive'.[4] In reality, whilst learning to construe history method in this way, the adolescent is either forced back upon his own preconceptions—which he may insist upon having 'deduced' from the evidence—or, more productively, upon questions and possibilities suggested by the teacher. Even at stage III, therefore, teacher intervention is at a premium; the pupil cannot yet be left to rediscover Thucydides' footsteps. There is no suggestion that any special kind of thinking or reasoning is involved in historical enquiry. The words 'deduction' and 'adduction' qualify types of arguments not mental processes. Historical arguments are necessarily deductive in the unexceptional sense that conclusions must follow from premises, but the terms of these arguments are often uncertain or contentious because we lack precise data about the contents of people's minds and are unable to reconstruct the actual structures and concatenations of events. It follows that in many, and perhaps most, historical arguments the key terms (or premises) are suppressed or uncertain. The historian, therefore, is concerned to *adduce* key terms and values for his arguments, to reconstruct intentions, interactions and saliences in respect of which actions become intelligible and events causally explicable.

One characteristic of the adductive method is that instead of drawing analytical, and hence tautologically true, inferences from evidentially supplied premises,[5] the historian more usually utilizes evidence to *reduce the uncertainty* attaching to particular questions. Some 14-year-olds are well able to abstract this feature of history method from exercises structured so as to emphasize it, for example:

(The Sutton Hoo unit) involved...constructing theories about a burial...A map showing the area in which the ship was found would explain a lot more about the vessell...(and) could help narrow the truth down.

If we assume this boy to be proposing the 'elimination of possibilities' in the phrase 'help narrow the truth down'—a reasonable supposition in view of his earlier reference to 'constructing theories about a burial'—he has grasped that the impossibility of 'right answers' in history does not compromise the possibility of 'worthwhile explanation' and 'justifiable assertion'. Strictly speaking 'right answers' may be found in history but without our being privileged to claim their discovery. The concept of the 'right answer', of 'accurate description', is therefore redundant.

History is the only empirical discipline in which NONE of the *facts* it seeks to establish and explain are given by direct sensory observation. History uses evidence, depends upon evidence, but is not *about* the evidence. We can make statements about evidence, and about the accuracy and comprehensiveness of historians' use of evidence that are different in kind from statements made about the past evidenced. If someone challenges what we say about the evidence, we settle the matter by *showing* him the original. If someone accepts the existence and content of a given corpus of sources but chooses to question what we say about the past, we are reduced to arguing the logic, the plausibility or the economy, of our case. 'Correct assertions' can be made about evidence; but about the past evidenced our statements are only ever more or less justifiable.

Ideas About Historical Sources

At stage I uncertainty = ignorance; at stage II uncertainty = lack of (reliable) evidence; at stage III uncertainty follows from the methodology of the historian and is conceived as inhering in the nature of the historical enterprise because this is now seen to involve the interpretation of data and the testing of hypotheses against evidence; the lesson of the sources has ceased to be self-evident, for example:

SUB: You look at the event and work backwards.
INT: How?
SUB: ...I'd think I'd make two or three suggestions and then test them by looking at the evidence.

This is the stage III response par excellence. It is not always so obvious what the pupil is saying, nor that he is fully aware of what he is saying. The following extract, for instance, is from a girl who may have hit upon a stage III idea by accident not design:

> *SUB:* I think you have to look at sources...look at books and documents and things...you have to...have a lot more facts...(...)... If somebody wrote a letter that you had been to London (= If someone wrote a letter to you from London?)...and you thought that person had caused a fire, you could look at the letter and prove he couldn't have been the cause of the fire. You've got to work it step by step and use the evidence.

The essential points of this somewhat confused argument are clear enough: the historian has an idea, that person 'p' started a fire, and tests this hypothesis against the available evidence.

A perhaps unintended feature of the above example is that the historian is shown using evidence to *disprove* a hypothesis, but one very unexpected finding is the frequency with which adolescents advance a version of the *falsification postulate* namely, the idea that evidence is used to *eliminate* rather than verify hypotheses, for example:

> *SUB:* You look at evidence and probably make an educated guess. (The phrase 'educated guess' was very common among pupils in one school).
> *INT:* What makes the guess educated?
> *SUB:* There are differences between picking a guess out of a hat and using the evidence to make an estimation.
> *INT:* How would you use the evidence to make an educated guess?
> SUB: You look to see which evidence led to one answer and which to another...see which had *most* evidence pointing to it...You've got to check on the evidence to see which could be false.

This boy is tentative to a fault, failing to perceive that evidence allows us to reject propositions with more confidence than we can ever *affirm* them, and he cannot, in consequence, be said to have a particularly secure grasp of the concept. Nonetheless, he may be said to possess a conception of history method transcending the commonsense constructions of every-day experience. He is beginning to see something of the historian's world, if but dimly and from afar. It is surprising that so many students come to think in this way especially since they frequently advance these views in schools in which teachers deny having taught them to evaluate hypotheses. Perhaps the approach transfers from Nuffield Science? Or perhaps some children are able to reinvent the wheel?

Ideas About What Historians Do

The major advance at stage III is that the historical detective is now seen as doing much more than scouring records in order to unearth the 'truth' about the past. Like Sherlock Holmes, he has a *method* and is no mere beachcomber along the shores of time. Conclusions are now *inferred* rather than *read off* from sources. If the product of the historian's labours is still thought of as 'true' in a sense uncomfortably close to that of the mathematician and physicist, the past is no longer construed as speaking for itself in any directly accessible fashion.

Less impressive is the detailed exposition of how these sophisticated strategies may be operated in practice. Few have any ideas as to how the historian formulates hypotheses, for example:

INT: How would the evidence allow you to test them (your ideas about what happened)?
SUB: Some would fit and some would contradict it.
INT: Where would you get the suggestions from—you want to test?
SUB: I'd look at the probabilities.
INT: What are they?
SUB: What's most likely. (Further questioning gets nowhere).

The historian may be unsure about the precise facts of the case, but the pupil assumes 'what's most likely' to be directly given. No less naïve are ideas about exactly how evidence is used to test hypotheses. Despite having worked with source materials, some adolescents persist in the use of language more appropriate to the chemistry laboratory, weighing evidence by counting sources pro and con some particular proposition, for example:

SUB: You could sort them out into sets...(...)...and see which was the heaviest reason as in a balance.

This boy understands that evidence can point in more than one direction but advocates a crudely numerical decision procedure. More sophisticated, but still mechanistic, is the quest for *maximum coherence*, what one boy called looking 'for common denominators' in evidence. At its most elaborate, this technique (which the evidence of public examinations proves adolescents can operate as well as discuss) amount to a holistic approach wherein all data are simultaneously considered and a 'best possible fit' adduced. Large numbers of pupils can make progress with these techniques, but few develop a fully refined *adductive* methodology. (More will undoubtedly do so given advances in materials and teaching).

At stage III, the pupils' ideas about the evaluation of evidence are also more developed. Here, too, self-conscious methods supersede stage II intuitions. In the following extract, for example, the pupil has discovered the simple procedural rule of checking provenance:

Questioning people for and against Richard (III) was difficult because before we could question them we had to look at their background and find out what they were like, and if they were unreliable we could not trust them.

Typically here too, the request for provenance is somewhat mechanistic and betrays little real understanding of what might be involved in looking 'at their background'. This girl has barely escaped the shadows of stage II thinking.

The principal deficiency in stage III conceptualization, and the root of the rigid and mechanistic approach to evidence, is a failure to apprehend the significance of a source having been produced in the past. Historical detective exercises are approached in exactly the same way as are contemporary simulations. A dawning awareness of the *historicity* of historical data is the significant development at stage IV.

Stage IV: Awareness of the Historicity of Evidence

At stage I historical knowledge is seen as *given*; at stage II it is something to be *discovered*; the stage III thinker sees it as having to be *worked out* by rational process; and at stage IV written history is beginning to be recognized as no more than a *reconstruction* of past events, a reconstruction, moreover, which makes visible connections and continuities, moralities and motives, that contemporaries would not have perceived, nor perhaps have understood. Implicit in this conception is the recognition that the methodological problems inhering in knowledge of the historic past are more profound and far-reaching than those attaching to the recent or personal past. A Sherlock Holmes with antiquarian interests ceases to model for the ideal historian.

Interpretation of interview data stands in perpetual danger of either exaggerating or underestimating adolescent thought. Interpretation of lower levels is more likely to 'write down' children's arguments; interpretation of higher levels is more prone to the converse. The danger derives from the fact that the objects of construction are footnote commentaries upon pupils' ideas, statements as to what responses presuppose and entail rather than directly aver. This is necessary since conscious theorizing and well-wrought philosophy cannot be demanded of 15-year olds; but it may easily lead to some elaborate conceptual artifice being spun around an ill-considered and intellectually empty conversational ploy, for example:

> *SUB:* In history (in contrast to science) you have to work backwards.
> *INT:* Why?
> *SUB:* You can't repeat what happened the first time.
> *INT:* How would you work backwards?
> *SUB:* If you have a thing and you know what caused it you then go and find what caused that...and so on...You've to take different steps...(...)...You must use common knowledge...You can see actions and then reactions—and then you look for motives.

This girl is quite clear in her own mind that because the past is not replicable, experimental re-enactment will not work in history. But she is very uncertain as to what is actually involved in 'working backwards'. Causation is her first touchstone, and when this looks like dragging her down to a dark and muddy bottom she lets go to clutch for preference onto something called 'common knowledge'. This may signify 'commonsense' but, just possibly in view of her succeeding statement, it may mean 'knowledge of what makes people tick'; if so, she is on the verge of grasping that the historian must do more than *compute* probabilities on the basis of *best fit* with available evidence, that he must also make sense of the material from a perspective *imputed* to his predecessors. Having consciously repudiated experimental re-enactment and, thereby, put the methodological problems of history in contrasting focus, the student may be making assumptions consistent with *empathetic reconstruction* the method par excellence of history.

She may, on the other hand, be casting around for something to say and, having run up a causal cul-de-sac, have recalled in desperation her teacher's emphasis upon people and motivation.

Even more dubious is the interpretation of illustrative material. Concrete examples may be little more than rote regurgitations of past lessons, demonstrating memory rather than generalized historical understanding. The following extract, for example, records conversation with a student who, having outlined the historian's need to reconstruct motives, offers an instance of how this might be done:

INT: How would you try to find out what those motives were?

SUB: ...I'd think about the realistic possibilities—for example, for an invasion there's differences in ideas, natural resources ...land...(and on?)

INT: How would you come to a decision when you seem to have a lot of 'realistic possibilities'?

SUB: I'd study the backgrounds of the countries and you'd trace over previous disputes and find out what they were in need of...

It is easy to imagine how this boy's teacher may have taught the Schools Council Project 'Arab-Israeli' unit. Nevertheless, there is no alternative but to take the extract at face value, and this reveals an able boy explaining how the historian generates hypotheses (significantly called 'realistic possibilities' not just 'ideas' or 'guesses') from analysis of historical context.

The presumption of contextual knowledge in history method is fraught with epistemological hazards, the most obvious of which is the danger of *infinite regress* if the possibility of secure knowledge of the past is thought prerequisite for finding out about the past. (If there is a problem in the determination of events at Lexington Green, can the relevant contextual 'knowledge' be considered any the less problematic?) This peril only obtains, however, if, with Ranke, we pretend to 'tell it like it was', if we say of historical narrative, 'This is an accurate description of the case' instead of advancing the more modest claim: 'We are more entitled to present this story than any other; this is what we are entitled to *say* about the case in question'. Dickinson, Gard and Lee, make a similar point:

> '...knowledge in history is acquired only through evidence, but only where there is prior knowledge of the past can any particular piece of evidence be used as such.
>
> The resolution of this paradox lies in recognising...that history is an ongoing public tradition...The works of other historians are not just second-best sources of information, but part of a common framework in terms of which historical questions, interpretations and evidence are given meaning. It is not simply information which is at issue here, but a whole way of looking at the world.'[6]

It is precisely because primary evidence needs to be indexed by means of secondary sources (contextual knowledge amounting to nothing other than witting or unwitting acceptance of secondary material) that *uncertainty* is built into the fabric of an academic enterprise that involves accepting a library of published texts in order to rewrite a single volume. The fact of there being no escape from this procedure, the lack of any ground that close examination will prove bedrock, also explains why the historian is committed to *reconstructing* rather than *describing* the past.

We may find a Popperian analogy helpful here: 'The empirical basis of objective science has nothing 'absolute' about it. Science does not rest upon solid bedrock. The bold structure of its theories rises, as it were, above a swamp. It is like a building erected on piles. The piles are driven down from above into the swamp, but not down to any natural or 'given' base; and if we stop driving the piles, it is not because we have reached firm ground. We simply stop when we are satisfied that the piles are firm enough to carry the structure, at least for the time being.'[7]

These epistemological questions fret few adolescent minds, however. Context is seen or assumed to matter for more naive reasons, for example:

> *SUB:* (Explaining how he would use evidence tending to support more than one version of events). I'd look at their ideas ...and would look at some different incidents which might offer some guidelines.
>
> *INT:* How would you do this?
>
> *SUB:* I'd try to find out as much as I could to judge their reactions.
>
> *INT:* Can you think of an example?
>
> *SUB:* ...Yes, did the Arabs and Jews...were they...couldn't they get on because of race or religion? You might look to see how each

reacted before to people of different race and then to different religions...It could give you a lead.

The example is ingenuous, sufficiently so for it to be confidently ascribed to the pupil not his teacher, but nevertheless exemplifies the use of data for comparative purposes with references to the historical context.

Stage IV thinking about the importance of contextual knowledge in an evidence-based methodology is limited in a number of ways. First, the adolescent's view of what counts as relevant historical context is a severely restricted one. The importance of immediate *situation* may be appreciated, but the significance of the wider social and cultural *milieu* is rarely seen. Thus, when studying emigration from early nineteenth-century Britain, even the most able 15-year-olds will neither use nor regard information on political, religious and industrial developments excepting when exercises are specifically designed to turn attention in these directions. Equally myopic is the disposition to use knowledge of antecedent but not of succeeding events when engaged in source-based work.[8]

Second, the stage IV thinker is not always sure whether or not contextual knowledge counts as 'evidence', and if so, of what sort. He often fails to recognize such knowledge as 'secondary source' material, especially if presented to a different format—without the heading 'Source J', 'Clue 3' or whatever, and with no attribution of provenance—or if dredged from the recesses of his own memory. Even when background information is categorized as secondary source material by the pupil, he remains unsure as to whether it should be subject to evaluative scrutiny.

Ultimately, the student must learn that *the range of convenience* of an enquiry determines what information he must ground in primary sources and what superimpose upon analysis of secondary sources. Before this point is reached, he may have to learn the more subtle craft of reworking secondary narrative, but this too seems considerably in advance of stage IV conceptualization as here described. A more mature understanding of what 'contextual knowledge' is and how it can be used may need to wait upon such conceptual achievements.

Finally, the pupil who construes at stage IV is limited in his ideas of how contextual knowledge may be used.[9] Pupils at stage III can use background information to pose mechanical questions about provenance. 'Who wrote S?' 'Is this author to be trusted?' and so on. At stage IV they can, without being specifically instructed to do so, consider the particular circumstances under which a source was produced, querying the intended audience, the author's access to information, his purposes in writing and what would be considered relevant and irrelevant, etc. But these questions are almost invariably posed with source *evaluation* in mind. The pupil seeks to establish the *reliability* but not the *meaning* of what is said. Rarely does he ask, 'What would these words have meant to people living at the time it was produced?' (Archaic and specialist terminology is dealt with by dictionary definition in exactly the same way as other big words in the adolescent's expanding vocabulary—'demesne' is learned like 'valency'). Meaning is assumed to be *constant in space and time* and the adolescent perceives no need to *interpret in context*; if he can make sense of a source this is seen as *the* sense of the source. This is not to say that able 15-year olds cannot attempt reconstruction of the values and beliefs, logic and perspectives, of people of a different time and place, for they certainly can do so, but they are less disposed to empathetically reconstruct the situation in which evidence may have been produced and will only apply contextual knowledge of values and ideas to source interpretations if presented with material that cannot be readily assimilated to a twentieth-century world view.

Given these limitations, how should the teacher present contextual information to students engaged in source-based work? The following suggestions may prove useful:

(i) Background information should always be presented as secondary source material and never as extra-evidential data. Pupils may be encouraged to regard what they themselves remember as secondary material, and may even be requested to present it as such.

(ii) Exercises using 'primary', 'secondary' and 'primary and secondary', sources may feed into discussion of how each might be used. Pupils below stage IV conceptualization might find such discussion too confusing to be of use.

(iii) The teacher should note that background data can relate to source-based exercises in different ways. It can relate to the topic under investigation or to the sources used in the investigation. It can relate to the topic by widening the investigator's in-depth understanding of social and cultural setting or by reminding him of developmental context, of the topic's location in a time-line. Contextual information may be applied to sources as an aid to interpretation or in order to assess reliability and authenticity. It is important to note that these areas are not equally accessible to children at any given level of conceptual attainment, to limit exercises to consideration of one area at a time, and to render the nature of each task as visible and unequivocal as possible.

(iv) Background information should be limited and highly selective. This means, of course, that the student will possess pre-selected evidence rather than background knowledge, but it is essential for him not to be swamped with 'background noise'. Irrelevant material is difficult for adolescents to handle and, if presented too early or in too large amounts, degrades the pupil's capacity to make sense of what he is doing.

Notes

1 DICKINSON, A.K., GARD, A., and LEE, P.J. (1978) 'Evidence in history and the classroom' in DICKENSON, A.K. and LEE, P.J. *History Teaching and Historical Understanding*. Heinemann.
2 Secondary Education Council. (1985) *Draft Grade Criteria*.
3 HEXTER, J.H. (1971) *The History Primer* Basic Books.
4 BOOTH, M.B. (1980) 'History teaching in the U.K., past, present and future' *Australian History Teacher*, 7.
5 Of course, *some* use of evidence is classically deductive.
6 DICKINSON, A.K., GARD, A. and LEE, P.J. (1978) *op. cit.* p. 10.
7 POPPER, K.R. (1959) *The Logic of Scientific Discovery*. Hutchinson, p. 111.
8 There are exceptions to both rules; some 15-year-olds do use knowledge of period as well as of local situation, and some set evidence in its full developmental context, but this is rare.
9 No account has been taken of the use of contextual knowledge as background information since this is tantamount to the student writing a secondary source from memory and employing it in conjunction with others directly presented.

4   Children's Concepts of Empathy and Understanding in History

Rosalyn Ashby and Peter Lee

Synopsis

This chapter offers a brief examination of what is and what is not involved in the concept of empathy in history and its connections with historical understanding. It proposes the possibility of establishing a set of levels for the analysis of children's ideas of what is involved in empathy, in the light of recent and current research. A provisional and tentative outline of such a set of levels is exemplified by transcripts of children discussing past institutions and practices. Some consequences for teaching are considered.

The Nature and Value of Empathy

During the last decade 'empathy' has firmly established itself as something which has an important place in history. It is a major item among 'History 13–16' objectives, and an important target in project examinations. It turned up—perhaps less successfully—in more traditional (but for some teachers apparently not traditional enough) AEB 'O' level examinations. It has a place in the national criteria. It appears increasingly in the literature of history education.

Yet despite all this, and despite the fact that 'empathy' has on the face of it achieved the status of a technical term in history, it is surprisingly difficult to pin down its meaning, or to get any agreement among teachers or examiners as to how it should be taught, or what sort of tests might validly assess it. In reality 'empathy' is still at best a shorthand term for a cluster of related notions, and 'empathy exercises' cover a range of tasks with very different goals. The purpose of this chapter is not to offer definitions, or to map out a viable concept of empathy, but to explore children's ideas about what is involved in understanding other people's behaviour in the past, as manifested in their attempts to make sense of alien institutions and actions. Nevertheless, it is obviously difficult to say anything at all about any of this without at least some more or less dogmatic statement about our own presuppositions.

Empathy in history is an achievement: it is where we get to when we have successfully reconstructed other peoples' beliefs, values, goals, and attendant feelings. To say that a pupil has 'empathized' (if it is to say anything sensible—or grammatical—at all) is to say that he or she is in a position to entertain a set of beliefs and values which are not necessarily his or her own. It is not to say that the pupil has gone through any particular—let alone special—process. In general empathy in history rests on evidential reconstruction, but although this must be broadly inferential, it does not have to involve formally articulated reasoning rather than intuitive leaps, sudden flashes of inspiration and the like. If someone wishes to convince us that a reconstruction of (say) some historical agent's beliefs and values is correct, he or she must set out in a relatively formal way the relationship between the evidence and the reconstruction. But this does not mean that in setting out why we should accept the account, the historian is telling us that the process by which he or she achieved the empathetic reconstruction was itself a piece of formal, methodical reasoning. Equally, it does not rule out such a methodical, conscious process of inference either. Empathy, to reiterate, is an achievement, not a particular process.

What sort of achievement is empathy? Entertaining the beliefs, goals, and values of other people or—insofar as one can talk in this way—of other societies, is a difficult intellectual achievement. It is difficult because it means holding in mind whole structures of ideas which are not one's own, and with which one may profoundly disagree. And not just holding them in mind as inert knowledge, but being in a position to work with them in order to explain and understand what people did in the past. All this is hard because it requires a high level of thinking.

Genuine difficulty of this kind must be distinguished from other problems which are often discussed in the context of empathy. Because empathy is seen as a mysterious process, it is frequently suggested that it is virtually an impossible task. How can we get into another mind, feel other people's feelings, really *identify* with others? Or, put in a 'harder' technological idiom, how do we get inside the 'black box'? There is no black box to get into. We understand people every day without having to cope with any of these misplaced and misleadingly phrased questions. We ascribe intentions, grasp motives, infer beliefs and goals on the basis of what people do and say, and for the purposes of our understanding, what people do counts more than what they say. In any case what they say is part of what they do. What is said and what is done only make sense because we have some overall grasp of the workings and conventions of language and the social world. Hence people's intentions are not the private contents of black boxes, but part of their doing things which have public meanings. It is only because we normally understand what people are trying to do that some people are able to disemble and mislead. The problems in achieving empathy are a result of the complexity of mind, not its essential privacy.

In history of course the problems are compounded by the uncertainties of the remaining evidence. It is not so much that we cannot cross-question people in the past, but that the public and social meanings of what they do are not necessarily the same as ours. We sometimes have to reconstruct a whole way of life at the same time as we make sense of the actions which are part of it and artefacts which are all that remain of it. This means that we can seldom be sure that we have got things right; but seldom being sure is no special problem for empathy, but part of the situation of historical research in general.

For history as part of education, perhaps the most important task is to help children acquire a disposition to empathize, and to develop strategies for its successful achievement. 'Helping children to acquire a disposition' may sound like training them into habits, and no doubt there will be something of this in effective teaching. But it also means getting children to understand what counts as empathy, and why it matters—what difference it makes. Pupils who understand this, and have learnt the kind of moves which help them to achieve empathy, have not just taken a step forward in their history, but are more likely to be able to cope with the present world.

People who can see how what they do affects other people—what it means to other people, how it looks from someone else's point of view—can of course make use of their achievement for good or ill. But we have all met in school and among adults the kind of blindness to the consequences of actions which leads us to ask 'How could anyone do that to someone?' It is easy to make absurdly optimistic claims here: that terrorists and vandals would shrink from what they do if they could understand the consequences for others. (Even to talk about stopping 'terrorists' and 'vandals' in this simplistic way is, of course, to beg a host of questions.) But there seems to us a clear sense in which children (and adults) make disastrous mistakes and do terrible things because they simply cannot envisage what an injury, an insult, or even a death may actually mean in terms of the experience of other people. This is a *cognitive* deficit, not necessarily a moral or emotional one (although it may be those too). People working at a Piagetian concrete-operational level in some particular context will not go beyond the immediate evidence directly presented to them: any damage they have done beyond what directly confronts them will be—so long as their thinking remains at that level—literally outside their ability to grasp. We have no space to develop these sketchy claims, and they need much qualification. Nevertheless, there seems to be the basis here of a claim that the dispositions and strategies learnt in history lessons have an immediate importance outside history; history is not inert and arid, but affects the whole way in which we see the world—past, present and future.

This is even clearer when the task is to make sense of comprehensive ways of life which at first sight appear alien and unintelligible. Again it is easy to make simple-minded and grandiose claims—that prejudice against other cultures or ethnic groups will be dispelled by empathy exercises in history at school. People's views are in large part based on material interests, fear, and their social relations with others: the presentation of rational alternatives in education is often almost powerless against all this. It remains true, however, that *unless* we can get children past the stage where the alien is seen as stupid and inferior, there is little chance of progress towards genuine understanding.

Investigation of Historical Empathy in Pupils

What evidence do we have about children's abilities, dispositions and strategies in this area? There is a vast amount of relevant work in general cognitive and developmental psychology, the best guide to which is still Margaret Donaldson.[1] In history there has until recently been much less attention to children's thinking and ideation in empathy and understanding than to their ability to handle evidence. In the last decade, however, the emphasis has begun to shift, and there is a growing body of research evidence which provides a basis for tentative suggestions about children's ideas and strategies in the face of the incomprehensible past. Early work generally used pencil and paper tests and closely followed the categories of children's thinking developed by Piaget or Peel.[2]

The most important of these investigations were those of Hallam and Thompson, both of which contained elements which touched on empathy and understanding.[3] Hallam's work was particularly interesting in that taped interviews with subjects provided some of the data. The difficulty in history is that while written tests can provide data on children's conclusions, it is much harder to obtain clues as to how the children got there. In any case even the best written tests can only give a rough picture of what children think, and if their writing is much below average the test will give very misleading results. Dickinson and Lee's Jutland test did provide some evidence about how children coped with a series of actions which they at first found hard to make sense of, but this was because a great deal of preliminary interview work was done which helped to establish certain statements in the written responses as reliable indicators of particular lines of thought, and because the written tests were more complex (and clumsy) than usual.[4] The questions also included a reflexive element, where children were in effect persuaded to comment on their own earlier answers.

Denis Shemilt's important *Evaluation Study* of 'History 13–16' covered most areas of pupils' ideas about history, and in so doing collected an impressive range of data on children's assumptions about empathy and understanding in history. In particular the use of detailed and often quite substantial interviews offered a wider and subtler insight into children's concepts than any study before it. Meanwhile Dickinson and Lee, in an attempt to get a much more detailed picture of children's thinking in action and at the same time avoid the problems inherent in interviews conducted by adults (leading questions, inadvertent reinforcement of certain responses and suppression of others, and the generally directed nature of the interaction) made a number of television recordings of small groups of children attempting to understand Anglo-Saxon oath-helping and Spartan education.[5] It is this technique of televising small group discussion which the present authors have developed and extended during the past three years (1982–85), and which has provided the examples offered in this chapter.

In essence the technique we have used is the same as the one described in 'Making Sense of History'.[6] The main differences are that we have used the video-camera much more extensively, recording children working on ordinary classwork exercises as well as on specially constructed tests—we now have hundreds of hours of tape—and that we generally leave children to work entirely on their own, with no adult in the room at all. The groups usually consist of three pupils, partly to make sound pick-up simpler, and partly because a group of three tends to produce shifting patterns of argument and tension in a way that groups of two or four do not. The school in which we work is the Bramston School, in Witham, Essex, an 11–18 comprehensive with an attached sixth form centre shared by the other comprehensive in the area. The intake includes a large proportion of pupils from two London overspill estates, and many of the children's families retain close links with the east end of London.

The exciting and encouraging feature of recent research is the way in which two independent approaches to children's ideas about understanding problematic actions and institutions seem to suggest very similar—although still highly speculative and tentative—conclusions. The system of levels suggested by Lee in 1978, and empirically supported by Dickinson and Lee in the Jutland test, was in many respects given independent support by the much more extensive work of Shemilt's *Evaluation Study*.[7] The latter went well beyond the relatively narrow compass of Dickinson and Lee's work, but the similarity in the concepts underlying the basic steps in children's ideas about empathy and understanding is very marked, as a glance at Shemilt's categories in 'Beauty and the philosopher' will show.[8]

On the basis of the evidence provided by all this work, and our own detailed investigation at Bramston, we have constructed a set of categories for the development of children's understanding of, and strategies for achieving, empathy.

Before we set out the list of categories, some cautionary remarks are in order. The categories represent a *logical* hierarchy, in that successive higher levels subsume or replace the ideas of lower levels, and permit new questions which open up new strategies for understanding. When children employ them in their encounters with the past, the assumptions made at lower levels create difficulties and contradictions which are progressively reconciled by the assumptions and ideas available at higher levels. But this is *not* to say that the categories constitute a *developmental* hierarchy. It *may* be that children tend to employ certain basic sets of assumptions in trying to understand the past, and hence it may be possible to talk of a particular child as being, on a range of tasks, at (say) level three. There is some evidence that there is, at any given moment and on any given task a ceiling on the level of ideas a particular child can call upon. But even if this were true, it would be highly misleading (and potentially disastrous for teaching) if it were understood as licensing the allocation of a child to a *stage* in anything like the Piagetian sense.

The most important reason for caution here is that although children's ideas may form connected clusters analyzable into a logical hierarchy, those ideas are not static or fixed. In the first place children's organizing ideas and assumptions vary with content. There is some evidence from our work, and much more from elsewhere, that familiar content is likely to be tackled at a higher level than unfamiliar content.[9] In the second place, lower level ideas are unstable because they produce contradictions and anomalies, with the result that the actual process of grappling with alien institutions or strange actions can move children up through the levels. At the same time, collision with especially recalcitrant features of the alien behaviour when the children are relatively firmly attached to lower level ideas can have the opposite effect, and force children back down the scale. In addition, where pupils are working with one another in small groups, it is even more likely that there will be shifts up and down the scale of levels.

The categories we offer, then, are very tentative and preliminary. Levels one and five are rather more clearly defined than the intermediate levels, and much work needs to be done before we can be sure that children's ideas go together in the ways we suggest here. It is worth repeating, however, that there are clear signs of convergence between the main strands of research in this area, and this may justify some degree of confidence in the validity of these interim remarks, and optimism as to what may be possible in the future.

Most of the examples we will give here will be from a test asking children to explain Anglo-Saxon oath-helping and the ordeal; this test has been described in more detail elsewhere.[10] Although we have material from a variety of other tasks, it is simpler where possible to draw comparisons and illustrations from one context. This is not the whole story, however: at the present stage in our work we lack tests that pick out important indicators with any degree of sophistication. Since the Anglo-Saxon test was devised as a pilot to provide experience on the basis of which to develop more sophisticated instruments, it has been used in a variety of schools and situations, and as such offers clearer examples of issues we wish to raise. Readers will nevertheless be aware that what they are being offered at this stage is selective exemplification, not conclusive evidence, let alone 'hard data'.

Level 1—The 'Divi' Past

Actions, institutions, etc., seen as unintelligible. People in the past were in an important way mentally defective ('divi', 'thick'), because they failed to adopt obviously 'better' courses of action. Sometimes this failure is seen by pupils in a very general way as a function of time and evolution: the further back we go, the more stupid (primitive, ape-like) people can be expected to be. Patently people in the past were not as *clever* as us anyway, because they lacked aeroplanes and television, thought the world was flat, and had inadequate standards of hygiene and medicine. But often the failure of past agents is more specific—they embark on courses of action which anyone can see will not work, and omit to do what anyone (more particularly the pupil) can see needs doing. The real basis of all this is the inability of the pupil to recognize that people in the past often could not know—either in general or in the details of the situation in which they were called upon to act—what the pupil now knows and takes for granted. Add to this pupil's inability to envisage the inherent complexity of human institutions and interactions, and the past becomes a catalogue of absurd behaviour, to which the only possible reaction is one of irritated incomprehension and contempt. At this level the additional difficulty that people in the past saw things very differently from us, and had different values, goals and expectations, begins to enter the pupil's calculations only as part of the *problem*, not as the first step towards attempting a *solution*.

Children responding at level one to the problem of understanding why the Saxons used oath-helping and the ordeal to decide if someone was guilty or innocent typically express a clear conviction that the whole business was stupid.

> *Andrew:* So you're guilty anyway…you haven't got a chance of getting out of it. (They all agree).
> *Mark:* They should have a proper trial like we have now.
> *Andrew and Robert:* Yeah.
> *Mark:* 'Cos, 'cos…
> *Andrew:* Have a jury and see if we're guilty or *not* guilty. (Aside to Mark) I've never been there, I don't know if you have Mark?
> *Mark:* B ___ has. (A reference to another boy in the class). (They decide you're bound to sink in the ordeal of cold-water).
> *Mark:* So either way you're going to get had up for it.
> *Andrew and Robert:* Yeah.

Robert: (Reads sheet under his breath, then continues) Say you got two people and they said they were five each, so that makes ten...

Andrew: Ten.

Robert: You could be innocent, and they could be telling the truth...

Andrew: (Wagging his finger at Robert) *But*, we need twenty-two shillings, 'cos their wage (sic) is twenty.

Mark: We've got to clear it.

Robert: But how do *they* know he's inno...he's guilty?

Mark: That's what I mean, you can't really decide.

Andrew: You can't...he's not going to get away with it.

Mark: What's the point of sticking him in water?

> (3rd years, bottom band, receiving help
> from Special Needs Department).

There is no sign here of any strategy for constructing some kind of rationale for what the pupils see as absurd behaviour—for trying to discover why people could have thought such institutions appropriate. The institutions are considered quite independent of other beliefs, values and material conditions: it is not just that children have no knowledge of the latter, but that they do not see any reason to try to find anything out about them. They all agree with Mark that 'they should have a proper trial like we have now'—as if such procedures were transferable without reference to any material or social context. Oath-helping and ordeal are weighed up as technical devices, and found wanting. They are assumed to be serving the same functions as our equivalent institutions, only badly. Consequently the children are drawn into a discussion of the practical workings of the system, which are in their eyes not merely irrelevant to their putative function, but disastrous in simple practical ways too.

Time and again children at this level come back to their belief that oath-helping is an easy way of 'getting away with it' and the ordeal is impossibly dangerous ('You're not going to survive anyway'). Because the boys already quoted have no strategy for relating Saxon methods to a wider context, and are quite willing to believe that people in the past were capable of almost any kind of absurdity, even clues to links with other beliefs are swallowed up in their general derisory assessment. Hence, the fact that the accused in ordeal by cold water would undertake a fast and drink holy water before undergoing the ordeal is seen as just another foolish practical mistake.

Robert: Yeah, that's stupid though...

Mark: Yeah, but just 'cos you don't eat yer food don't mean you're going to prove...

Andrew: ...you're not guilty.

Mark: (Simultaneously)...you're not guilty, does it.

Robert: I know!

Instead of suggesting a way forward a potential clue becomes just another part of the same incomprehensible problem. The obvious consequence is a rejection of the whole institution as self-evidently absurd.

> *Robert:* So what do we...what do we say about it?
> *Mark:* Well, there's nothing...
> *Robert:* Load of rubbish?

The same pattern is apparent with three top band third year pupils.

> *Sophie:* That sort of thing we wouldn't be doing nowadays 'cos we're not that stupid nowadays...
> *Mark:* (Laughs) Exactly!

They have the same problem with potential clues:

> *Matthew:* ...it's got 'the priest would ask God to accept him if he was innocent or cast him out if he was guilty'—and that was, that's really a bit stupid 'cos, some of the things, like say if the, say if the um person got thrown into the water, couldn't swim or something, you know, he'd drown.

And there is the same assumption that our own institutions could be switched back in time, regardless of context.

> *Sophie:* It's stupid though, ta..., taking your hand out of a pot of boiling water and taking out a stone. Well I never, you might as well just do it, you know, like a proper court.

With another group of top-band third years the idea of fasting is even more dramatically incorporated into the problem, rather than being harnessed to a solution.

> *Maria:* I don't understand...um, how they can, putting, doing this fasting for three days, I don't see the point of that really 'cos it, and then drinking the water, unless it's just a sign of holiness, it hasn't got anything to do with being innocent or guilty I don't think.

A comment from a second year middle-band group sums up the kind of desperate condescension which comes over tolerant but exasperated children at this level:

> *Celia:* Really, really they got that way, because that was the first way they thought of.

The conviction that the Anglo-Saxons were in a quite fundamental way *backward*—in a sense which typically combines technological simplicity with mental retardation—comes through in numerous exchanges.

> *Robert:* How do they know you only went down one and a half metres?

Mark: Yeah.

Andrew: Good question.

Mark: Perhaps they measure it. And in them times *was* it a metre or centimetre or millimetre?

Andrew: Yeah, we don't know nothing about that way of jumping in the water and that sort of thing and sinking.

Robert: No, 'cos the river might be five metres.

Mark: No but how do they know it was five metres? They might not've invented five metres or centimetres...

Andrew: Yeah.

Mark: ...in that time.

(Bottom-band third years).

The point that once the accused man had sunk sufficiently to be proven innocent he might be pulled out of the water is completely missed, even though the group has centred its discussion on the measurement issue. Instead doubt is cast on whether Anglo-Saxons could manage measurement, given that they had probably not invented metres. The assumption that people who sink far enough to be shown to be innocent were then left to drown is extremely widespread, and tenaciously held (even when put under direct pressure from teachers asking whether it made sense).

Sophie: I was just thinking about this...cold water. Like he's got his hands behind his back, so he's going to drown anyway, isn't he.

Mark: Probably...sort of get him out I suppose...(Grins to show he thinks it a bit unlikely that anyone *will* get him out).

Sophie: I know, but they, they wouldn't know how long it would take, would they?

(Top-band, third year).

The assumption that the Saxons failed to understand basic practical facts about human physiology defeats the glimmering of an idea that an innocent man might be saved from drowning. The same point is made even more explicitly by a top-band first year group.

Scott: But we *know* that nowadays if you ain't got air you're dead, but they didn't, didn't they (sic).

Even the assumptions about inferior Saxon technology are more drastic than one might expect:

Sophie: And what about the boiling water, the boiling water—that could be hotter one time than another. I know it boils at a hundred centigrade, but um...

Mark: They wouldn't be able to get it that high, actually, would they, not, not in them times.

(Top-band, third year).

Level 2—Generalized Stereotypes

Actions, institutions, etc., understood by reference to a 'conventional' or stereotypical account of people's intentions, situations, values and goals. The 'conventional' element includes stereotyped role descriptions (or extrapolations from such descriptions), the ascription of very generalized dispositions, and assumptions based on 'merely conceptual' understandings of intentions and situations. The use of personal projection to explain actions or institutions is more typically a sign of the next level (everyday empathy), but routine projection based on stereotyped roles or conventional classification of situations unsupported by evidence as to what the particular situation was, are indicators of stereotype empathy. In general no attempt is made at this level to distinguish what people now know and think from what people in the past knew and thought, or between their values and ours. There is sometimes, however, reference to major differences, but this recognition is used as an explanation of how people could be so stupid, not to explain the institutions, practice or action itself.

At level two children appeal to religion to explain the strange character of trial by ordeal, but the reference to religion is general and stereotyped. The assumption is that *any* religious person who believes in God will as a consequence accept almost any absurdity if it is done in the name of religion. Hence the Saxons would quite happily allow innocent people to sink and then leave them to drown, *because* they were religious. Pupils thinking like this make no detailed explanatory connections—or at any rate, no consistent explanatory connections—between the religion involved as the explanation, and the actual practices of the ordeal. Specific evidence as to how the Anglo-Saxons saw things is ignored, because religion explains it all and there is no need to go further. Belief in God explains how people could be so silly.

The three top-band first-year boys already quoted decide early in their discussion that religion is the key. But one of them is not sure that this has really sorted matters out.

> *Colin:* (Turns and addresses the camera to conclude the discussion so far.) We think that it is religion.
> *Simon:* Somebody go and get No. 2 (the second question).
> *Scott:* No.
> *Colin:* Shall I go and get No. 2?
> *Scott:* Well, not yet, 'cos we haven't really *explained* it—we just said...
> *Colin:* Yeah I know, we, we explained it...that they do that, because of their religion.

Colin and Simon join with Scott in reiterating relevant details of the ordeal, but somehow although they can see that religious beliefs are central—

'they're going to think that God cures them or saves them from drowning'—religion only serves as a stereotype to explain how the Anglo-Saxons could have been so stupid, not how the ordeal might have made sense. 'Religion' explains how people could watch an innocent man sink, and then drown. It also explains how the Saxons could, despite the repeated evidence of their senses, go on thinking that God would intervene.

> *Colin:* They, they believed in God, and they're going to think that God cures them or saves them from drowning or whatever test they...
> *Simon:* Yeah.
> *Scott:* Cos, say that in the olden days we think it's religion because God and all that lot all their...beliefs...
> *Colin:* ...believed it—by nearly everybody...
> *Scott:* ...by near-enough everybody and that was why in everyday life like say, we don't, not all of us go to Church: then, *everybody* went to Church...

Religion is finally invoked almost in desperation.

> *Colin:* ...like if, that one where, that where there's a hole in the ground, they're going to do it, because like it *must* be their religion because it says themselves, it's a...I mean, how else would somebody sink if they were innocent...
> *Scott:* Well *everybody* sinks if you're alive.
> *Colin:* No hang on, sink if you're innocent or float if you're guilty or whatever it was...
> *Scott:* Yeah, that's what it was.
> *Colin:* Right; they're not going to believe *that* like, if, unless it's religion—you know what I mean?
> *Scott:* Mm.
> *Colin:* So they've got—it's *got*, it's *got* to be religion.
> *Scott:* Yeah.

A similar pattern emerges with a group of second year (middle-band) girls:

> *Jody:* Yeah, but what if some people don't believe in God then?
> *Tina:* Yeah but you'd have to, otherwise they don't wanna spend...
> *Celia:* Otherwise you wouldn't have a Saxon Court, would you?

Asked whether a Saxon would have explained oath-helping and ordeal in the same way as they (the pupils) have explained it, Jody replies: 'No, because he believed in God, so he would've believed it wouldn't he.' Towards the end of the discussion which then develops, the following exchange illustrates elements of generalized stereotype empathy, and at the same time indicates the instability of this level:

> *Jody:* The difference is...would be that they believe in God and we don't believe in God but they...*they* believe that God does everything, like, if um, like the stone or the brick or whatever goes to two metres they reckon that God done that, but *I* don't.
>
> *Celia:* Well, if you, well if...no really, really the difference is that everybody believed in God, where now, not many do.
>
> *Jody:* Well *I* believe in God...but I don't believe that God done *that.*

In this passage Celia remains at level two. Jody, on the other hand, has problems precisely because she is not prepared to accept a stereotype of religion. On the basis of her own experience she wants to distinguish between belief in God, and belief in the kind of direct divine intervention which seems implicit in trial by ordeal. This suggests that Jody's position is highly unstable, and she may be on the verge of a level four response to the problem.

This sort of connection between level two and level four is frequently discernible in the Anglo-Saxon trials test, and suggests a possible weakness in the current form of that test. But it is only partly a test weakness: it is also indicative of a genuine instability in level two, which can push children into level four just as easily as it can force them to come up with explanations of a level three kind. It will be clear that even a slight movement on the part of the first-year pupils quoted above towards a more careful examination of Saxon religious beliefs would move them from level two to level four. (This connection will be raised again in the context of level four).

Level 3—Everyday Empathy

Actions, institutions etc. understood by reference to evidence of the specific situation in which people found themselves, but the situation is seen in modern terms, with no distinction made between how we see it and how contemporaries would have seen it, or between what the agent(s) knew and what we now know. Nevertheless, there is a genuine attempt to reconstruct salient features of the particular situation, and this is coupled with a general awareness of the kinds of ways in which people might react, and frequently with some form of personal projection: what would it have been like for me if *I* had been there? This mixture of generalized awareness of how people react and personal projection can appear similar to the stereotyping of level two, but differs from the latter in its much closer application to the particular circumstances and people involved.

At level three in response to the practical difficulties of the ordeal, children look for explanatory ideas in their own experience, without appreciating the differences between their own beliefs and values and those of another society. The ordeal in particular is frequently seen as a form of punishment, and of course this raises problems of fairness in an acute form. The group in the following excerpt takes a step towards clearing up these problems, without abandoning the assumption that the Saxons must be doing what *we* would be doing if we behaved in that way.

Gary: Why did they use them? (Ordeals).

John: I know why, because um, if this is as unfair as *we* seem to make out it is, no-one's going to steal anything...

Gary: Oh yeah. (They develop this new idea excitedly).

John: ...because someone's going to bring...

Gary: So...

John: ...because someone's...

Gary: ...someone's...going to be scared...

John: ...someone's going to see them...

Gary: ...going to be scared they'll get caught...

John: ...because someone will get caught...

Gary: ...so they won't use it.

John: ...and they're going to go through this ordeal whether they're innocent *or* guilty aren't they.

(After a further brief exchange along the same lines the explanation is spelt out).

Nick: First of all, you know, they had the oath-helping and then they found people was getting out of it too easy...

John: Yeah.

Nick: ...so they *did* do that, you know, to make it a bit harder on 'em...

John: Yeah.

Nick: ...so they wouldn't try and do it (the crime) but um, I still don't think, you know, trial by ordeal is very fair.

John: I think...I think...

Gary: Yeah but they used it because it...

Nick: ...to scare 'em.

Gary: ...it's going to scare 'em, stop 'em from doing it.

John: It's, it's a real, um, defence, sort of um, oh, what do you call it...a...a deterrent.

Gary: A deterrent, yeah. (Gary and Nick grin at the word).

John: It's a deterrent, that's what it is really.

(Middle-band, third years).

Children working at this level draw heavily and directly on their own experience of life. They are able to take into account other people's positions and circumstances, but interpreted in terms of their own values, beliefs, fears and goals. To the extent that these appeal to common features of human experience they are able to make real progress in understanding the past, but there are obviously limits to such an approach. Many of the strengths and some of the limitations are apparent in this discussion (by bottom-band second-years) of people's possible reaction to enclosure in the eighteenth century.

> *Tony:* Yeah, rich people, they could, they could afford to give people lots of money, and say, if I give, if I give you say, a hundred pound, you'll, you'll be on my side...
>
> *Gareth:* Yeah.
>
> *Tony:* ...and say it's my land.
>
> *Gareth:* And all these high lawyers and court judges will get on their side.
>
> *Tony:* And they can get, and they, and they can get, they can um hire out all their high lawyers and everything, and they can afford to go to Parliament and all that, and the poor people they ain't got no say in it, they can't afford to go to Parliament and all that, so when rich people, um, say, 'Oh, this is my land', the poor people can't say, can't say, 'No it's my land', 'cos, the rich people've got all the lawyers 'n that to say 'Yeah, this is, er, his or her land'.
>
> *Gareth:* Yeah.
>
> *Tony:* Know what I mean?
>
> *Gareth:* I reckon, um, 'cos all these high people are their friends, they go drinking with 'em nearly every day, you know, meeting them social like. (Turns to Sarah). Sarah?
>
> *Sarah:* Well, they get to know all the rich people same sort of things *you* said...
>
> *Gareth:* Right. (Reads) 'What different type...'
>
> *Sarah:* Come on!
>
> *Gareth:* OK.
>
> *Sarah:* (Reads) 'You are a villager, with no title deeds to the land you farm, you farm; tell your story.' We've got to do this properly now. (Looks at Tony and waves a finger at him). Tony?
>
> *Tony:* Right.
>
> *Gareth:* Describe what you feel like.
>
> *Tony:* Well, if I was, er...
>
> *Sarah:* You're meant to be...
>
> *Tony:* ...an old farmer, and people took my land, I'd be very upset and I'd...really try to get it back, but...I wouldn't have any chance I don't reckon, 'cos, say if a rich person took it, like I said before they can give plenty of money to say (inaudible) say 'This is my land', and they can buy land and everything, and...and I just, I think that's not right.
>
> *Gareth:* No.
>
> *Sarah:* (Inaudible—agrees?)
>
> *Tony:* I think everyone should, I reckon everyone should have a job and all that.

Gareth: Yes, I reckon, um, they're not going to take any notice or bother about a um little nobody like us, like a small farmer, whose um only right is he's farmed it for, his family's farmed it for a few hundred years.

Sarah: (laughs).

Gareth: (Inaudible very brief remark).

Tony: He might've been the only one left in the generation, in his family...

Sarah: I'd be, yeah, I'd be...

Tony: ...and they can't, and...say his father, and his father after that, and his grandad's father...

Sarah: Mmm, I'd be really mad, (inaudible)...

Tony: ...and then...

Sarah: ...try and get it back...

Tony: ...they, *they* all might be dead...

Sarah: ...get a (inaudible).

Tony: ...and they can't say 'Oh I had this land before and I gave it my grandson' and all that...

Gareth: 'Cos they ain't got no deeds, anyway...they've all taken them up (inaudible)...

Tony: Yeah.

Sarah: What I'd do, I'd be really furious, I'd get, try and get a petition to the...Parliament.

Gareth: Wouldn't work, 'cos there's loads of rich people, wouldn't er...

Sarah: Yeah I know, and I'd try and do anything...

Gareth: Yeah 'cos all them little farmers haven't got no other thing to do and they'll all be unemployed.

Sarah: I'd be sick.

Tony: What do *you* reckon they'd do, Sarah?

Sarah: I just said...

Gareth: You'd feel really ill, wouldn't yer. No other job, and you don't, you'd been doing that all your life and um...

Sarah: Now let's talk about *it*, without the, we've done all the questions, let's just talk about it.

Tony: You can imagine if, er...

Gareth: Some pers...

Tony: ...we were, we were living in that time...

Gareth: ...Some sick person come along, and turfed you out of yer 'ouse...

Tony: Yeah, you, you wouldn't be 'ere now...

Gareth: ...crushed it and built a multi-storey car-park over the top of it.

Sarah: Yeah, 'cos that's the same sort of thing, only *nowadays*

Gareth: (simultaneously)...it wouldn't be much fun then!

Sarah: It's like if they bashed down some, one of our houses, and they put er...well, anything there.

Gareth: Yeah, and they didn't give you no money, nowhere to live...

Sarah: No, and you was out like a...

Gareth: ...and all your furniture and stuff was...

Tony: And you said 'Oi, where's my house?' and they just said 'Aah, don't worry about the 'ouse, you'll, you'll find another one mate'...

Gareth and Sarah: Yeah.

Tony: ...and they won't take any notice of yer...

Sarah: No.

Gareth: It's like if they sack you and don't give you no notice then um, all yer assets, all your furniture, your car, are all owned by the company...

Sarah: Yeah.

Gareth: They turf you all out, you know...

The children's own experience of authority and their chances of resisting it come through very strongly:

Tony: If I was a villager and um, the Council took my land, I'd be very upset, and I'd try and get a petition, and try and get into Parliament, and, I'd get as many people as I can, to sign it, and I'd get a load of people to come with me, and um, see if I could get my land back, but I wouldn't have a chance.

Level 4—Restricted Historical Empathy

Actions, institutions etc. understood by reference to evidence of the specific situations in which people found themselves, with the recognition that these cannot necessarily be characterized as we now may characterize them, partly because we may know things people in the past did not or could not know, and partly because their beliefs, goals and values were different from ours. Where individual actions are concerned, pupils are able to understand that intentions are likely to be qualified, and to begin to follow some of their ramifications, redescribing the intentions in ways which indicate general awareness of longer-term goals (where appropriate). Understanding of institutions is likely to take the form of an attempt to reconstruct some kind of rationale in terms of goals directly connected with the overt and explicit function of the institution. The workings of the institutions tend to be appraised in terms of their efficacy in contributing to the manifest functions of the institution, taken in relative isolation from its wider context. The same narrow focus is employed in the assessment of gains and losses accruing from possible alternative sets of behaviour. Pupils at this level accept that people in the past saw things in a different way from us, but cannot take this much beyond the specific circumstances in order to relate these differences to other beliefs, values, and material conditions. Hence understanding of items of behaviour and institutional or social practices is potentially unstable. Pupils may still resort to exasperated and condescending criticism of what they see as futile, unintelligible beliefs, or ignorance; and these beliefs will be precisely those which underlie the differences they have just cited in arriving at an understanding of the institution. Only when everything can be seen in a wider context will this instability disappear, and attempts to reconstruct that wider context are the mark of the next level.

Children working on the Anglo-Saxon trials test seldom stay at level four for long, and it is harder to exemplify level four responses than those from other levels. This is partly because the interaction between children trying to work out a solution drives them rapidly beyond a level four response (once they have grasped the fact that Saxon views and circumstances were radically different from their own), and partly a result of the actual material. In the Jutland test employed by Dickinson and Lee children could provide a reasonably adequate and self-contained explanation of Jellicoe's behaviour without going outside the immediate context of the battle. In consequence there were a great many responses which clearly distinguished the agent's point of view from the historian's, and yet did not see the wider strategic considerations which in the end were essential to the proper understanding of Jellicoe's conduct of the battle. Take this answer by a fifth year pupil to the question why Jellicoe turned his fleet away from the Germans during the battle of Jutland:

> Admiral Jellicoe turned the fleet away from the Germans as he probably thought they were launching an all-out torpedo attack on the British fleet, because he had been informed that the Germans had developed a system of concealing the torpedo tracks, and if this was the case, the fleet would have been unable to avoid the attack and suffered severe losses.

Asked what Jellicoe was trying to do in the battle—as a whole, not just in turning away—the pupil does not fit the tactics of the battle into the wider strategic context and hence remains at level four.

> The battle was meant to be a pitched battle with a decisive victory for either the British or German fleet. The original idea was 'all or nothing' with the complete destruction of one of the sides. Normally such a battle would have been continuous fighting but Jellicoe probably tried to use new tactics to combat the new unknown naval tactics of the German fleet, as from the very start it was meant to be a trap, but this went wrong. Once the German main fleet had forced its way through the front of the British fleet it was severely punished by the

bulk of the British Fleet. More confrontations occurred with the German fleet attacking and even turning around in one move and disappearing. After Jellicoe's turn away the British tried to cut off the German's retreat and probably gain the decisive win that was expected, but this failed in the confusion of the night.

There is no sign here of an awareness of the importance of the navy to Britain as a means of maintaining control of the sea, and with it the defence of trade and the blockade of Germany which were so vital to the British war-effort. Information on this was available, but simply not harnessed to understanding what went on at Jutland.

In dealing with Anglo-Saxon oath-helping and the ordeal, children find it hard to provide an adequate explanation simply in terms of unpacking the implications of religious belief. The assertion that everything was a result of religion—the stereotyped response of level two—needs only a small nudge from someone in a group to open up a close examination of *how* religious beliefs could make sense of the practices under discussion. Jody's remark (quoted already in the section on level two) 'Well *I* believe in God...but I don't believe that God done *that*' is characteristic of the beginnings of a move to level four.

It *was* religion that explained these strange goings-on, but not any old religion, and not *our* religion. At level four the distinction between what we believe and what people in the past believed is made in a clear way, and is something to be examined, not just further proof of the idiocy of our ancestors.

Laura: It's obvious that they were really good believers in God, because it says here you could ask to go to the ordeal.

Jayne: Mm.

Maria: If you was a really good believer in God you'd probably choose the first um ordeal...

Jayne: Holy water! There's no such thing!

Maria: ...drinking holy water.

Jayne: All it is just a glass of water.

Maria: Yeah, but it's blessed by the priest isn't it.

Jayne: What good's that going to do?

Maria: Well...if you believe in God...

Jayne: (Inaudible).

Maria: Yeah, but if you believe in God...

Jayne: Oh yeah, it'd work, but...

Maria: ...You'd think it would work, and you, you'd believe that you were going to come out.

Laura: How would they know that God accepts them for innocent...or guilty?

Jayne: I dunno.

Maria: Well you, if he, no, if he d..., if he is accepted as innocent by God and then, then he's, when he's thrown into the hole filled with water, he'd sink lower than the two metres, but if he was proved, um, guilty by God then he won't sink lower...

Jayne: No.

Maria: ...and that's the way that they can tell.

(Top-band, third years).

This is a complex interaction, and Jayne seems to be thinking in level one terms. Maria, on the other hand, is distinguishing between how *we* would regard the religious rites, and how the Saxons might have taken them. In particular she is trying to establish the particular connection between general religious beliefs and the actual workings of the ordeal. This is an important sign of level four thinking. It is not consistently maintained in this group's discussion, but this is not surprising given the age of the pupils concerned.

Pupils seldom stop here. Once the real differences between people's beliefs and values in Saxon times are seriously taken up, the wider social context and material conditions are required to provide a framework in which to set those beliefs and values. The natural progression is to level five.

Level 5—Contextual Historical Empathy

At this level pupils attempt to fit what is to be understood or explained into a wider picture. Where information or evidence is lacking, they may fall back on speculation which may even involve a degree to circularity: these people *must* have believed p^1 and been in circumstance c^1 to have found it possible to believe p in circumstances c, and it is therefore p^1 and c^1 which allow us to understand how they could have done x. The point is not that at this level pupils get things 'right'—much still depends on the information available to them or on whether they have sufficient evidence to arrive at something approximating to an adequate account. It is the strategies employed, the grasp of what has to be done in order to achieve understanding, which determines whether pupils are at level five. There is a clear differentiation between the position and point of view of the historical agent, and that of the historian; between what the agent knew and what we know; between the beliefs, values, goals and habits enshrined in a past institution or social practice, and those which are prevalent in our own society. There is an attempt to set the problematic action or institution in a wider context of beliefs and values, and often an attempt to link it with the material conditions of life. It is not assumed that an action or institution is to be understood only in terms of what it appears or claims to concern itself with: pupils at this level often suggest implicit goals and latent or even hidden functions. None of this means that the past is above criticism:

pupils at this level may still want to stand back and apply current standards of rationality and knowledge in assessing actions or institutions. At level five, however, this is done in the clear knowledge that their own standards are likely to be different from those of the past.

Because responses at level five begin to weave together different strands to produce a coherent overall account, we will begin by quoting a continuous passage of discussion to illustrate the ideas involved. (The group is from a top-band third year class).

Tim: Well if you were honest, and people in the village thought you were honest, they'd swear by you, wouldn't they? (Jason points out that there would be much less chance of getting people to swear for you if the crime was serious.)

Lawrence: I think what the main reason was, right, that they believed in God, you know, everybody probably believed in God and that, right, and it also says that...they er, an oath was like swearing to God that you were telling the truth, right...

Tim: Mm...

Lawrence: ...so what they reckon, is that, if you're, if you're telling the truth to God...

Tim: Mm...

Lawrence: ...you're telling the truth to the rest of the people.

Tim: Yeah, no-one would lie to God, God was all-powerful...

Jason: Yeah.

Tim: ...he'd know if you lied and you'd be in trouble.

Lawrence: Yeah.

Jason: And it was a very...very closely-knit society wasn't it.

Lawrence: Yeah.

Jason: So, if um, if you did try and do something, chances are *someone* saw you.

Lawrence: Yeah.

Tim: True.

Jason: So, er...

Tim: Your guilt, that was to do with God as well...

Lawrence: Yeah.

Tim: ...because you couldn't fool God.

Lawrence: No.

Tim: ...if you were guilty you'd fail the ordeal.

Lawrence: Yeah. (Long pause). Do you reckon it worked? (Tim and Lawrence laugh).

Jason: Yeah and er, the ordeal was, um, sort of if you were guilty, then God would...punish you...

Lawrence: Yeah.

Jason: So really sort of they believed that your fate was in God's hands.

Lawrence: I mean, although they were probably intelligent they probably didn't have the...they believed in God of course...

Jason: Mm.

Lawrence: ...so, they thought, if God's so clever and powerful, we'll let him do the judging, and we'll carry out the punishments, if need be.

Tim: Yeah, it's just the way they interpret what God says...

Lawrence: Yeah.

Tim: ...so to speak.

At this level there is both a readiness to look behind the institutions for alternative explanations, and an unwillingness to make easy criticisms.

Jason: ...These, um, people that are actually in the courts deciding that they were guilty, and er the people who gave...the oaths were usually the um, they're...

Lawrence: Yeah.

Jason: Sort of, if um, if they didn't like someone, they could quite easily um, sort of...

Tim: Oh.

Lawrence: Oh yeah.

Jason: Make sure that enough people, um, said that he was guilty, and that not enough people said he w...he um, wasn't guilty...

Lawrence: Yeah.

Tim: Mind you they were all petrified of God's wrath so they wouldn't do any...they wouldn't do anything to, um, upset him, so...

Jason: I know but...

Tim: You'd get a *few* who'd do it for money or fear of something but most people wouldn't.

Lawrence: You had to swear that you wouldn't though, didn't you.

Jason: Well that, well that um...

Tim: You'd be *petrified*—if I lie, God will strike me down and kill all my family and ruin my fields and everything.

There is an awareness of the importance of differences in context between now and then:

Jason: Then of course these days there's um, they've got a better system of policing and government and er...um...

Tim: Well, perhaps not better, more organized.

Jason: ...there's also, there's, there's fam...family um allowance, things like that; there's benefit schemes for older pensioners, and things like that; there's, all, all different types of insurance that if something gets stolen, so, so we, we wouldn't have to worry, but in those days they didn't have any of that so, obviously er, it would've been perhaps more serious then, than it would be today.

Instead of the feeling that nothing makes sense—which is so often apparent at earlier levels—at level five the presupposition of rationality is strong enough to get the support of an argument that is very nearly circular:

> *Lawrence:* I mean it depends if you believe that God would've intervened. It depends on your beliefs really.
> *Tim:* Mm.
> *Lawrence:* I mean they all believed in God in those days, so they held true...
> *Tim and Jason:* Mmm...
> *Lawrence:* I mean, as far as it goes, I mean, probably the same percentage of people got off...
> *Tim:* ...as do now.
> *Lawrence:* Well yeah, the same perc...the same percentage of people got off, as were guilty; so it seemed fair.
> *Tim:* Yeah.
> *Lawrence:* I mean, if , say the courts here, every...everybody that was tried was found guilty, right...
> *Tim:* Mm...
> *Lawrence:* ...you'd soon think there was something wrong with them.

Comparisons with the present put the past on an equal footing:

> *Tim:* Mind you, sometimes our trial can be unfair—completely.
> *Lawrence:* Yeah.
> *Tim:* It just depends who's on the jury. It just depends how *they* interpret the signs from God.

There is a genuine willingness to switch perspective:

> *Tim:* They'd probably say that their system then, with God, is better than ours, because well people can lie, people can...
> *Lawrence:* Yeah.
> *Tim:* ...muck around with the truth, but God...
> *Lawrence:* But God doesn't.
> *Tim:* No. They'd probably say theirs was better than ours.
> *Lawrence:* Yeah.
> *Tim:* Just depends where you've been brought up, or when...

Finally, our own institutions are also seen as historical products, subject in their turn to the judgment of the future:

> *Lawrence:* What I reckon right, is the system was as fair as the, as the current culture would allow.
> *Tim:* Yeah.
> *Lawrence:* I mean, I mean they weren't dim, I mean they still had the same capability for intelligence...

Tim: They just didn't have, hadn't had enough time to develop it.

Lawrence: Yeah, I mean like our age...I mean, say the technology goes further, right, and you have brain-tapping systems, right, that just, a sensor on your head...

Tim: Yeah.

Lawrence: ...and it reads your brain cells: 'I did it', 'I didn't do it', simple as that.

Jason: It's like lie-detectors isn't it.

Lawrence: Yeah.

Tim: Except more...

Lawrence: I mean if they could get them working properly...that'd be...

Tim: Or, even working...

Lawrence: You wouldn't need courts would you.

Tim: They'd say our system was archaic and unfair.

Lawrence: Yeah.

Tim: Just like we're saying *theirs* is. (i.e. the Anglo-Saxon system).

Teaching for Empathy

Denis Shemilt has elsewhere listed and evaluated the most important different kinds of empathy exercise, and Dickinson and Lee have attacked inadequately structured exercises, suggesting some criteria which genuinely useful work should meet.[11] There is not space here to pursue those issues further. We will conclude our chapter instead by looking briefly at the kind of teaching approaches which might best advance children's conceptual development in this area.

It would be misleading and premature to offer confident, straightforward advice. We have our own guesses, however, and two different lines of approach suggest similar practical steps. In the first place there is a long tradition of experimental work and theoretical argument suggesting the importance of social interaction, and especially peer-group interaction, in enabling children to achieve higher conceptual levels. For all his concentration on the child's physical environment—the manipulation of objects—Piaget constantly stressed the importance of decentration, and sometimes suggested that discussion among equals was crucial for this.[12] In the last decade or so there has been increasing interest in the way in which social interaction affects cognitive development, and although it is too soon to set out conclusions, there is a good deal of support for the view that interaction between peers can be a powerful agent of such development.[13] The importance of conflict of view in children's interactions is still a matter for argument, and so are the conditions under which gains are most likely to be achieved.[14] For history teachers, however, it is perhaps most interesting that it does not matter if all the partners in a discussion are equally wrong, provided that they are wrong in different ways.[15]

At this point the research evidence connects with the other approach: our own experience of watching many hours of recorded discussion, and of talking with teachers who have begun to try similar work for themselves. Of course such anecdotal and personal evidence has no claim over other people's experiences, which may be quite different. But where many teachers' practical classroom experience is consonant with research evidence, even if that evidence is still partial and tentative, there is reason to think further investigation worthwhile. It seems to us that children often reach higher levels of understanding when arguing out a problem among themselves than they would achieve on their own, provided the problem is one they have some strategies for tackling. And this is not just true of small-group-work, but of class-discussion too, provided the teacher is prepared to tolerate error, value the various contributions of all pupils, and refrain from early intervention with corrections or the 'right' answer.

This too ties in with recent experimental work. Numerous studies of interaction between parents and children or teachers and children, attempting to test a wide variety of hypotheses, have turned up (almost as a by-product) the negative conclusion that an instructional and didactic approach is relatively ineffective. Such approaches are particularly weak if they remain entirely verbal. There is evidence that 'what proves to be effective is not telling the child the right answer, but guiding him or her towards the right considerations'.[16]

Traditional history teaching has always (rightly) been cautious of new approaches which appear to allow children to get things wrong. History is a public form of knowledge which, although it offers no certainties, has standards and criteria which are not matters of mere personal preference or whim. It is important that children begin to grasp these, but equally important for us to realize that simply telling children what we believe is the right answer will defeat even that goal. Encouraging children to argue out difficult problems, and allowing them to suggest interpretations of people's behaviour in the past which are—to the best of our knowledge— wrong, is not pandering in some muddle-headed way to mushy child-centred theorizing. Provided we do not jump in too quickly to correct children, the conflicts that arise between their different perspectives help them to see that there *are* standards, and that their own interpretations are not necessarily either the same or as good as those held by other members of the class.

Such teaching demands immense restraint and patience, but the rewards are enormous. To begin with, it is possible to spend time discovering how children see things, without feeling guilty that too little ground is being covered. In the end it is more interesting listening to pupils and trying to understand why they see things as they do, than it is to hear one's own voice trying to push them into giving the right answer. Secondly, once one understands what sort of conceptual level they have reached, there is some chance of gearing one's teaching efficiently to moving them on. Thirdly, it allows the teacher to take children's views seriously, and to give them all chances to make their own points. Pupils stop trying to guess what teacher wants them to say, and say what they think is important. The teacher's interventions are frequently questions, asking for elaboration, pointing out ambiguities and inconsistencies, and drawing attention to possible consequences which may be unacceptable to the pupil promulgating the original point of view.

This sort of teaching takes time to develop—it is no use expecting a third-year class to adapt to a sudden switch in approach. But if children in the first-year are given exercises in which they have to decide what policies to pursue as Governor of Roman Britain, or what strategy to adopt in order to save Wessex from the Vikings, or if they are asked to explain what the Anglo-Saxons were doing in trying people by oath-helping, and if they are encouraged to argue out the strengths and weaknesses of each others' suggestions, then there is an opportunity for the history teacher to see where his or her pupils have got to, and a chance to help them move forward. Historical understanding has to be built slowly alongside the approaches which most effectively develop it.

Notes

1 DONALDSON, M. (1978) *Children's Minds*, Fontana.
2 INHELDER, B. and PIAGET, J. (1958) *The Growth of Logical Thinking*, Routledge and Kegan Paul, PEEL, E.A. (1971) *The Nature of Adolescent Judgement*, Staples.
3 HALLAM, R.N. (1966) *An Investigation into Some Aspects of the Historical Thinking of Children and Adolescents*, unpublished MEd thesis, University of Leeds. See also his 'Piaget and thinking in history' in BALLARD, M. (Ed.) (1970) *New Movements in the Study and Teaching of History*, Temple Smith; and (1967) 'Logical thinking in history', *Educational Review*, 19, 1967. Most of Donald Thompson's work remains unpublished, but see his 'Understanding the past: Procedures and content' in DICKINSON, A.K., LEE, P.J. and ROGERS, P.J. (Eds), (1984) *Learning History*, Heinemann Educational Books.
4 DICKINSON, A.K. and LEE, P.J. (1978) 'Understanding and research', in DICKINSON, A.K. and LEE, P.J. (Eds), *History Teaching and Historical Understanding*, Heinemann Educational Books.
5 DICKINSON, A.K. and LEE, P.J. (1984) 'Making sense of history', in DICKINSON, A.K., LEE, P.J. and ROGERS, P.J. (Eds), *op. cit.*, LEE, P.J. (1978) 'Explanation and understanding in history', in DICKINSON, A.K. and LEE, P.J. (Eds), *op cit.*
6 DICKINSON, A.K. and LEE, P.J. (1984) *op. cit.*
7 SHEMILT, D. (1980) *History 13–16 Evaluation Study*, Holmes McDougall.
8 SHEMILT, D. (1984) 'Beauty and the philosopher: Empathy in history and classroom', in DICKINSON, A.K., LEE, P.J. and ROGERS, P.J. (Eds), *op. cit.*
9 WASON, P.C. 'The theory of formal operations—A critique' in GEBER, B.A. (Ed.), (1977) *Piaget and Knowing*, Routledge and Kegan Paul. See also DONALDSON, M. (1978) *op. cit.*
10 DICKINSON, A.K. and LEE, P.J. (1984) *op. cit.*
11 SHEMILT, D. (1984) *op. cit.*, DICKINSON, A.K. and LEE, P.J. (1984) *op. cit.*

12 INHELDER, B. and PIAGET, J. (1958) *op. cit.*, chapter 18. Piaget as much more specific in his earlier work on moral judgment, which is obviously concerned with human affairs rather than physical objects: PIAGET, J. (1932) *The Moral Judgement of the Child*, Routledge and Kegan Paul, p. 409.
13 LIGHT, P. (1983) 'Social interaction and cognitive development: A review of post-Piagetian research', in MEADOWS, S. (Ed.), *Developing Thinking*, Methuen University Paperback.
14 Is the effect of conflict of perspective best understood as decentration through a conflict of centrations, or as a way in which children acquire an objective cognitive attitude—recognizing the existence of public criteria for judgment?
15 LIGHT, P. (1983), p. 72.
16 *Ibid.*, p. 79 and 83.

5   *Empathy as an Objective for History Teaching*

Christopher Portal

Synopsis

When empathy is specified as an objective for history teaching it is not always clear whether a particular kind of knowledge is involved or, alternatively, whether empathy is an heuristic process which can stimulate or reinforce other forms of historical thinking. The latter view is argued here: that empathy is a way of thinking imaginatively which needs to be used in conjunction with other cognitive skills in order to see significant human values in history. Suggestions are made as to how empathy may be given greater emphasis in history teaching to achieve a dialectical relationship between imagination and cognition.

What Empathy Is

The term 'empathy' (*Einfühlung*) derives from German idealism of the nineteenth century and was seen by Wilhelm Dilthey as an essential element in 'understanding' history or any of the human sciences.[1] As in the natural sciences we need evidence and the use of rational processes to relate it to the questions we want answered, but social studies carry an extra dimension—broadly that of the meanings carried by language. Words still in use today, such as 'marriage', 'rebellion', 'heresy', may be found in sources from the past, but they will often have important differences of sense from how we would now define them. And this is not a minor matter, confined to the semi-technical vocabulary of social institutions; it applies to every aspect of life and thought. So the historian's first task is precisely 'interpretation' (as Dilthey insisted). It is necessary to establish what people thought was going on and how they saw their own range of options before any explanation of their motives has a chance of success.

It must be stressed that 'interpretation' in this sense applies as much to actions as it does to words and to articulate concepts, as much to customary social behaviour as it does to the individual point of view.

A modern definition of empathy is to grasp imaginatively 'the thinking, feelings and actions of another and so structure the world as he does,'[2] to which corresponds, in historical terms, Collingwood's belief that the historian should reconstruct and 'rethink' the opinions and purposes of people in the past.[3] But such an historical achievement presumes a high level of expertise in a whole range of historical skills; although empathy may be a necessary element in such insights, it is confusing to regard as empathy everything concerned with understanding historical ideas. Collingwood did not use the term empathy (although 'rethinking' implies something very like it) and more familiar mental operations such as inference from evidence and from background knowledge will play a part in every historical reconstruction.

The role of empathy in understanding the ideas of the past is to project ourselves imaginatively into the historical situation and to use 'our mind's eye' to bring into play the standards of intuitive observation and judgment which we have developed in everyday life. It is possible to recognize in this way what 'makes sense' in an alien world by implicit analogy with our own way of looking at things. At this stage we may be a long way from the authentic thoughts of the past, but the attempt to apply our own categories can show us what 'doesn't work' as well as those aspects that do.[4] Given such stimulus we may, as we do so often in daily life, arrive at a new and more challenging hypothesis to account for behaviour that is otherwise strange and inexplicable.

Projective imagination supplies a whole range of detail about the possible outward appearance of things—characteristic features to which we should be immediately sensitive in our own lives. Such emotionally charged elements, rather than formal concepts verbally defined, become the symbols of intuitive thought, and it is by such a route that our grasp of other people's feelings may be direct and immediate (although not, of course, infallible).[5] Eisner has drawn attention to this aspect of learning— 'expressive' as distinct from 'instructional'[6]. This is the dimension of intellect upon which aesthetic judgment is formed and from which we attain the general sense of direction that leads us to *ask* the right questions, prior to working out the answers by conscious reasoning.

Examples of Historical Empathy

In order to demonstrate the nature of empathy and how it contributes to interpreting the past I have selected from the work of two eminent medieval historians. The episodes appear difficult to understand because they do not rest upon the presuppositions of our society, each being concerned in some way with religious ideas of people living in the thirteenth century.

Sir Richard Southern, in writing the biography of Archbishop Anselm, is faced with a letter written in a strangely emotional style.

> My eyes eagerly long to see your face, most beloved: my arms stretch out to your embraces. My lips long for your kisses; whatever remains of my life desires your company, so that my soul's joy may be full in time to come.

'It is extremely difficult' writes Southern,

> to give these words a sense that is at once plausible and sensible. The difficulty will be apparent when it is remarked that they were written to two young relations, aspirants to the monastic life, whom Anselm in all probability had never seen. Even if there were no other grounds for doing so, we must therefore, to some extent at least, exclude the natural sense of the words in explaining this and similar passages. Equally however, we may not explain them in a purely symbolic sense. They are distantly, but only distantly, reminiscent of the *Song of Songs*, which provided the best authority for the expression of spiritual love in terms of physical union...(Anselm) bends his mind to the contemplation of an ideal image, he attaches it to himself with passionate intensity, he defines its nature, and he gives it a name. Here the name is that of a friend...When he wrote to his young relatives, Anselm's ardent response was excited by their monastic vocation and not by their personalities, of which he knew nothing.[7]

Here, the historian begins with the 'natural sense' of the words—how *we* might understand them if serialized in the Sunday newspapers. The suggestion of physical infatuation is then ruled out both on practical grounds (Anselm didn't know his correspondents personally) and from inconsistency with what else is known of Anselm. Southern considers and rejects the idea that Anselm is merely echoing the language of the *Song of Songs*, before reaching a conclusion incorporating knowledge of Anselm's character derived from many other sources.

The process of empathy has presented us with a paradox based on our probable misinterpretation of Anselm's words and, at the same time with the need to 'make sense' of this strand of his character and behaviour. Background knowledge of thirteenth century literary conventions is used to establish the extent to which Anselm is merely being imitative, while we return to what we might call second-order empathy to extract from all that may be known of his life and character the conclusion that he is really in love with the monastic vocation rather than with human individuals. Finally, although not within the extract given, the style of writing used here by Anselm is shown to have become widespread and more typical of a later generation. An idea reached largely through empathy is thus incorporated in a wider web of historical reasoning.

Le Roy Ladurie devotes a chapter of 'Montaillou' to 'the shepherd's mental outlook', addressed to the question 'how the people of Montaillou saw the meaning of their lives'. Among these people he selects one shepherd as the focus upon which to reconstruct a typical philosophy and, first, establishes what is known about his personality.

> Pierre Maury is the easy-going hero *par excellence*, the embodiment of cheerful openness towards the world and other people. When he greets anyone, even someone he scarcely knows and whom he has good reason to mistrust, he welcomes him with a ringing shepherd's laugh. Arnaud Sicré, the secret informer (of the Inquisition), is greeted like the rest...

Le Roy Ladurie then turns to the foundation for such *sangfroid* on Maury's part.

> Two citizens of Montaillou...asked Pierre Maury 'How is it that you dare to live in Fenouillides when you are being sought for heresy?' Pierre replied 'I might as well go on living in Fenouillides...; for no one can take away my fate. And I must bear my fate, whether it be here or there.'...The idea of ineluctable fate pursued Maury in all his subsequent travels...
>
> 'From where could Maury have got this idea of fate? From his friends the Cathars?...If we set the Albigensian (i.e. Cathar) influence aside we may easily compare Pierre Maury's idea of fate with similar notions popular among the various cultures of the western Mediterranean...Finally we may recall that Pierre Maury was a mountain shepherd, and it was these 'great shepherds of the high mountains' who, before the Renaissance, gave in their calendars the most complete version of the relationships uniting macrocosm and microcosm...We should also note that Pierre Maury's sense of destiny had no connection with absurd superstition. One day...Bélibaste was anxious because he had seen a magpie cross his path three times...Pierre laughed at him; 'Guillaume, take no notice of signs of birds...Only old women bother about such things.'
>
> Pierre Maury's sense of fate was thus not vulgarly magical but loftily philosophical. In him as in others it is simply a very old peasant idea quite natural in societies where there is no growth and where people literally have no choice.[8]

As with Anselm, we are presented with the actual words of Maury and with the impression he made upon others, as far as these can be established. Our possible reaction that he was merely superstitious is examined and rejected, as is the idea, drawn from background knowledge of the period, that he was simply copying the beliefs of the Cathars. The 'loftily philosphical' interpretation is empathetic again, drawing upon our ideas of what such philosophy entails but, in this case, also guided by sociological conclusions as to what is typical among peasants. As with Southern's remarks about the later influence of Anselm, so Le Roy Ladurie concludes with reflections about the influence of societies upon beliefs which could not have been available to the characters of his story. Thus we may see how empathy is employed at important stages of historical thinking, but not to the exclusion of other sources of interest and as one element among others in reaching conclusions in which empathy as such is transcended.

The empathetic element common to the two examples is the interpretation of an individual's viewpoint in a way that moves from our normal but anachronistic terms of reference (personal attraction; absurd superstition) through generalized influences of the period (imitation of the Song of Songs or of the Cathars) to what is characteristic precisely of the individual or social group at issue (enthusiasm for monasticism; philosophic fatalism). Empathy as a skill must therefore comprise both the evocation of a personality from the clues presented by the sources from the past and the process of refinement of this evocation into a consistent character in an authentic context.

Empathy Among Other Historical Skills

In an interesting article about historical imagination,[9] Vivienne Little sees the importance of empathy in its power to reveal to the historian the feelings which may often be as important as thoughts in motivating human activity. This must be right as far as it goes, but there is also the dimension of feeling-based intuitive thinking which the practice of empathy may stimulate and whose main historical function would lie in the generation of 'hunches' (intuitively based hypotheses) about motivation and meaning. Little writes 'Empathy is an heuristic device which the historian abandons when it has done its work, just as the builder removes his scaffolding. Its work is to aid the faithful reconstruction of the past...'[10]. As an aid to learning rather than its product the term 'heuristic' applies precisely to *any* separate academic 'skill'. It is surely a commonplace that in real learning such skills must act in combination and that their separation for the purposes of teaching or examining is justifiable only as a pedagogic (or heuristic) device, whether we are concerned with empathy or with more systematic operations. But I think Little is implying that empathy is ephemeral in a way that other skills—the bricks and mortar of historical reasoning, perhaps—cannot be. The test here is whether the products of empathy can be recognized among other elements in the historical reconstruction, and it is my contention that this is very much the case. In the elucidation of the state of mind of Anselm or of the mountain shepherds we have noted the interaction of sensitivity to nuances of person and situation with background knowledge and more general theory, but in each case we are left with a personal standpoint which we must be able to occupy imaginatively so that it all makes sense.

If then we accept empathy as a respectable feature of historical thinking—albeit a somewhat elusive one—the question arises as to how much weight it should be accorded in any scheme of study. Such questions do not perhaps allow of very precise answers, and we find ourselves at the present time adopting somewhat arbitrary emphasis for the number of different aspects of history we are able to identify. Traditionally, the study of people might be recommended for the junior and less specialized classes, while the work of historical specialists at examination level became increasingly abstract and analytical. Where a skill-based syllabus has become important to the survival of the subject, empathy generally appears as one among half a dozen or so historical skills to which approximately equal weight is accorded. But, even here, empathy as 'odd one out' among skills of an entirely predictable kind may find itself in the position of an optional extra.

Following, however, Vivienne Little's demonstration that imagination is an essential ingredient of all historical thought,[11] there seems to be some danger that this may be the casualty of over-emphasis on the practise of precisely defined skills. Although not the whole of imagination, empathy is one aspect of it and perhaps the most obvious form of imagination to apply to most of the topics and exercises commonly encountered at school. From this it might follow that provision for empathy ought not to be a discrete section of the syllabus devoted to 'depth-study' or some biographical topic, but rather a characteristic dimension of each of the other historical skills. So, instead of having 'empathy exercises' as such, the importance of empathy would appear in the method used for the presentation and teaching of evidence work, explanation, etc. By introducing into all such work the circumstances and points of view of particular people (real or imaginary according to the circumstances of the class and the topic) history's characteristic alternation between imaginative speculation and methodical investigation would be preserved and the weight given to empathy would reach something like 50 per cent.

Teaching Empathy

Given that there is a case for according more weight than is customary to the use of empathy in learning history, the question arises how to stimulate empathy and how to obtain from it the greatest contribution to historical understanding.

From the account of empathy above, it will be clear that one mode of teaching will not be appropriate for the several different kinds of insight and experience involved; it will be necessary to cater for the exploratory stage of personal projection, for background knowledge of what is typical of the situation, for the opportunity to identify with a particular subject or group through authentic detail. Thus the empathy-based course will not be entirely fragmented, since progression of this kind will involve the study of a single topic in some detail; it will also include scope for the inclusion of other historical skills.

Provision for the first stage of empathy, that of projecting one's own ideas and feelings into an historical situation accords quite well with the characteristics of the 'new history' as active learning. What will make one's pupils more active and more interested in a topic will make accessible to them a whole range of language and ideas which they will have developed informally in their homes and among their peers—for them a far richer and more stimulating register than what Barnes has called 'the language of secondary education'.[12] There is no mystery how to set about this; indeed the stimulus to empathy provides a rationale for activities such as simulation, site-visits, drama, art-work and informal group work which are often advocated pragmatically in their own right. On the same grounds, topics with an immediate appeal or which are relatively easy to visualize may provide good foundations for empathetic work. Here I have in mind the study of pupils' family history, of topics growing from the collection by pupils of relics and momentos from home or a study of the immediate locality.

However, there is one essential requirement over and above that of a pupil-involving lesson—there must be an element of paradox at some point where our scheme of things does not account for the behaviour of the past; the problem of the trial by ordeal is a case in point[13], as would be the infatuation of Anselm or the complacency of Pierre Maury. So, not every topic will serve, and simple exploratory activity, whether based on an 'age', on a locality or upon a subject such as family records will be found insufficiently stimulating to develop empathy.[14]

It has been said that the test of an historian's recreation of his characters was whether he could 'hear them talking'.[15] The ability to imagine the topics of conversation, the various points of view typical of different social groups and the terms in which such opinions might be expressed involves immersion in historical sources to a degree beyond the resources of a school history course. Yet, the recognition of what is typical of the age or the situation is a necessary ingredient for developing empathy. As suggested above, this will form a spontaneous standard of comparison for the expert historian (influence of the Song of Songs, comparison with the Cathars), but the school student will also need enough information to distinguish the period he is studying from his own. Although important for empathy, this aspect of study is not necessarily empathetic, so that relevant background material may be provided through any convenient materials and teaching methods. The main danger here is to revert from the empathy-base to a mere survey of a period. Rather, therefore, than imposing a 'background' course through set text and exposition, it will be preferable to build a collection of reference materials in the shape of selected books and worksheets to be drawn upon when needed. A programme of work might with advantage make provision for the study of such materials at an appropriate stage, but leave the actual choice open to negotiation between pupils and teacher as the interests of the pupils require. The ideal material to provide this kind of background would be, of course, a wide range of contemporary sources, such as may nowadays be obtained at very moderate cost from the archives departments of local government. For use in this way the materials would require editing and presentation so as to underline those aspects of the age regarded as typical and different from the present (the purpose of this activity would not be seen as 'discovery-learning'); they should also prove a stimulus to empathy in so far as they are colloquial and as they can be selected for detailed description of the physical aspect of things.

As an example of the power of eye witness description to evoke a typical situation consider this brief passage from Cobbett's *Rural Rides*:

> Go down into these villages, view the large, and once the most beautiful, churches; see the parson's house, large, and in the midst of pleasure-gardens; and then look at the miserable sheds in which the labourers reside! Look at these hovels, made of mud and straw; bits of glass, or of old off-cast windows, without frames or hinges frequently, but merely stuck in the mud wall. Enter them, and look at the bits of chairs or stools; the wretched boards tacked together to serve for a table; the floor of pebble, broken brick, or the bare ground; look at the thing called a bed; and survey the rags on the backs of the wretched inhabitants...[16]

The invitation 'to go down', 'to view', 'enter them', although open to Cobbett's contemporaries to follow literally, may also be taken as an imaginative tour, guided and supported by Cobbett's sharp observation.

Having 'projected' our contemporary ideas into an historical situation, having identified aspects of that situation which do not respond to modern values, and having absorbed a good deal of background material from carefully selected resources, the development of empathy now requires the presentation of a particular person or situation in terms that extend beyond the merely typical to encompass the unique circumstances of the case. The choice of a suitable assignment will clearly be of critical importance, where the burden is to resolve a genuine dilemma from the past and to create consistent motivation rather than simply adopting an individual viewpoint for description. Here the problems embodied in a particular narrative from the past will embody implicitly both the standards of its own time and also the essentially historical qualities of selection, explanation and attribution of value without which a story cannot be told. Recreation of a particular trial might, for instance form the conclusion to work on the idea of the ordeal; a series of pictures, as perhaps selections from the Bayeux Tapestry, could require interpretation as a coherent sequence of events; Bamford's description of the Peterloo meeting[17] might be used to prepare a legal defence of the radical leaders who were later to be prosecuted.

Probably the most favourable vehicle for empathetic work is the two-sided narrative where the inadequately empathetic relationship between the historical participants leads to misunderstanding, conflict, even to tragedy. For example, wider publication of the Aztec *Codices* now allows us to follow the thoughts and plans of Motecuhzoma in his dealings with Cortez and to follow the Aztec version of events as expressed in their terminology (subject of course to translation).[18] This story offers a wealth of vividly described incident for use as stimulus to empathy and as starting points for developing plans, reports and confrontations, taking the standpoint of one side or the other.

Motecuhzoma interprets the invasion as a visitation of gods, so he

> sent captives to be sacrificed, because the strangers might wish to drink their blood. The envoys sacrificed these captives in the presence of the strangers, but when the white men saw this done, they were filled with disgust and loathing. They spat on the ground, or wiped away their tears, or closed their eyes and shook their heads in abhorrence. They refused to eat the food that was sprinkled with blood, because it reeked of it; it sickened them, as if the blood had rotted.[19]

It is hard to imagine more completely opposite interpretations of an event than were made here by the Aztecs and the Europeans. The standpoint of Cortez's party would not be hard for modern pupils to share (although the Spaniards were not particularly squeamish when it came to dealing with their own captives); the Aztec position will require more preparation, although the single phrase 'as if the blood had rotted' reveals a normal attitude of enjoyment of the consumption of fresh blood in such circumstances. Based upon passages of this kind, groups of pupils could prepare reports upon Aztecs and Spaniards as seen by the other group, perhaps also comparable reports upon each group made from our own standpoint. Taking such appreciations into account, each group might develop general principles for dealing with the other side, as a preliminary to subsequent study of the events that followed.[20]

Conclusion

What then is the significance of elevating empathy from a marginal position among teaching objectives in history to one of predominance? There is no doubt that many imaginative teachers will find themselves in the position of Moliere's Bourgeois Gentilhomme who found that he'd been talking 'prose' all his life, but without the need to classify it in this way. If it were merely a matter of terminology, there would be nothing to gain from the introduction of a novel and sometimes elusive concept. However, the teaching of history is not universally imaginative. Understanding of the importance of empathy as a dimension of *every* historical topic and situation would do a great deal to underline the humane quality of history, as a subject concerned primarily with the intentions and actions of human beings and the ways in which these purposes interact and influence each other. Such emphasis would be an advance upon the acquisition of 'fact' or of second-hand opinion which may still fill students' notebooks or upon the mechanical comprehension exercises which can dominate the worksheet.

However, most readers of this book will be familiar with the 'new history' and, in particular with the work of the Schools Council History Project which has done so much to support the development of 'new' history in schools. For such readers history will no longer seem in danger of atrophy for want of mental activity; the model of 'detective-work' stands at the centre of a refurbished subject concerned very largely with the handling of evidence. It can hardly be denied that the change is salutory, but there is also a danger; in making of history an actively rational subject it is possible to overemphasize the objectivity and the stability of the judgments it may lead us to. Such a positivist interpretation of history is misleading and excludes aspects of intuitive insight into the existence and coherence of mental worlds other than the one we happen to inhabit; aspects of thought and judgment essential to history as such. Empathy is not, perhaps, the whole existential dimension of history, but to make ample provision for its development may be seen as a valuable heuristic; a way of teaching which will maintain the imaginative aspects of history against other competing influences.

Notes

1 PORTAL, C. (1983) 'Empathy as an aim for curriculum: Lessons from history,' *Journal of Curriculum Studies*, 15, 3, pp. 305–6.
2 NATALE, S. (1972) *An Experiment in Empathy*, NFER, p. 16.
3 COLLINGWOOD, R.G. (1946) *The Idea of History*, Oxford University Press.
4 See the examples quoted by ASHBY and LEE, above, pp. 74–8.
5 DUNLOP, F. (1984) *The Education of Feelings and Emotion*, Allen and Unwin, p. 78.
6 EISNER, E. (1982) *Cognition and Curriculum*, Longman.
7 SOUTHERN, R.W. (1963) *St. Anselm and his Biographer*, Cambridge University Press, pp. 72–3.
8 LE ROY LADURIE, E. (1978) *Montaillou*, Scholar Press, p. 130.
9 LITTLE, V. (1983) 'What is historical imagination?', *Teaching History*, 36, pp. 27–32.
10 *Ibid.*, p. 31.
11 *Ibid.*, pp. 28–30.
12 BARNES, D., BRITTON, J. and ROSEN, H. (Eds) (1969) *Language, the Learner and the School*, Penguin, pp. 53–62.

13 See above, pp. 67ff.
14 For further discussion of this point see C. SANSOM'S chapter in this volume, pp. 116–141.
15 I have always attributed this aphorism to G.M. YOUNG in *Victorian England* (1936) Oxford University Press, but I am now unable to find the words quoted. A full statement of Young's empathetic view of historical study appears on p. 185 of the above work.
16 COBBETT, W. (1853) *Rural Rides. Vol. II*, Dent (Everyman), p. 266.
17 BAMFORD, S. (1893) *Passages in the Life of a Radical. Vol. II*, Fisher and Unwin, chapter 25.
18 LEON-PORTILLA, M. (1962) *The Broken Spears*, Constable.
19 *Ibid.*, p. 33.
20 Further suggestions for teaching empathy will be found in the booklet *Empathy in History* (1986), SREB.

Section B

6 Making Sense Out of the Content of the History Curriculum

John Fines

Synopsis

Being asked to write about the content of the history curriculum, I turned again to an image that came to me many years ago: it is just like trying to stuff a barrage balloon into a Gladstone bag, with the train already prepared for leaving the station. The too-muchness of it all is perhaps the most impressive sensation, the smallness of the space allocated a close second, but possibly it is the haste of the operation that we all recognize, racing like demented jockeys for 1945 (or whenever the syllabus ends), feeling that there might be a winning-post after all.

Yet there are other problems, for the debate on the content of the history curriculum has gone on for many years now, and there are many positions held in the battle for the one true curriculum. For twenty years the 'skills merchants', offering a curriculum that would leave people able to do things rather than just knowing facts, seemed to be holding the fort with spirit. Then new troops, claiming to be in support, moved up, firing concepts into the arena, urging that history should teach our children basic organizing principles that were essential to the understanding of the world at large. They wore the same history uniform, but in their rearguard came people who cried that history should not be taught for its own sake but for wider educational purposes, for understandings about humanity, morality, society and (whisper it not in Gath) politics.

This war over the history curriculum went largely unquestioned for it is fun taking sides, and sniping the greatest sport around; but it doesn't take a masterly intelligence to realize that you can't do history without content, without facts, that the practice of history is inextricably bound up with knowing history. On the other hand it is perfectly clear that there is no point in history in knowing what, without also knowing how: unless you are that mindless heap of junk, a computer, you simply cannot merely know about the battle of Hastings, for example, for to know about it at once promotes reflection, and that reflection cannot be restrained within the confines of that one battle itself: the mind flies off to general ideas about rights and duties, promises, kingship, power, and violence, human folly and the clash of cultures. There is no true separation of content from skills and concepts, to separate them involves ripping to pieces the very fabric of history itself.

Thus I shall be talking of 'content' in this chapter without reference to uneasy attempts to demarcate factual information from skills and concepts, but as the whole content of the curriculum, a living, working process rather than a dissected dead body.

One aspect of the last twenty years of debate about the shape of history in schools has been an attempt to reduce the subject to logical dimensions, to set it in some kind of hierarchical order, to see it as an adult, comprehensible and well-ordered process. Although I have had some part in this myself, I have very great doubts about its utility when one is thinking about how children learn their first history. In effect I believe there is a logical fault in the attempt to impose a logical pattern on children's learning—a paradox I must try to explain.

Of course men and women are compulsive pattern-makers, arranging, ordering, sequencing, they push their material around until it makes some kind of sense to them. But the sense they are making is the sense of someone who has completed a very long journey, which has involved not just school learning but also a wide range of maturational experiences. The pattern made by those who have arrived (by diverse routes) at an acceptable result does not necessarily make sense to those starting out on that journey. The only sense it can make is if you want to impose exactly the same scholastic, emotional and social experiences on the children that the deviser of the curriculum had. Professor Elton's sense of the past began as the child of an ancient historian in Prague. Mine began as the son of a railway porter in Lincoln. He is a fine Tudor historian, I am a rotten one, but we can't make Tudor historians by shipping them off to Prague University's Department of Classical Studies in search of fostering.

Children's learning processes are not logical, indeed they frequently seem quite jumbled, incoherent, inexplicable, zipping backwards and forwards without any pattern at all. 3z seemed yesterday to understand the whole process, to have made a major breakthrough in learning, yet this morning they have turned, as if by magic into a bunch of untamed, sullen, silly animals. We search for a reason, and none comes, for there isn't a clear answer to be found, there are no stages of learning, like platforms on the way up the wall of civilization (oh Arnold, you have a lot to answer for), securely achieved, ready for the next climb. There is no sequential development that makes sense to our eyes; we are lucky in classrooms if we can apply a few broad and general propositions, observe some overall tendencies (and often they don't apply to individuals), living in hope and trust that it is all worthwhile.

The reader may find these statements anti-intellectual, perhaps anti-educational, certainly quite gloomy; but I think teachers will recognize them as realistic. If we are to set out on a trip to find a history curriculum, we cannot expect order and good sense to prevail. In every way, I believe that to teach children effectively we must somehow divest ourselves for the time being of our learning and our scholarly habits of mind, accumulated with so much effort over so many years, and stand beside the children who know so little, who have few developed abilities, are subject to pressures we forgot about years ago. Above all we must remember that they are not there by choice, we are. Long ago in Lincoln my peer-group was perhaps 1300 pupils: all got history taught to them in some shape, but only four went on to university to study it. Of that group of four, I alone remain teaching it. I must constantly question my right to teach history to all pupils, and the stance from which I teach it.

This leads us to a major question about the status of what we teach (for if it is not important then we must at once pack up and stop). Perhaps this should be a matter for philosophers to enquire into, but I think history teaching has had its fill of philosophy. Perhaps a time will come again when it is useful to invite the philosophers back in, but the damage done to the subject by the last major interruption is incalculable. So I intend to ask the question 'does historical knowledge matter?' for purely pragmatic reasons in a purely practical way. It may seem that at this stage I shall be entering the debate between factual content and skills and concepts once more, but what I am really after at this stage is the status of historical information in the context of learning. One might ask similar questions about skills and concepts in a skills-dominated or concepts-dominated curriculum, but I ask them here about the facts-dominated curriculum because that is largely what we have on our hands, in ninety eight schools out of 100.

So, should I feel in some way ashamed when all I can recall about the Directoire is that they invented knickers (I don't even know that, I am assuming, making connections)? Maybe the reader will find that a typically frivolous and flippant remark, but let me tell here a story that puts it a little into context. Many years ago when the Schools Council still existed, and overlooked all sorts and conditions of examinations a paper was put before us as a sample of what the less able might be tested upon. Then (as now, alas) the assumption was that because they couldn't write well they should do multiple-choice questions (which demand an infinitely greater expanse of pure historical knowledge than a formal essay paper does). One of the questions was 'who invented the flanged wheel?' I slowed up business a little by enquiring mildly whether any of the distinguished gathering actually knew the answer to this little question. None did. I slowed business some more by asking whether anyone cared. Not a person there could persuade me that this piece of knowledge was worth knowing *as such*. It was inert, non-functioning knowledge, and as it stood, quite worthless.

Now there are situations in which such knowledge may be applied, and indeed situations in which lack of such knowledge can be a serious embarrassment. If I have presented myself to Magnus as a wheel man, well not knowing matters there. If I am at a conference on Russian history in this century and cry out merrily 'Djugashvili, who he?', why, then it matters. If at a party I find myself unable to understand what is going on when the baroque is mentioned, then I am embarrassed. In effect inert knowledge is of value for the self-announced expert and for those who inhabit a particular cultural milieu (usually, but not always an elite).

But we are not in the business of creating experts nor are we, I hope, continuing the old-style snobbish education of the grammar schools in which the cultural information was passed on for recognition purposes only. Can you recognize a post-card illustration of a Pinturiccio at twenty paces? Good, you are a member. Can you spell the name and give the dates? Good, go one step higher, friend. You can now come to our parties.

Is this unfair, this description of historical knowledge of this kind as essentially bunk? I think not, for such knowledge, known in these ways can be very dangerous, because it is not true knowledge, very frequently as mythical as Robin Hood. Is Magna Carta really important? Well, if you know that it had a legal life of ten weeks, you start to think better of it. What about Habeas Corpus, great defender of English liberties, our gift to a wicked world? We don't actually operate it here, and it was passed by the crookedest Whig peer of them all (and my goodness wasn't that a high distinction?) acting as teller and counting at least five more votes than were cast in its favour. So what does knowing about Habeas Corpus *mean*, where is its value, when does it matter? I am prouder of knowing that the stetson hat was invented to cure TB. That fact quite moves me.

Knowledge only matters in a context, it cannot live in a vacuum; its reality consists in the need you have for it, in the use you want to put it to. Let me give a practical example: I was recently asked to do some demonstration lessons using the Schools Council Project materials on Richard III, and when I reread the pamphlet I became uncomfortably aware of why all the lessons I had seen using that pamphlet had failed. I am second to none in my admiration for the project, but those materials are terrible: they assume that having a hunch-back matters (which is pretty hard on hunchbacks, the kindest bookseller I ever knew was one) and they assume that you can find out who murdered those dratted princes. Pure piffle—history is not about detection, never has been, never can be. Clearly the only worthwhile question to ask about Richard III is what happened in those hectic months between the death of Edward IV and the death of Buckingham, and how that knowledge might make some sense of how Richard behaved. How did Richard tumble into kingship—did he fall or was he pushed? Did he react wildly, or did he plot? Was there some sort of a plan, or was what happened the unexpected result of a nexus of forces? These are real questions, they are historical questions, and we do have some chance of answering them, but to answer them we need facts—lots of them, all set out in careful chronology, for in this case time matters greatly. We must go back to Miss Hanham and Mr Wolffe and look hard at what difference it might make if Hastings were executed on the 13th or on the 20th.

The students who watched me teach were somewhat astonished to find the arch-hater of historical facts presenting children with a detailed chronology of the subject, carefully grubbed from the remoter shelves of academe, and proclaiming that the booklet wouldn't do because it told us too little information. No doubt some of them (and some of the children) thought I was showing off my knowledge, but it is important to say that knowledge is not for all time. I hope I forget it, I don't want a cluttered mind, I don't want to win competitions. But when I need knowledge, when I want to put it to some use, then it has real status, and only the best and fullest sets of materials will do.

Thus I am no despiser of information: I love it as all historians should, and have a huge appetite for it. To illustrate my meaning about knowledge in use, let me provide an analogy (I suppose I should call it a model, these days): the reserve of historical information (in libraries, archives, museums, wherever) is rather like a wood store, where all types are kept, all shapes, all sizes, because all is worth preserving (why even sawdust may be glued together to make blockboard). The good craftsman will know his yard, appreciating its value, and he will never throw anything away, always be collecting. But the yard doesn't dominate him, he rules it, makes it serve his purpose: his own skills and the demand for them are what condition the enterprise, they are what make sense of this heap of junk. Given a job to do, he first hunts around to see whether there are materials there to complete the task (not all jobs may be done). Some jobs need oak, some require big stuff, some are inlay-work, some veneering. Some craftsmen work to the market, knowing what they can do best, knowing what will sell; others lavish endless hours on careful work that will spin no money at all. But all need the woodyard, and upon the quality, suitability and strength of the woods will depend success.

Maybe the reader will sniff in all this heady talk of craftsmanship that I am reviving the old heresy of turning all children into practising historians. I hasten to disavow this always ridiculous assertion. Children cannot be historians in the same sense as university professors can, nor should they be. If our aim in teaching was to produce historians, then one look at the over-crowded profession, and its regrettably low standards of all sorts of behaviours would turn us away at once. No, we are after experience of using information because that is the only way that sense may be made: learning is not just by doing, it is essentially about doing, it gives the power to do, and each time we waste children's time by telling them things, letting them copy, making them learn by heart, then we are avoiding that action which is at the very heart of the learning. In a moment, when I have stopped being negative, I hope to expand on what that action is for.

But first we must pause to do Quixotic battle with three desperate enemies of a good history curriculum which are ever present in the wings of change, and need constantly beating down: I speak of nationalism, breadth and development. A brief tilt at each, and then I promise to be positive.

Under nationalism I want to include a whole load of isms. I rejoice in the Foreign Office comment on the Molotov-Ribbentrop Pact—'all their isms are now wasms'. For wasms are surely what we want: does not the whole of human experience shout aloud against that vaunting pride in your own side, whatever it may be, British, white, Christian, men, and should we not simply stop now? Well not according to our new criteria, I read, where the elect nation is given special protection, presumably on direct orders from above? How strange it is, when Sweden, after years of ideological commitment to teaching children only the history of modern China and India, has now turned full circle to look again at itself, of course most dispassionately. But no to isms, even to flash and trendy isms—feminism may take its place in this queue, and no cries of 'unfair' will move me, this is a principle.

Secondly let us say no to 'breadth' (which sounds like a motto for slimmers) in the sense that Tout originally saw it. Breadth was a feeling that real history implied an attempt to swallow all of it, however superficially treated, so that students should do ancient, then medieval then modern (although in his day there was no attempt upon the contemporary world). The lads who survived this course could have in their final year a taste of 'depth' which involves really knowing about something, however small it might be. Real knowledge, of course consists in knowing how little you know, how far there is to go, still at the end of the day, but perhaps that kind of knowledge is reserved for the very good PhD, the *gloria cum laude* boys. Tout's ridiculous notion of a curriculum governed by this first breadth then depth notion has done infinite harm to history teaching in schools. It turned history into a race which nobody could ever win, with the teacher getting faster and faster the nearer the exams they get, leaving out greater and greater chunks of reality in the hopes of making it to the winning post. Fast history teaching leaves out all the best bits, the stories, the detail, the rambling by-ways which intuition tells you to follow. Fast history tells lies, for it paints history not as it is, confused and confusing, bedraggled and messy, gloriously cluttered, inexplicable and maddening, and sorts it all out into one almighty washing line with only the pegs left in place. More of this later, in a more positive vein.

But first a third no, this time to development in history, which has many roots: some in good old Whig history, in the progressive view of the story of how dreadful savage cave men grew steadily and slowly until they got to be beautiful and perfect old us; it also grows from Toutism—if you teach a 'breadth' curriculum then chasing development through it is a secondary product; above all it comes from the dreaded 'lines of development' notion that did so much harm to history in the immediately postwar period. Recently Schools Council history has added weight to this notion, taking it on board for its history of medicine project. Denis Shemilt, in demonstrating with great skill what children could logically deduce about the processes of time and change from this experience, gives it a spurious glamour, but to show that children can manage to work out some positions *vis-à-vis* cause and effect does not prove these are worthwhile things to learn about, or that they are specially to do with historical learning.

In fact I would suggest that this is very dangerous ground indeed, for even in areas where a developmental model might seem appropriate (the most obvious example being the history of Parliament) we find false logic at work. Simon de Montfort had really nothing in common with William Ewart Gladstone, even though the latter thought he did. There is not growth in the history of Parliament, however much people want to show it that way. Certainly we can observe through many years a determined continuity, a reluctance to change, a tendency to hang on to past ways in the face of the whirling crises of the everyday world. But to stalk development in this way is once again to tell lies about the past: it may be convenient in the text book to block all we know or want the pupils to know about Parliament in the nineteenth century in one chapter under one heading, but such change as did occur in the nineteenth century was intimately associated with all the other aspects of life, and the only thing that demarcates parliamentary history effectively is its institutional reluctance to face change. We cannot take a longways slice out of history and thrust it upon the unsuspecting public: that is a lie.

But enough for the time being of negative bluster (clear signs to the reader that I fear the challenge of saying something positive on this knotty matter). The first positive proposition I want to push is the reverse of my second negative, anti-Toutian statement. I believe the history we should present to children should be depth, by which I mean real history. In universities we often comment on the success of special subjects where third year students suddenly come alive because we allow them to get at the real meat of history, the documented, detailed, slow and thorough study of something that clearly defines itself. The students enjoy their work and clearly do better than before, and I ask 'why can't we let them do this kind of work all the time—why must they be forced through endless trackways of mediocre failure before the few who survive to the end are given the rewarding plums of the real stuff?' Good question, but one rarely answered, for it turns the whole of the curriculum neatly on its head. If first and second year university students should be able to study in depth, why not children too?

Much of the experience of what I have called 'fast history' is indeed an experience of mediocre study in which failure is guaranteed. We tackle a patch of history so fast that nobody can catch it, understand it, enjoy it, and all the students look fools when they answer their tests because we haven't given them time to be anything else. By the time one or two of the brighter ones are getting a grip on one subject, and feeling some confidence in it, beginning to perform rather well, we whisk them on to the next, where they can look foolish all over again. I am not a great believer in conspiracy theories, but if history teachers really wanted to fix their pupils into the role of permanent inadequate idiots, then they couldn't have chosen a better way of doing it than to move through a breadth curriculum at speed.

So a hey! for the slow, thorough specialized study that we would normally associate with higher levels of learning; but immediately we must add two further propositions. First of all I think it vital that we have variety in the curriculum, for pupils can't learn if only one dimension is being examined. They will frankly grow very bored if one topic is spun out at too great a length, and they will revolt if the next topic turns out to be a mirror-image of the first. Good for them, they are wise about their own learning: pace and challenge are major requirements, they need constantly to turn corners and bump into something new.

This is not that easy for a teacher to manage. We all have our specialisms, special areas of knowledge, special interests and particular delights: the pupils get to recognize these quickly. At first they can be fun, and a strength, but the teacher who is always 'going on' about Henry VIII, or the teacher who will always stray onto battlefields whatever the topic in hand soon becomes a bore. Those who tell teachers to teach what they themselves are interested in are talking about first lessons only, in my experience. We have, in fact a duty to present to pupils the many-faceted nature of our subject. What are some of the necessary constituents? Here we will meet with disagreement in detail, but what follows might make a first stab at such a list.

First of all I want to sketch in two major dimensions which in their contrast seem to me to hold together the dynamic of the subject: I believe when we come to study history we need to discover something strange and distant and also to study something very close and familiar. In that statement the reader will at once see bound up the war between local and world history in the syllabus as well as the relevance argument of the values of the recent as against the values of the long dead. These are the two great arguments in the field, yet I would not pose them in that form, for I think they are unanswerable; I cannot judge Tutankhamen against Mubarak in terms of curricular value, nor can I honestly say that the parish church on the corner is of greater importance than knowledge about Mr Deng's China. Greedy as I am, I want them both.

The demand for both types of history might evoke a number of responses, but two major ones must be dealt with here. First of all there are the advocates of a coherent curriculum who will say that it will confuse the children if you dash from one disparate subject to another, and that it is better to stick to one thing. In answer to this I would say that I want to do every topic thoroughly, and I would want to demonstrate the interrelationship of the various topics under study. And the evaluation of the Schools Council 13–16 Project showed quite clearly that children did not worry when faced with a four-fold history curriculum.

The second challenge might be to say that this is to use history in an anthropological rather than in an historical manner, thus denying the integrity of the subject. That one is harder to get away from, for I do believe we have much more to learn from anthropological approaches to the humanities curriculum than Bruner had to tell us. What is different, however, is the material and our ways of using it, and if these remain strictly historical and the intent remains historical, then all will be well (and fascinating as anthropological reports may be, they have proved as charmingly unreliable as any historical controversy, and I do believe history to be more interesting, if just as messy).

The important constituent in holding these two dimensions together in some sort of real focus is discussion and comparison. Thus it is not enough to go from a phase of oral or family history about the recent past of our own locality to the wildly different story of Cortez and Montezuma; what we must do is to reflect on both, to do this rigorously and repeatedly, and to look in a comparative vein all the time. We must say to the children that the problems we had when the two old ladies we interviewed disagreed violently about Mr Churchill are similar in some respects to the problems of the different story told in Cortez's letters to his king from that we found in the Aztec pictograms. If we do not stop to reflect in this way then all the learning will be lost, will seep away, leaving vague memories and the question 'whyever did we do that, at school, and why did we work so hard to have nothing explained in the end?'. We must test, not the knowledge of the children, but the quality of their learning, and how fast and in what directions it is growing.

Thus far with the positive: the curriculum must be detailed, specialized study of the distant and the local, with full examination of all the implications. Let us get a bit more practical: just what shall we study? There are a number of possible constituents here, but not all are equally attended to at the moment: our history in school is often the history of events, ideas and institutions (that is, a very abstract rather than a concrete selection) and we often leave out those noble constituents of older, out-moded histories: people and places.

Fear of Carlyle (a perfectly natural condition, but one hard to cure) has driven historians away from biographical approaches. 'Great Men' (although not yet 'Great Women') histories are derided, and the role of the masses, of trends and tendencies, of revolutionary forces as major instruments of change are regularly stressed. Now I would accept that there were times when Disraeli was no more than a leaf blown by the winds, and that at other times the grand puppeteer had a few hands up his own coat, but take Disraeli away from history and what is left crumbles into a much less orderly and comprehensible scenario (which is probably a fair thing) but also one that lacks the verve and interest he supplies. I don't wish to worship him, put him up for a role model, or suggest that he was more instrumental than in truth he was, but I don't wish either to steal him from pupils' experience of history either. So let's us have some biography.

Let us also have some geography. It is astonishing that so many schools teach history and geography as if they were cognate subjects, and so many of our French masters of the Annales school tell us how desperately important a sense of place is, and yet it plays so little part in our teaching. To many students of medieval history Byzantium is more of a concept than a place, and for the Russian Revolution, well the Finland station may raise the image of a book rather than a real place of railway trains. I think we need to see places (in photographs and maps if not on trips) in our history almost as much as we need to think about the time that history took to happen. How different might the history of sixteenth/seventeenth-century Europe be in school if seen in the context of Venice, Antwerp, Amsterdam, Hamburg and Bremen? I know it all seems as old hat as biography, smacking of those little grey volumes on medieval towns or the green and black Stories of the Nations we see mouldering in second-hand shops. Perhaps their time has come again.

This is not, of course to decry the other components listed above. We do need to study some of the prime institutions of world history, we need to be learning about farming and village life, about food and its place on the world stage; we need to know about factories and cities, about all kinds of governmental constitutions and instruments; we need to know about things that connect and divide us, about exploration, warfare and travel. These great overarching concepts in history should be by no means ignored in curriculum building, but let us, for the children's sake, take the abstractness out of them, put the stories back in. We can, indeed, look at international relations, but not in the first instance merely as an idea: look instead at the astonishing story of the Congo crisis, and then, on the basis of interesting knowledge draw out in discussion some of the more general principles that may be learned from such a study.

We are beginning to fill out the content of the curriculum in relation to principles: let us now add a third, the vital quality which history illuminates is the nature of change. I have talked a little about this before, and it will be clear to the reader that I am slightly ambivalent on the subject. Change in revolutionary circumstances is interesting to look at and often useful, but it is by no means typical, and it is unwise of the curriculum builder to be over-impressed by the noise and bustle of a subject. The change that is important is the change induced by ideas, that slow and anxious accommodation to the new by those who wish to continue just as they were, but know that something has to give. Thus the notions unleashed by Marx, Freud and Darwin were much more significant in terms of real change than most of the great events of the last 100 years. To recognize the nature and power of class in shaping society, to see man as the most recent part of many millions of years of development in the context of the survival of the fittest, to unleash the yoke of inhibition man has borne before, these ideas (however simply and therefore sillyly expressed) have changed the world dramatically, and should be the subject of study.

My penultimate dimension of curriculum building is one that could cause lots of debate: I believe that if we wish to use history to teach children effectively about humanity, what human nature is, how it works, its problems and possibilities, then we require a moral focus. I really do seem to be dragging history teaching back into the nineteenth century with a will, don't I? Yet I am unrepentant: I believe children need to find out about human behaviour and they need to study many examples of many different types of behaviour, and of course reflect upon them and discuss them fully. To do this in a perfectly objective, so-called 'scientific' manner is quite impossible even if it were desirable, and I doubt that. We must judge, we must order, we must arrange, we can't stop ourselves doing that, it is part of our nature, an habitual pattern that comes with our thought processes. Children who are growing up into a baffling world where laws and commands seem to conflict with behaviours all the time ('BE QUIET' bellows the teacher) need to find out first what is fair, then what is wise, then what is right and finally what is just—find it out for themselves, I hasten to add, not have it thrust upon them as a ready-made code of conduct. History provides an endless sequence of examples on which we may draw, ranging from St Francis right through to Hitler. In our days we feed the children quite a lot about the bad end of the scale (why does almost every pupil get a dose, however small of Hitler, I wonder?) but very little of the good. Is it that history teachers fear to look like nineteenth-century Sunday school teachers, fear the children's conventional mockery of the good, the wise and the just? Perhaps a little of both, but I believe we must learn to cope with both fears if we are to offer children a good diet of examples on which to cut their wisdom teeth, on which to learn how to make judgments.

Lastly, perhaps the most obvious dimension of them all: all the time, in every aspect of their work, whatever it might be, children should be learning how to find out, how to cope with materials from the past, how to assess their findings, how to use them to make their own historical statements. When people ask about the real worth of history in the present-day vocationally oriented curriculum, I tend to use this as a prime statement, for it really does answer the question. To give a pupil the chance to learn how to find out information; to give him the confidence to deal with a lot of material and learn to analyze it; to give him some of the skills needed to judge the relevance and validity of the evidence that he finds; to give him the power to pull this all together into a convincing and coherent statement—these are no mean gifts, and though they are here specific to history, they contribute notably to the whole school curriculum, and relate immediately to major educational goals.

So these are some of the dimensions that structure the choice of content in any history curriculum. They point towards a set of educational aims, and perhaps it is time to formulate these more precisely. There are not many, but I find them important in governing my own choice of material. I want to imbue children with:

(a) a sensitivity to the hugeness and complexity of problems, with a willingness to admit that it is not easy to get things right, however much you might want to, and however clever you think you are. A properly educated person will not feel that peace could be available in Northern Ireland by banging a few heads together and sitting around a table with a crate of Jameson's to hand;

(b) a knowledge about humanity, about suffering and achievement, about order and disorder, about good and evil; some feeling for how things tend to happen, how they got the way they are;

(c) some understanding of the difficulties involved in getting at the true story, how things really happened, who was responsible and why. I want children to begin to feel for the provisional nature of historical statements, to understand the need to interpret, to question, to analyze and to rebuild the story for oneself;

(d) an enriched and inspired curiosity about positively everything from simple scandal right through to the meaning of world religions, and the confidence to let that curiosity flow and feed on finding out;

(e) some security of spirit from the knowledge of the times out of which we have stepped, what lies behind our births and origins. A delight in the past, a desire to preserve and treasure the past.

What help is all this, you cry—I read thus far in the hope that you would present me with a curriculum, with hints about *what* to teach, and now, you rat, you are ducking the great question once more. Well yes, I am, regretfully. Wherever you turn there is too much history to teach, and there are no ways inherent in the content itself for judging its value. Whatever you teach you are leaving out a host of good things. Anything in that great toy box of the past will do, we must judge alone by fitness to purpose. Choose your own historical content, then, but know above all what you want it to do for your children.

7   Concepts, Skills and Content: A Developmental Approach to the History Syllabus

Chris Sansom

Synopsis

Recent research has identified some patterns in the development of children's understanding of the 'tools of thought' of history—the concepts of time, evidence, change, causation and motivation. With an understanding of these developmental patterns, we can use them to structure our syllabuses so that we provide our pupils with thought-experiences which systematically develop their concept structure. This aim can be applied both to the history syllabus in the broad sense and to the design of smaller units of work, examples of which are given in some detail. This type of approach gives our pupils tools for survival and growth, and puts history teaching in a key position in the school curriculum.

The Tools of the Historian

When we are teaching our pupils about the past, we are using and thus leading our pupils to use ideas about the way things happen in the world, and ideas about how we know about things in the past. These ideas structure and give meaning to the events of the past. Labbett (Fines, 1983) suggests that it is profoundly unhistorical to present our pupils with those meanings in their study of the past without giving them the opportunity to explore and develop the structures and meanings for themselves. In this way, for the pupil as well as the adult historian, the 'rules of thought' which govern historical thinking—concepts of time, evidence, causation, change and motivation—turn information into historical knowledge. In other words if we wish to develop an understanding of history in our pupils, it depends on that understanding being historical, that is, informed by historical procedures and organizational concepts.

Of these, it is the concept of evidence that has attracted the most attention so far in the 'new history'. Pupils have become accustomed to handling primary sources of various kinds and to coming to conclusions from them about the past. Pupils' skills in the use of historical sources are actively developed in many history syllabuses and in some of the newer textbooks; what is more open to question is whether the concept of the nature of historical knowledge that those pupils have is actively developed. To do that requires some sort of developmental sequence in the understanding of evidence, which can then be built into the syllabus or resources.

It was this search for 'what should my pupils do first, and what should they do next?' in the area of evidence evaluation that led me into the investigation of current research into pupil thinking in history, and towards some of the implications that I attempt to develop below.

The problem of developmental sequences is not restricted to the idea of evidence. The ability to handle historical sources and to evaluate them as evidence is only a part of the historian's armoury. His task is to come to conclusions about the interrelationships of events in the past. Those inter-relationships are structured by two separate but related conceptual tools— the idea of change over time, and the idea of causation.

Each of these has a further concept associated with it: change has as its adjunct the idea of development or progress; and causation when applied to individuals takes on a more personal aspect in the idea of motivation.

I see it as a major part of our role as teachers to structure our pupils' work in history in such a way that in each of these concept areas there is a developmental sequence, the effect of which will be to raise the level of the pupil's conceptualization of what it means to use the term 'cause', 'motive' etc.

My aim in the following pages is to examine the nature of these developmental sequences and to suggest ways of building them into our history syllabuses so that as we teach our pupils the content of history, we also increase their ability to use in their own thinking its organizing concepts and thus to think historically.

What Does Historical Thinking in Children Look Like?

Research based on a Piagetian framework produced some pretty depressing results when applied to historical thinking. By the early 1970s the idea was common that the abstract and logical explanatory thought that is needed to do well in the hypothetical and deductive world of history does not develop fully in children until about the age of 16—if at all. The majority of our pupils were said to be thinking at a concrete operational level and were thus ill-equipped to meet the demands of any secondary school history course, let alone one that stresses concepts, issues and the testing of hypotheses against evidence.

Recent writers have cast doubts on the usefulness of these findings that children can't do history till they are about 16, and have supported their criticisms with research which has made the picture rather more clear and rather more hopeful.[1]

These research findings enable us to state that:

(a) The ability to think in an historically sophisticated way develops gradually in our pupils over the ages 10 to 18.

(b) There are no clear 'breakthrough' points, but by age 14 to 15 perhaps 40–50 per cent of our pupils can operate at a sophisticated level some of the time.

(c) The ability to respond at a high level is present in some pupils at first year secondary age, and may not be present in 18-year-olds studying for 'A' level.

(d) Where there was a 'control' group, a significant minority achieved results as good as those of the 'experimental' group—but only when asked deliberately probing questions.

We can conclude, then, that our pupils come to us in secondary school with a clear potential for historical thinking, which grows during their adolescence.

While the research identified a number of factors which indirectly influenced the performance of pupils in tests which assessed the sophistication of their ideas about the nature of historical thought, the most important were the teacher and the course. In his work on the evaluation of the Schools Council History Project, Shemilt found that pupil success was linked with a strong collaborative department which saw history as a problem-solving exercise and the teachers as a curriculum development team, and with energetic, knowledgeable and intelligent teachers—but successful curriculum development in many areas would claim that too! Booth (1980; and in Fines, 1983) makes several comments on the success of the teacher who values creative, independent and open-ended thinking, encourages the development of concepts through open-ended discussion and is, in general, enthusiastic and skilful in the classroom.

But it is not just the quality of the teachers that has made concept/skills based courses successful. It may seem an obvious point to make, but time and again the research reports conclude that a raised level of abstract conceptualization in pupils is linked with a course structure specifically designed to develop skills and concepts.

Teaching methods which include discussion by groups of pupils, and allow them to bring out their false assumptions without being 'put down' (Dickinson and Lee, 1978); encouragement to work out, discuss and refine thoughts and ideas (Thompson in Dickinson, Lee and Rogers, 1984); the concern of the teacher with weaving together knowledge, concepts, cognitive skills, empathy, interest and personal experience (Booth, 1983); a discussion/document/picture based programme specifically spiralling concepts and limiting content (Rogers, 1979); a course which specifically focusses on concepts of change, causation, development, evidence, etc (Shemilt, 1980): all these are thought to play a very important role in producing the main effect noted by the researchers—that the skills and concepts of history *can be* and *were* effectively taught, and that children's thinking was developed by the teaching.

The Development of Concepts

One of the most important aspects of the more recent research has been a homing in on the way in which children 'make sense of' the concepts of change, cause, motive and evidence. Shemilt in particular has analyzed some 150 in-depth interviews with carefully matched Schools Council History Project and control pupils, probing the answers given by his subjects in previous written tests. The interviews were intended to be non-threatening, but to push the child to 'explain what he means by...' until the limits of his capacity to make sense are reached. This yields rich, fascinating data but is very difficult to quantify, and it does not produce statistically verifiable results; what the interview analysis technique gives us is the possibility of making a judgment about the assumptions the subject brings to his understanding of history. By collecting a large number of assumptions about, say evidence, or cause, we can then begin to map out the different ways children construe the rules of the game.

Over ten years of research, patterns have begun to emerge which Shemilt describes as 'conceptual maps'—descriptions which point up key features in the ways pupils think about each of the concepts. He has set out schemes of pupil perceptions of the idea of cause, change, motivation and evidence which give an indication of the possible levels of understanding that we are likely to meet: the boundaries between these levels are not precise—these are points on a continuum—and pupils are not consistent in their levels of understanding. What does emerge in particular is that only at the lowest levels are pupils thinking in a directly unhistorical way; mostly their thinking exhibits an imperfect but developing set of theories about how things happen—a set of 'tools for thinking with' which can develop through the experience of thinking about historical materials.

It is difficult in a few words to do justice to the subtlety of Shemilt's analysis, but I feel it is important to our understanding of our pupils' thought to attempt to summarize his conclusions.[2]

Causation

Level 1
There isn't a 'logic' of cause in history—things happen without relationship to each other, and there isn't a problem. The story 'unfolds' but doesn't develop.

Level 2
If it was caused, it had to happen—sees causes as a string of units, the 'sum' of which is an inevitable event; a mechanistic view.

Level 3
Causes rather like forces interacting in *combination*; we can't know all the causes and give a comprehensive and final picture of reality; events are unique because the complex interaction of factors is unlikely ever to be repeated.

Level 4
Causes like a net: and the relationship of the knots to each other can be as important as what the knots are; the dimensions and properties of causal factors, and the relationships between them, change with time.

Change and Continuity—The Analytical Aspect of Time

Level 1
Changes are unrelated; they do not transform the story.

Level 2
(a) Change is a series, a long causal chain extending back to a 'first cause'.
(b) *Everything* which happened in the past is an antecedent to the present.

Level 3
Historical change as the gradual transformation of a situation; only some aspects of a situation change, and then may do so trivially or radically.

Motivation and Intention as Explanations of the Past

Level 1
A patronizing attitude to the past—they acted like that because they were stupid/earlier than us/not as developed.

Level 2
Attribution of motives but in a vague, generalized or stereotyped way—'because of his character', 'because of religion'.

Level 3
Attribution of specific motives, but from a twentieth-century viewpoint: the feelings could be equally valid in a different historical situation.

Level 4
Sees the need for the reconstruction of historically apt motives: 'what would be different in my feelings living at that time, in that situation?'.

Level 5
Sees the difficulty of using sources from a different world as evidence for the attribution of motives, feelings, etc, in that world.

Evidence and Historical Method

Level 1
Evidence = information; it's true because it's there to be known.
    At this level, pupils see evidence as a jigsaw of facts with pieces missing, see no need for supportive evidence and make no sense of contradictory evidence.

Level 2
Picture of the past reconstituted from evidence (rather than reconstructed on the basis of evidence); the evidence is there to be discovered, and when you've discovered it, it gives you the answer. Evidence is a superior form of narrative.

Level 3
Historian has to work out conclusions, reduce his uncertainty. Evidence more like a book of sums than an answer book.

Level 4
Realization of importance of context and historicity of evidence: historian's job is reconstruction.

    What are the developmental implications of these 'levels'? It seems to me that they are sequenced descriptions of a dynamic thinking process rather than stages of mental development. If we think of historical understanding as being built up in a pupil by the cumulative experience of the historical thought-processes he has been through in tackling historical problems, then a pupil has the potential to show sophisticated historical understanding from the start, but at any particular point in his historical education reaches a more or less limited understanding which can be described approximately by one of the levels. Development of his understanding to a further level is dependent on further process-experience at or around the appropriate level. The levels of understanding are thus a guide for sequencing and structuring the processes of thought we want our pupils to go through, rather than absolute intellectual stages through which their minds develop.

Table 1 is an attempt to summarize the research findings described above. Reading down the columns we have typical concept-development stages which represent the 'ways of thinking about things' that we want our pupils to make their own. While it is unwise to read too much 'parallelism' into the horizontal levels, I would hope that at least some pupils were already beyond the preliminary level on arrival in secondary school, and that all pupils would reach at least the third level before giving up history as a school subject.

Building 'Process' Into the Syllabus

Whenever pupils are engaged in work on an historical topic there are two types of learning outcome: *knowledge of the content or concept* under study and *experience of the process* of historical thought. I think the primary implication of the research described above is that these process-experiences are vital to the development of historical understanding— indeed in a sense they *are* historical understanding in that children's concepts of what historical explanation is all about rest on the experience they have had of historical thought.

There is a strong similarity apparent between this 'historical thought in action' and what Hexter (1972) has called the historian's 'second record'—his 'skills, the range of his knowledge, the set of his mind...and experience' (p. 104). Dickinson, Gard and Lee[3] emphasize the public and open nature of this second record, which, while it allows room for the subjectivity that gives originality to an historian's work, also includes 'the shared understandings and procedures characteristic of a public form of knowledge' which in particular govern the way historians use their sources to validate their statements about the past. While Dickinson, Gard and Lee are concerned primarily with historical evidence in the second record, I think they would agree that the assumptions about how humans behave, encapsulated in the historical concepts of motivation and causation, and the assumptions about events and time that we make when using terms like change and development, are equally part of the second record, part of the experience of thought in action that we use when talking about the past.

Table 1: *Concept Structure*

| Level | **Concept** | | | |
	Causation	*Motivation (Empathy)*	*Evidence and Knowledge*	*Change, Development, Continuity*
Preliminary level	Story just happens: fact = cause	People in the past were underdeveloped	Evidence = information about the past	Discontinuous eruptions of events
Basic grounding	Causes as a series	Generalized motives	Evidence needs collation by historian to turn it into knowledge	Change and progress uni-directional and linked
Minimum competence	Causes interacting	Specific motives	Evidence can be misleading and needs interpretation	Change not always equal to progress
Further study	Causes nesting	Historically apt motives	Evidence gives us provisional knowledge	History a gradual transformation, always changing
Advanced	Causes bound to period; historiography of causation	Sees difficulties of attributing mentalité from evidence	Knowledge a best possibility validated by context of evidence	Different rates of change going on simultaneously, with links forward and backward in time

For the entries in this table I owe a considerable debt to the work of Shemilt.

What is happening when a pupil is thinking about a problem in history and trying out an historical concept on some new material?

I think we can sum it up like this:

(a) An historical concept (in the broad sense, for example, causation) is an assumption in the pupil's mind about how the world works and what kind of knowledge we have of it.

(b) We have some evidence for the type of assumption he is making from the ideas he expresses about the past and the way he handles particular examples of historical thought—his second record in action in the process of thought.

(c) Thought in action is an interplay of skills, experience and new material which is given structure by the concept assumptions; in the process of that interplay the structure may be modified—an assumption about the nature of history and the past may become more complex and sophisticated, more like that of a mature historian.

The mechanism of the learning that is taking place is thus an interplay of skills, experience and material which modifies the concept structure of the pupil; the mechanism of teaching ought then to be *the provision of experiences which modify the pupil's concept structure through the exercise of his skills on historical material.* The nature of the experiences we should provide depends on the level of sophistication of the pupil's concept structure and the point on the developmental sequence towards which we are trying to bring him.

These experiences must now become the building blocks of our syllabuses—the ways our pupils are dealing with historical materials must be specified as systematically as the content of the materials has always been. The following tables attempt to provide a blueprint or framework for the construction of the process aspect of a syllabus.

Each table takes as its starting point the developmental concept structures summarized in table 1. The various levels of each concept are linked to sequences of skills in use of evidence, empathy and chronology which relate to the appropriate level. The final column of each table suggests a process or exercise by means of which the chosen level of conceptualization may be developed or reinforced.

The suggested thought-process is not, of course, the only possible one in each case; it is, however, a reminder of the interplay of skills and concepts and embodies what the research would lead us to think of as most fruitful in the development of our pupils' perceptions and understanding of the procedures of history and the organizing concepts of causation, motivation, change and evidence that lie behind those procedures.

It is the 'big conceptual questions' then that should guide our selection of content, and it is the same big conceptual questions inherent in the content that justify its selection or retention. Any content unit will have a

Table 2: Concepts, Skills and Processes: Causation

Concept Level	Appropriate Skill Levels			Examples of Process
	Evidence	Empathy	Chronology	
Story just happens: fact = cause	Comprehension and deduction of story from one or more sources	This is what they did	Events in order; sequencing of sources	Describes events
Causes as a series	Recognizes causal statements as such	Can see individual actions as causation	Can give date, how long ago, century, age-name	Answers 'why did it happen' by list
Causes interacting	Infers causes from primary sources. Compares and correlates statements about cause	Can relate individual actions to causes	Can locate event in period and relate to other events	Multiple answers showing interaction of causes
Causes nesting	Can differentiate actor's and historian's views of causes	Can assess relative importance of individual motive and attitude as a cause	Can place event clearly in broader period context	Differentiates long and short term, cause, condition and contingency
Causes bound to period; historiography of causation	Can relate causation explanations to historiography	Empathy becomes part of reconstruction of past, explaining models of mind within which causes and motives operate	Recognizes historiographical significance of periodization	Differentiates historians' views of causation

Table 3: Concepts, Skills and Processes: Motivation (Empathy)

Concept Level	Appropriate Skill Levels			Examples of Process
	Evidence	Empathy	Chronology	
People in the past were under-developed	Recognizes then-now differences	Recognizes 'strangeness' of actions	Events in order; sequencing of sources	Notices differences, strangeness of actions
Generalized motives	Can identify attitude or opinion in a source	Recognizes possible but general attitudes and motives	Can give date, how long ago, century, age, name	Explains reasons for actions—vague and generalized
Specific motives	Can infer motives and translate attitudes expressed in sources	Can attribute specific motives to individuals	Can locate event in period and relate to other events	Imagines self in situation
Historically apt motives	Can relate inferences about attitude and motive to context of sources	Limits selection of motives by knowledge of period and evidence	Can place event clearly in broader period context	Attributes attitudes by reference to norms of past period
Sees difficulties of attributing mentalité from evidence	Clear view of problems of inference and translation of motives from sources	Empathy becomes part of reconstruction of past, explaining models of mind within which causes and motives operate	Recognizes historiographical significance of periodization	Historian's remoteness from actors clear in writing

Table 4: Concepts, Skills and Processes: Evidence and Knowledge About The Past

Concept Level	Appropriate Skill Levels			Examples of Process
	Evidence	Empathy	Chronology	
Evidence = information about the past	Comprehension and translation of information	They were 'different'	Events in order; sequencing of sources	Accumulates information from sources
Evidence needs collation by historian to turn it into knowledge	Inference, collation, colligation of sources; awareness of gaps and irrelevance. Primary/ secondary distinction	They were like us	Approximate dating of sources. Accurate sequencing	Works things out from sources. How do we know?
Evidence can be misleading and needs interpretation	Primary/secondary nesting; fact/opinion; attitude, emotive language, propaganda, bias, authenticity; types of source—general	Imagines self in context of period	Uses dates in evidence and argument	Criticizes and rejects some sources. Biased = unreliable
Evidence gives us provisional knowledge	Overlap of primary/ secondary. Typicality. Corroboration, reliability and purpose of historian. Value of bias. Types of source—specific	Steps outside self towards person in period	Establishes chronology as part of evaluation of evidence	Demonstrates points by reference to sources. Relates to background knowledge. Goes beyond information given. Assesses utility of source for purpose
Knowledge a best possibility validated by context of evidence	Selection, editing, referencing, evaluation of source's use of evidence	Difficulty of interpreting a mentalité	Time is a construct of the historian	Reconstructs temporal and social context, analyzes alternative possibilities

Table 5: Concepts, Skills and Processes: Change, Development and Continuity

Concept Level	Appropriate Skill Levels			Examples of Process
	Evidence	Empathy	Chronology	
Discontinuous eruptions of events	Sources used 'end-on' or individually	Recognizes 'strangeness' of actions	Events in order; sequencing of sources	Makes lists of events in order
Change and progress uni-directional and linked	Differences between sources	Recognizes stimulus in motives	Time lines, scale—AD/BC, age, name, century	Can see uni-dimensional trend in events
Change not always equal to progress	Inferences about trends from sources	Specific attitudes and motives	Period names, detailed time lines	Can see trends in developments
History a gradual transformation, always changing	Linking of sources to infer multiple or independent trends	They had good reasons for being different	Can handle several time scales at once	Can separate change from progress. Can recognize continuity
Different rates of change going on simultaneously, with links forward and backward in time	Seeks evidence for continuity, etc, actively in use of sources	Can we be certain we know what it was like?	Change/development/ continuity are historians' constructs	Demonstrates strands of change, continuity, etc, clearly in writing

Table 6: Framework for a One Year Course[4]

Type of Unit	Concept Area	Main Skills Areas
1 Development study	Progress/continuity/change	Chronological; academic, use of evidence, empathy
(This could take the form of a 'theme', for example, transport, or a 'period', for example, early man, or an 'attitude' study, for example, immigrants in Britain 600 BC – 1984 AD)		
2 'Turning point' study	Causation, motivation	Use of evidence, empathy
(for example, the Renaissance, the Industrial Revolution)		
3 A 'mystery' or 'contrast'	Empathy, motivation	Empathy, use of evidence
(for example, why did they behave in that way at that time or why did they behave differently from us? 'patch')		
4 An evidence study	Evidence/knowledge of the past	Evaluation of evidence

spin-off in other conceptual areas but a major feature of the process-based syllabus is that it provides a structure by means of which a clear balance can be kept between the concepts, and a clear relationship between concepts and skills, and thus helps to ensure our syllabuses are developmental in a fairly systematic way.

We have to fit together concept development levels, appropriate skills and the materials and resources we have available or can design for ourselves. We have to be aware of needs for balance and variety, of the possibilities offered by the local area and by current concerns, and we are faced with the constraints of time, money and examination syllabuses. I offer here some suggestions for syllabus strategy—a general scheme, a specific example and an analysis chart.

Table 6 is a suggested framework for the history syllabus: a progression in which each section of the course includes specific elements. Table 7 is a practical example of how topics, concepts and skills can be united in one year of a course: the layout attempts to specify the main concept level aimed at within each topic, as well as the skills to be developed or consolidated and some of the content-concepts.

The format is one that may be useful to teachers in analyzing their own courses and a blank version of the same table could be completed as an analysis of an existing or planned syllabus or scheme of work.

Designing Work Units

The success of a process-based syllabus depends heavily on the quality of the thought-processes the pupils experience in tackling the work set by their teachers. The quality of design of individual work units is thus very important. I want to consider again the principle of developmental

Table 7: Example of a Third Year Syllabus

Time	Topic	Main concept and level	Subsidiary Concepts	Skills				Content concepts
				Evaluation	Empathy	Chronology	Academic skills	
7–8 weeks	Renaissance and reformation	Causation—interacting, nesting. Causation—individual role	Change Motivation	Use of sources Dating of sources from internal evidence	Attribution of specific motives	Revise: AD/BC. century, Ages Intro: period names. Time line of events. Source dating	Explain set of causes. Narrative of events	Nation, science, art, factor, conflict, Protestant, Catholic, gen us, church, abuses, reform.
7–8 weeks	Nature of evidence	Evidence—types of, collation of, inference from, interpretation	Change	Dating of sources, types of sources, translation inference, primary/secondary		Sequencing, dating of sources	Translation, inference, research	Document, artefact, accounts, relic, record, authenticity?
7–8 weeks	Industrial Revolution	Causation: multiple, nesting. Motivation—specific, historic	Change Evidence	Use of primary/secondary sources	Imagine self in context of period, explain differences	Detailed time line. Interaction of time scales. Conventional period and names	Use of specialist terms, synthesis of explanations in essay form, making notes	Revolution, industry, transport, slum, laissez faire, population, reform, propaganda.
7–8 weeks	Problems of evidence	Evidence misleading; purpose of historian		Spotting fact, opinion, attitude, emotive language, contradiction etc		Dating of evidence	Express attitude in own words	Fact, opinion, attitude, corroboration utility, reliability emotive.
7–8 weeks	Twentieth century	Causation, change	Evidence	Use of current media, evaluation of media.	Explain differences in view, attitude	Detailed chronology of an event	Research skills. Arguments for and against a view	Politics etc.

(Two full hours a week over 40 weeks: 3rd year of a 7 form entry 11–18 comprehensive) sequencing as it applies to sub-divisions of the syllabus which can be as small as a single exercise or as large as several weeks' work, but which can be seen as a unit developing a specific historical concept.

There are certain criteria which should be built into work units:

(a) Each one should be concept specific—that is, should aim to develop the understanding of one of the major historical concepts; and it should be explicit about the type of thinking which is its focus.

(b) Each unit should have a definable place in a sequence of concept-development.

(c) Each unit should focus on one or two of the levels within a concept; it should include work which reinforces a concept level or work which aims to advance understanding of a concept or preferably both.

(d) It should recognize the historical skills appropriate to that level of concept, and include practice at those skills, as well as their application to a new situation.

(e) A unit has both broad and limited objectives: the limited objective is that the pupil should experience the thought-processes embodied in the unit (if he doesn't, the unit is inappropriate to his conceptual needs); the broad objective is that the pupil's understanding of an historical concept should develop, either in level or in breadth.

(f) The end product of the unit, the pupil's work, should include some answers which give evidence of his current level of understanding of the broad. historical concept in question, as well as being open to assessment on some of the other criteria commonly in use relating to the skills and the content of the unit.

The development of these broad procedural concepts is the aim of our teaching. The objective of each work unit should thus be to encourage in the pupil the application of his second record and skills to some historical material in an historical thought-process; the process thus becomes the key to the design of the unit, and ensures that the outcome, the work produced by the pupil, is concept-related.

It also serves—very importantly, too—in building up historical understanding in the propositional sense, and thus helps to 'fill in' the pupil's second record that he takes on to further historical experiences. It is important to remember that any work unit, even one that is purely concerned with information and concepts of a propositional nature ('know that...'), also carries with it conceptual assumptions of a procedural nature; whether we like it or not, those assumptions will become part of the second record—so we need to be aware of them, particularly where we are concerned with the nature of causation and the status of our knowledge about the past. A process-led work unit is one that is designed specifically to enable pupils to explore ways of thinking about the past, as well as to explore the past itself.

Examples of Process-led Work Units

Let us now look at some ideas for work units which could serve to develop the main historical concepts over a longer or shorter period. Most of these examples could be used in years 1–3 of a secondary school.

Change, Development, Continuity and Time

Exercises in years 1–3 need to focus on concrete manifestations of change and on linking the details of visual materials with time-words (ages, periods, date-related concepts such as 'industrial revolution').

It is possible to make up a wide variety of work units on the *'pictures of change'* principle. Two simple examples are: a sequence of (reconstructed) figures of early man from Proconsul through to *Homo sapiens*; and a sequence of pictures of education in action, from a Greek vase through a monastery, an Elizabethan schoolroom, to early and later nineteenth and twentieth century examples. Such sequences obviously lend themselves to exercises such as 'put these in (chronological) order', 'discuss and research possible dates/period names', 'describe the changes', 'make inferences about the trends'. Basic skills of chronology and basic change-concepts are thus developed simultaneously.

It is also possible, even with these simple examples, to introduce a further 'push' to the conceptual levels: for example, the places appropriate to South African Australopithecus and West European Neanderthal Man are complicating factors in the sequence; and in the education example, medieval and industrial-revolution schoolrooms may give rise to an animated and quite complex discussion about change and progress, for example, individual tuition versus mass education. Study of the evolution of human life and culture provides an opportunity for introducing the idea of gradual and partial development at an early stage: at what point can we call early man human? Here are some possibilities:

When did man become human?

5,000,000 BP	Upright stance. Family groups. Communication?
2,000,000 BP	Use of tools? Enlarged brain, smaller jaw.
1,000,000	Definite use of tools. Communication by speech/language.
750,000	Use of fire. Enlarged brain.
500,000	'Culture' = technology shared worldwide.
c 250,000	Virtually modern skeleton and brain.
c 100,000	'Religion' = burial of dead with symbolism.
c 50,000	Physically 'Modern' *Homo sapiens*.
c 25,000	'Art'—carvings and cave paintings.

This way of thinking about change is pretty abstract for 11–12 year olds—but has resulted in some excellent discussions. It helps the pupil to present, like the historian, an 'evaluated profile of time'.[5]

It is probably better, though, to stick with fairly concrete examples when tackling ideas of continuity and here the local environment can provide many examples; it is very important to keep the level of conceptualization of change as high as possible, and to exercise chronological skills; a footpath is not just a piece of the past 'fossilized': it has links with fairly specific, datable periods of history, for example, early Middle Ages, Turnpike roads, the building of a housing estate; and while it is an example of continuity—still in use after hundreds of years—it is also an example of change in that its purpose for the community may be very different now (girls exercising their horses) from 150 years ago (short cut across fields from village to mill) and from 500 years ago (main route linking villages to market).

The following list of ideas about change has been produced as an introduction to the Schools Council History Project development study on Medicine through Time.[6]

(i) Things change at *varying rates*, sometimes quickly and sometimes slowly, for example, man has *evolved* over a *long period* of time, whilst the evolution of flight has been *rapid* and dramatic.

(ii) There is a wide variety of *factors* which have *stimulated* change. There is also a wide variety of factors which have *inhibited* change. The idea of *time* itself is liable to vary, for example, 1974 AD = 1394 AH = 5734 AM; change does not of itself mean that a thing is improved upon, for example, Ancient Jewish and Anglo-Saxon views of the universe—we know that both are wrong, so the ideas are *different*, there is a change, but *no better*.

(iii) Sometimes things change for the better—this is *progress* or *development*. Sometimes things change for the worse—this is *regression*. Change can be *intended* or *unintended*. Change can depend on *interacting* reasons. Not everything changes at once—some things do not change—this is called *continuity*. There can be chains of *cause and effect* where an effect acts as the cause of another change.

Perhaps an aim of our teaching about change should be that all pupils can apply the italicized words to appropriate situations by the time they finish studying history.

Causation

The idea of 'factor' and 'development' in the list above presupposes some sort of idea about causation. It is important to remember that we are working from a base level which does not see a need for the question 'why'?

Interviewer: If I drop this pen, why does it fall?
Subject: Because it got dropped.
Interviewer: Easy, yes!...Is it so easy to explain why the Second World War occurred?
Subject: Cos they had a fight.
(Interview extract reported by Shemilt, 1983b, p. 5)

As with the 'change' concept, failure to come to terms with the question 'why?' makes it impossible for the pupil to grasp the relationship of the story the historian tells to the reality depicted in it—the girl in the extract just quoted uses the word 'because' in a way that is very different from her teacher.

It looks as if our teaching about causation in the early years of secondary school has to be fairly basic, concerned mainly with identifying causal statements as such, and exploring the different sorts of causes and factors to which we can attribute responsibility for events.

Some types of work which would seem to contribute towards those ends are:

(i)   *'Detective' work*, in which pupils explore the kinds of questions historians can ask about an event in the past, as well as trying to give answers to them.

(ii) *Simulations*, in which several factors have to be manipulated to reach a conclusion, for example, the 'Seige' computer simulation, which can be followed up by an analysis of why the attempted strategy failed or succeeded, as well as which factors were important to the result.

(iii) *'Spotting the statement'* exercises—extract the 'who, where, when and how?' statements from a piece of historical writing, and examine the nature of the statements that are left—the 'why?' statements.

(iv) *Cause-effect matching*: match up items from a list of causes with items from a list of effects, and give an example which illustrates each pair (this works better with a development than an event).

(v)   *'Factors charts'*—devising diagrams which show the factors behind, or reasons for an event: these could eventually become quite sophisticated, identifying factors and causes of different kinds, for example, short-term and long-term; economic, political, religious, etc; necessary conditions, immediate causes, contingencies.

(vi) *'Case studies'* in which the justification for the exercise is the ideas it raises about the nature of cause and effect in human affairs. Possible topics are an event in the pupils' lives—a fight, an accident; an event in the news—especially if there is some controversy about its causes, as for example, the Korean jumbo-jet incident; and a study of different types of explanation of the same event—for example, a scientist's and historian's explanations of a death.

Evidence and the Kind of Knowledge We Have About the Past

The basic-level distinction between information and evidence, between 'what do we know?' and 'how do we know that?' seems to be one that emerges best through exposure to source material at an early   it would seem to me that exercises which push pupils into making inferences from visual or artefact sources will raise that distinction better than document based exercises, because the comparison in the pupil's mind between the source and the statement he has made is in itself a concrete manifestation of the distinction.

West, too, suggests that a basic grounding in the evidence concept can be built up in very young children by exposure to and discussion of historical objects and pictures. There is a wealth of material related to developing the concept of evidence and skills in handling and analyzing sources derived from his work with 8–13 year olds in West (1981).

The following sequence of exercises has been found to be useful in practice with third year pupils. The particular sources selected were *not* intended to relate to anything the pupils were studying at that time—they are examples which were intended as methodology exercises and as a spur to discussions of the nature of historical evidence.

(i)   *Different sorts of written sources*: a wide selection of source extracts was presented, with questions aimed at:
      (a)   Inference from the source.
      (b)   Things the source doesn't tell us.
      (c)   Problems in using particular kinds of sources.
(ii) *Primary and secondary sources*: links between secondary source statements and specific primary sources (as in 'What is History?' Book III). Picking out from an historical novel phrases likely to be based on primary evidence (easiest with physical descriptions, for example, Roman Army moving into battle) and suggesting types of source supplying data. Analysis of newspaper report for primary and secondary traits. Discussion of use made by historian of primary and secondary sources in research, etc. I think this is probably as far as the primary/secondary distinction can usefully be taken with third years—there is obvious scope, however, for further sophistication with fourth and fifth year pupils in discussing Schools Council History Project Paper II questions: I can recommend in particular the paper on the Charge of the Light Brigade ('O' level 1983).
(iii) *Fact and opinion*—the following exercise has provided many a happy hour of discussion with third years—and older pupils too:

> Which of the following are facts and which are opinions? Think about each one carefully.
>
> (a) Queen Victoria died in 1901.
> (b) Queen Victoria was a bad queen.
> (c) Marco Polo was an explorer.
> (d) Robin Hood was a famous outlaw.
> (e) The Romans were an important civilization.
> (f) World War Two started in 1939.
> (g) World War Two was caused by Hitler's invasion of Poland.
> (h) The Middle Ages began in 1000 AD.
> (i) The 'Middle Ages' is a term used by historians.
> (j) Historians have opinions.

(iv) *Attitude, tone, impression*: this type of exercise can equally well be used in or out of context: it is, I think, useful to distinguish between giving examples of attitude, tone, etc. *from* a source (which also gives practice in quotation skills) and describing (in own words) the attitude or impression conveyed *by* the source—a rather more difficult exercise linguistically, which stretches powers of abstraction and generalization.

(v) *Use of emotive language:*
    (a) Picking out from a secondary source (for example, an historical novel) words or phrases used by author to convey an impression. Discussion of nature of this kind of evidence; discussion of possible validation of such an impression in primary evidence.
    (b) Picking out examples of value-laden words from newspaper article or propaganda source. Discussion of how historian can use evidence of this kind leads to insights on bias and the historian.

(vi) *Reliability*: the main idea to get across at this stage is that reliability and the historian's purpose are inextricably linked.

(vii) *Vocabulary*: at this third year stage, and as a preparation for fourth and fifth year work, the use of the following terms seems appropriate: authenticity; corroboration; value-judgment; emotive language; attitude; reliability; propaganda; bias.

Empathy

The approach to empathy in the teaching of history has been analyzed in great depth by Shemilt[8] and I agree with his view that we should be concerned particularly with the role of motivation in human affairs and with the interpretation of human motivation as brought to us through historical sources. Many of the exercises commonly done under the name of empathy evoke responses at rather low level in the conceptual scales by requiring pupils to project themselves into the past and attempt to live out an historical experience. The child's lack of historical experience tends to result in the projection of twentieth century emotional responses onto an historical background. This is clearly an improvement on the levels of understanding at which the actions of people in the past are seen as stupid or underdeveloped, but how can we improve on such responses?

Shemilt[9] suggests that two types of exercise might structure the pupil's thinking process in such a way that the result is a consideration of motivation in its historical context. It is interesting to note that these exercises are very similar to those which led to such fruitful analytical results in Dickinson and Lee's research work (1984, chapter 5). The two types present pupils with an 'empathetic problem' either through the upsetting of a previously formed perception, or through a motivation puzzle.

(i) *Empathetic dilemma problems*
In the first type of exercise, pupils are presented with some materials from which they are asked to make a judgment about the likely action or reaction of a person in an historical situation. Having reached a 'satisfactory' solution, they are then presented with further sources which show the actual action—an unexpected one. The problem of resolving the misfit opens eyes to the position of the person in his motivational context.

(ii) *Empathetic comparison problems*
The second type involves a comparison—usually of the actions of a person in the past with the likely action of a modern counterpart. Again the historical character has to be understood in the context of his own time's perception of moral and political rectitude rather than that of the twentieth century. It is very pleasing to see this type of question occurring regularly in Schools Council History Project CSE and 'O' level examinations—particularly as this structure can be applied to many different historical contexts and still give results which are directly comparable.

The trend in empathy exercises is thus away from imagination towards explanation.

It is, of course, impossible for the teacher to produce an endless succession of process-led work units from his own resources and in his own time. Much of the time we are working from textbooks, sometimes from very old ones. We must always try, though, to be aware of the process implications of the things the pupils are doing, and plan their use of the materials, whatever they are, in such a way that the thought-processes called for are developmentally valid.

Many of the newer textbooks, especially for lower secondary use, incorporate an evidence based approach—but that doesn't mean they help our pupils to develop ideas about cause, motivation or change; and at times, the types of conceptual demand made of pupils using the books fly erratically and inconsequentially up and down the levels of conceptualization that pupils are capable of.

Even in a well thought out series such as *History in the Making* (Macmillan) there are opportunities missed in prompting the teacher to use the books in a process-led rather than a content-led way. As an example, take the section on Martin Luther in *The early modern world*. Over four pages the Luther story is told, with a nice balance of illustrative detail, narrative and background explanation (though a paragraph on the abuses of the church would have been useful); but there is no attempt to point pupil or teacher towards questions like 'What was the influence of William of Anhalt/the Renaissance/printing/etc. on Luther?', 'What outside forces made his protest into a revolution?', 'Was the situation or the person more important?'—questions that third year pupils will discuss avidly and which give them a fine example of the interlocking of causative factors with human personality and motivation in historical change.

Getting rid of the idea of a 'history textbook' and using a wide variety of books old and new and visual, artefact and even oral sources is an option that is increasingly being forced on us by the economic situation—we can turn it to our advantage if the 'process' aspect of the syllabus is the controlling factor in guiding pupils' work rather than the content of individual textbooks.

For example, a neat change/development exercise can be constructed from a text book account of the development of castles[10] if pupils can consider how the reasons for castle-building changed during the Middle Ages, and what factors influenced their design and construction at different times. The aim should always be to get the pupils to try to answer genuinely historical questions, rather than remain at the 'textual comprehension' level.

History in the Curriculum

The type of history syllabus advocated in this chapter implies an open philosophy of education in which the role of the teacher is to plan and resource intellectual experiences for the pupil, rather than to transfer specific knowledge. This is as much an historical philosophy as an educational one, since it is based on the idea that our statements about the past are provisional, open to question and made from within the framework of our own time and culture.

Responsibility for active thinking is thus placed firmly on the pupil, who should not be able to rely on the teacher for ideas—the teacher is instead a provider of tools for thinking with. The process-based history syllabus thus makes a contribution to the development of autonomy and self-reliance in pupils.

Apart from tools for thinking with in the more general sense, a study of history can give pupils tools for dealing with the affairs of the world beyond school.

There is a telling phrase in HMI's approach to this aspect of an historical education—'informed scepticism' is the attitude that they like to see history developing in pupils[11], through the opportunity for critical evaluation of sources of evidence: this is a tool which the pupil can carry out of the classroom into the media-dominated world, a tool of value even at the basic level of distinguishing between fact and opinion and spotting propaganda.

An other tool of thought hinted at by the Historical Association, is of equal value: the understanding of human society in action. We are failing our pupils throughout their lives if we cannot give them an understanding of causation, of how things happen in the world. What chance is there of changing your relationship with a world whose workings are a mystery to you? If things 'just happened' in the past, we can't do anything about the future either.

An understanding of evidence and of causation then, gives our pupils tools for handling their future. Through the study of history our pupils can develop a maturity of approach to their world.

It is not just this open philosophy which can give history a clear role to play in the school's broader curriculum: I think it will be clear already that there must also be an openness of teaching style and methods in a process-based history syllabus, an openness which links history with recent developments in the area of personal and social education, especially in the approaches characterized by the life skills and active tutorial work schemes.

Among the approaches that history shares with these areas I would include:

(i)   the building up of provisional answers to broad analytical questions rather than 'correct' answers to limited questions;

(ii)   the building up of these answers from more than one type of source and by participatory methods, for example, the sharing and pooling of ideas; discussion and oral work; drafting, comparing and reviewing;

(iii)   the teacher's role as a resource and a planner/manager of experiences;

(iv)   variety and flexibility of classroom activity, eg small and large group work as well as individual and full class work;

(v)   the educational value of the lesson activity is as much in the process as in the content, and several different levels of process-activity may be going on simultaneously;

(vi)   the developmental objectives of the learning experiences are specified as precisely as possible as well as the content.

We are in a position to be leaders of curriculum development in our
schools in moves towards giving the academic curriculum a central role not
only in the intellectual but also in the personal development of each pupil.
The concepts that structure our syllabuses—the tools of thought of the
historian—really are tools for survival and growth in the world of the third
millennium. No pupil should leave our charge without those tools.

Notes

1   There are useful critiques of the Piagetian approach by DICKINSON, A.K. and LEE,
P.J. (1978b) and BOOTH, M. (in FINES, J. 1983). For examples of recent research,
see DICKINSON, A.K. and LEE, P.J. (1978b), GARD, A. and LEE, P.J. (1978),
BOOTH, M. (1983a and 1983b), SHEMILT, D. (1980, 1983a, 1983b and 1984) and
ROGERS, P.J. (1979a and 1984b) and the present author's review of that research
SANSOM, C.J. (1985).
2   They can be found in full detail in the various articles and books listed in the
References. I am grateful to him for the opportunity to discuss his work with him
at some length, and for the use of a preliminary draft of the chapter that appears in
this volume.
3   In DICKINSON, A.K. and LEE, P.J. (1978).
4   The outline of this chart has clear origins in the Schools Council History Project
13–16, and in the units being developed by Boddington and Dawson for 11–13
work.
5   FINES, J. (1983b) [Is there no respect of place, person nor time in you?' in FINES,
J. *Teaching History*, Holmes MacDougall (a thought-provoking essay on change
and time).]
6   STEELE, P. (1982).
7   See chapter 3, above.
8   SHEMILT, D. (1984).
9   See pp. 120–1 above.
10   As provided in *Living History*, Book III, Holmes MacDougall.
11   Department of Education and Science (1977).

Acknowledgements

I would like to acknowledge the great debt that all teachers owe to the ideas of
others—in this case particularly to my former colleagues at Glossop School and the
ideas collected in Schools Council History Project 'Explorations' and the Schools
Council History Project Teachers' Guides.

References

BOOTH, M. (1980) 'A recent research project into children's historical thinking and its
implications for history teaching' in DANCY, J.C. (Ed.) *Developments in History
Teaching: Perspectives 4*, University of Exeter School of Education.

BOOTH, M. (1983a) 'Inductive teaching in history' in FINES, J. (Ed.) *Teaching History*, Holmes MacDougall.

BOOTH, M. (1983b) 'Skills, concepts and attitudes: The development of adolescent children's historical thinking. *History and Theory*, 22.

CHAPLIN, B.A. (1978) *History and Career Opportunities* (typescript issued by HML).

DANCY, J.C. (Ed.) (1980) *Developments in History Teaching: Perspectives 4*, University of Exeter School of Education.

DEPARTMENT of EDUCATION and SCIENCE (1977) *Curriculum 11–16*, Department of Education and Science.

DICKINSON, A.K. and LEE, P.J. (Eds) (1978a) *History Teaching and Historical Understanding*, Heinemann Educational Books.

DICKINSON, A.K. and LEE, P.J. (1978b) 'Understanding and research' in DICKINSON, A.K. and LEE, P.J. (1978a).

DICKINSON, A.K., GARD, A. and LEE, P.J. (1978) 'Evidence in history and the classroom' in DICKINSON, A.K. & LEE, P.J. (1978a).

DICKINSON, A.K., LEE, P.J. and ROGERS, P.J. (1984) *Learning History*, Heinemann Educational Books.

EDWARDS, A.D. (1978) 'The language of history' in DICKINSON, A.K. and LEE, P.J. (Eds) (1978a).

FINES, J. (1981) 'Towards some criteria for establishing the history curriculum', *Teaching History*, 31, October.

FINES, J. (Ed.) (1983) *Teaching History*, Holmes MacDougall.

HEXTER, J. (1972) *The History Primer*, Allen Lane.

HISTORICAL ASSOCIATION (1979) *History as a Preparation for a Career*, Historical Association pamphlet.

LALLY, J. and WEST, J. (1981) *The Child's Awareness of the Past—Teacher's Guide*, Hereford and Worcester County History Advisory Committee.

ROGERS, P.J. (1979) *The New History: Theory into Practice*, Historical Association pamphlet TH44.

ROGERS, P.J. (1984) 'The power of visual presentation' in DICKINSON, A.K. and LEE, P.J. and ROGERS, P.J. (Eds).

SANSOM, C.J. (1985) *The History Syllabus—A Survey of Recent Research and Its Implications for the Teacher*, Derbyshire County Council Education Committee.

Schools Council History (1981–to date) *Explorations* (SCHP and SREB).

SHEMILT, D. (1980) *History 13–16 Evaluation Study*, Holmes MacDougall.

SHEMILT, D. (1983a) 'The devil's locomotive', *History and Theory*, 22.

SHEMILT, D. (1983b) 'Formal operational thought in history' in FINES, J. (Ed.) *Teaching History*, Holmes MacDougall.

SHEMILT, D. (1984) 'Beauty and the philosopher' in DICKINSON, A.K. LFE, P.J. and ROGERS, P.J. (Eds).

SLATER, J. (1984) speech to Historical Association Conference 1984, *The Historian*, 2, Historical Association.

STEELE, P. (1982) *Medicine Through Time—A Pupil Handbook*, County of Avon Resources for Learning Development Unit.

WEST, J. (1981) *History 7–13*, Dudley Teachers Centre.

8   Extending the Principles of Schools Council History Across the Early Secondary Years

Christopher Smallbone

Synopsis

The central argument is that a history course for years 2 and 3 should be based on defined objectives, and content which relates to the achievement of these objectives, and that a chronological approach is not the best way to do this.

The history course should be seen in total as developing certain attitudes, concepts and skills. Content should relate to objectives, be relevant and develop the pupils' experiences. General objectives should be established which become specific objectives when applied to the course content. Criteria should be developed which establish the means to assess how much the objectives are being realized.

If all this is not done, those who opt out of history at the end of year 3 are being sold short while those who opt into a history course in years 4 and 5 are being ill-prepared.

Teaching History: the Theoretical Basis

The 'new history' which was to become embodied as the Schools Council History Project 13–16 redefined the experiences which history can and should provide for today's 13–16 year olds. History was to be presented not as a received story about the past but as a distinct form of knowledge with its own logic, methods and perspectives. The distinctiveness of history as a discipline within the school was no longer to be defined in terms of the subject matter but in terms of skills and concepts. Firstly, underpinning the whole course was the assertion that skills associated with historical knowledge are founded upon reason; the foundation of history must be a spirit of enquiry which involves the critical and discriminatory use of source material. Secondly, certain concepts were chosen as being essential to historical study and relevant to the personal and social needs of adolescents. Historical empathy, the role of the individual in history, causation and motivation, interpretation of current events in relation to the past, the historical context of our environment and development are examples of the concepts which were deemed to be both essential perspectives of the historian and relevant to the pupils of today. A traditional chronological syllabus was rejected on the grounds that no one period could adequately allow for the expression of these wide ranging concepts. The enquiry in depth would take the form of the study of a people of a different time and place which would encourage the pupils to develop a sense of period, to increase their awareness of beliefs, attitudes and values. The modern world study would aim to increase the pupils' understanding of how issues of the contemporary world are rooted in the past. 'History Around Us' would aim to heighten their awareness and understanding of the historical aspects of their environment. The study of development would focus upon change and continuity in time. The unifying framework for the whole course was to be the perspectives which gave history as a subject its rationale. The coherence was to be provided by the approach and by the conceptual aims, not by syllabus *content*.

Despite G.R. Elton's assertion that such 'academic' history is the 'wrong thing' to teach children the experience of the Schools Council History Project 13–16 is that such skills and concepts can be meaningfully taught. Elton argued that a level of maturity was necessary if oversimplification was to be avoided because history deals with the activities of men.[1] However the experience of the Schools Council History Project 13–16 would support Bruner's contention that it *is* possible to adapt sophisticated concepts to tender minds.

> If one respects the ways of thought of the growing child, if one is courteous enough to translate material into his logical forms and challenging enough to tempt him to advance, then it is possible to introduce him at an early age to the ideas and styles that in later life make an educated man.[2]

The evaluation of the Schools Council History Project 13–16 has shown that the pupils' understanding of

> Concepts like 'evidence', 'empathy', 'necessity' and so on is cumulative: concepts fit in to the Brunerian scheme of the spiral curriculum as ideas refined and reshaped on successive encounters throughout a pupil's school life.[3]

When correctly implemented history 13–16 offers the possibility of a quantum leap in pupils' historical understanding. It combines a coherent philosophy for teaching history as what Paul Hirst calls a form of knowledge with a materials supported examination framework within which serious curriculum development can proceed.[4]

Thus the Schools Council History Project 13–16 has achieved a significant shift in curriculum design away from content-oriented syllabuses towards a definition of the subject in terms of the perspectives of the historian. The enormous success of the Project in curriculum innovation has been achieved partly as a result of its link to public examinations. However despite the production of the 'What is History?' materials it has been left to individual schools to develop courses in the lower years of the secondary school. Clearly it is illogical and unacceptable to achieve significant curriculum change in years 4 and 5 but to maintain established practices in the lower school. Indeed it may well be that pupils will, regrettably, opt for other examination subjects and thus avoid the perspectives which history should offer them. It has been suggested that in the lower school a chronological approach should be maintained:

> Students need a background of information in order that they may appreciate chronological development.[5]

However a background of historical information will not necessarily result in increased understanding unless the conceptual awareness of the pupil is sufficiently well developed to achieve this. This contention would be supported by Bruner, who makes this very point that it is the 'ideas and styles' of a discipline which facilitate the basis of future learning. Further, it is doubtful whether chronology as a concept is developed by studying historical periods in chronological order. The overview of development which is surely implied by the concept of chronology is a most worthwhile objective which needs to be specifically encouraged and brought out by carefully planning the learning experience of the pupils. One way of achieving this which is popular with the pupils is to invite them to put a number of illustrations of, for example, homes or weapons into chronological order, explaining their reasons for doing so. Thus a framework of information should not be the basis of syllabus construction; by extending the objectives of the Schools Council History Project as the rationale behind the history course throughout the school one is:

(i) Preparing pupils thoroughly for the approach to be met in years 4 and 5—one has created a consistent sequential course throughout the school.

(ii) Opening the Schools Council's philosophy and approach to *all* pupils, whether or not they opt for history in years 4 and 5.

Having established the necessity for building one's course around defined objectives based on the perspectives which the subject may contribute in terms of skills attitudes and concepts, we may define these objectives as the following:

(i)   To develop an understanding of the nature of history, that it is not immutable but is an area of study which is based on the use of sources which leaves room for questions and speculations leading to informed opinions and judgments.

(ii)   To develop an awareness of change and continuity, to investigate the development of history.

(iii)   To develop an understanding of causation, to encourage the search for explanations and their multiplicity.

(iv)   To develop empathy for the past, to enter into an informed appreciation of the predicaments, attitudes and values of people in the past.

(v)   To develop a sense of chronology and time.

(vi)   To develop the skills of abstraction and the ability to locate information from sources of all kinds.

(vii)   To develop the skills of analysis: the ability to categorize observations; to recognize emotional content and bias, cause and effect, omissions and irrelevancies; to distinguish the verifiable from the unverifiable; above all, the ability to relate statements about people to evidence.

(viii) To develop the skills of evaluation: the ability to assess the authority of evidence and relate it to its historical context; to understand its meaning for and impact on the audience intended, recognize its bias and emotional content; the ability to evaluate human conduct in its historical context; the ability to test hypotheses.

(ix)   To develop the skills of communication: the ability to communicate in a variety of written forms; to present a case verbally, to pose questions, to discuss, and to listen; the ability to make valid historical statements, based on evidence, through art, craft and drama.

(x)   To develop the skills of synthesis: the ability to analyze facts in sequence; select evidence from a variety of similar sources, for example, a book, a newspaper, a personal memory; from conflicting sources. The ability to use historical data to make imaginative reconstructions, spoken, dramatic, written; the ability to construct hypotheses. Most important is the ability to organize material of the past into a coherent narrative. A good story is probably what first gripped the attention of young children about the past; it must continue to be a part of the teaching of pupils of all ages. Their ability to construct a good narrative should remain one of their own central responses to it.[6]

Strategies to Implement a Scheme of Work—One School's Approach

The Nature of History

When commencing a new course it seems logical to establish what the subject *is*. The expectations of the pupils are generally that history is an uncritical story of what has happened in the past. In the spirit of enquiry and exploration our history course begins by asking the question 'What is history?' and in a sense the whole history course is an extended answer to this question. The introduction aims to establish that history is about people, time past and using sources. The teaching strategy draws upon the materials and ideas encompassed in the Schools Council History Project 13–16; 'What is History?' and 'Place, Time and Society 8–13'. By discussing six pictures of historical characters central questions are raised such as: Is history about famous people or does it include ordinary folk? Why do we know more about some people than others? Can people be historical while they are still alive? Are women as important as men in history?[7] An interesting lead into the last question is to ask the pupils to name a famous character from history—the results are normally heavily weighted towards male characters. The second aspect of the introduction; that history is about time is explored from the starting point of recording the history of the lesson, the history of the pupils' day, the history of their lives. The pupils gain experience in recording events on a time chart and develop an awareness of the scale of historic time. To introduce history as a subject which uses sources to develop explanations we have adapted the Place, Time and Society 8–13 materials. Pupils, working in small groups, are asked to fully describe what they can see, and secondly to explain what it shows. They begin with a picture of what is to most people a foot. The more precise refer to a left human footprint in what is probably sand. Careful observation is a necessary precursor to full explanation, but the latter, for which the pupils use the sources as evidence is a higher order skill. What did the footprint mean to 'Robinson Crusoe?' for it is an illustration taken from Defoe's classic. The exercise is repeated with an illustration from Kenneth Grahame's *Wind in the Willows* in which Ratty and Mole, searching for Badger's house, are pictured looking at a foot-scraper in the middle of a wood. 'Don't you see what it *means* you—you dull witted animal?' cried the Rat impatiently. 'Of course I see what it means' replied the Mole. It simply means that some *very* careless and forgetful person left his door scraper lying about in the middle of the wild wood, *just* where its *sure* to trip *everybody* up. Very thoughtless of him, I call it, when I get home I shall go and complain about it—to somebody or other, see if I don't!'[8]

The 'rats' in the class will begin to use the observation as evidence. (If there is a footscraper it is reasonable to suppose that there is someone's home nearby—they have found Badger's house!).

A third, more complex exercise is now attempted which is the use of a picture of an overturned dustbin. A colleague's help was enlisted in the sketching of the contents of this bin, and once again the pupils are asked to describe what they can see and to draw conclusions from the debris about the inhabitants of the house outside which this bin was to be found. All pupils are capable of observing and recording the contents of the bin, many manage to draw conclusions about its owners. Some—but very few—even begin to evaluate this source by questioning the validity of the conclusions they have drawn. These three exercises, however interesting and motivating, are rather contrived and removed from the pupils' experience, so the next very popular development is for the pupils to bring in an historical object of less than fifty years of age. Once again they are asked to describe it and to explain what it tells us about life in the last fifty years. By doing this orally an interdependent atmosphere is created whereby the class becomes a forum in which members of the class contribute ideas and learn from one another. Such an atmosphere is essential if a spirit of enquiry is to prevail. The pupils are collectively using their objects as evidence. Some of them even begin to evaluate the sources, realizing their limitations. Others find the abstract thought required in seeking explanations is too challenging—and, while they are able to respond to structured questioning, they are unable to go beyond description when they attempt a written task on their chosen object.

History in our Locality

Having established the nature of history as a subject and the means of enquiry, it would seem to be appropriate to extend out from themselves to utilize and to widen their experience of their environment. In our area the salt industry has a great impact on the environment and we use this as a focus for our historical enquiry. Using sources of many different types we investigate how methods of extracting salt have developed. We reconstruct what life was like for a worker in the salt industry and draw out conclusions of wider significance about change and continuity generally and the importance of written documentation in our knowledge of history. A variety of sources is used—beginning with those which the pupils themselves have observed. Starting from the task that we need to be able to prove that the salt industry was the major reason for our town's development the pupils respond by contributing their observations of their environment. Some have experienced subsidence caused by the uncontrolled brine extraction which took place up until 1896. Many know of instances of people rising in the morning to find their garage has disappeared into a gaping hole! Some pupils have observed the specialized building techniques employed in building in the town centre. Others use place-name evidence, bring in photographs or interview ageing relatives who worked in the industry. The teacher needs to exploit all these contributions and collect any extra documents, photographs and artefacts which may help in reconstructing what life was like for a salt worker. The pupils gain practical experience of history—not as a story given by a book or by the teacher, but as a reconstruction using available evidence. And what of the evidence? There is very little until the seventeenth century, chiefly the remains of a lead salt pan from Roman times and the first written evidence of salt in the area from the Domesday Book. This, in itself, raises a number of questions. During this part of the history course pupils complete a number of written questions which demand comprehension of written and pictorial sources. Early in the course it is important to establish that written questions demand answers of differing lengths, that many questions need to be developed further to explore their implications (i.e. questions within the question) and that questions which ask for reasons are requesting a number of points in answer. The establishment of rigorous attention to detail is imperative very early in the course, and this should be borne in mind when written questions on sources are formulated. As the study unfolds pupils will explore the concepts associated with development. Changes will become apparent, but also continuity, for the process used by the salt industry changed very little, in essence, from earliest times up to the early twentieth century.

History in Another Time and Place: Enquiry and Empathy

While the salt industry is particular to our area, the important point of principle here is that history as a subject should not be remote from the pupils' own experience and existence. By choosing content which is familiar, one is taking the first step in overcoming problems in teaching history as a subject to school children. It helps to make the subject accessible and interesting so that complex concepts and skills can be taught successfully. The sources used are not abstract or removed from the pupils who are eased into the subject, moving from the known and into the unknown. They are then ready to study a period of history in depth, in order that they may gain an overall picture of the attitudes and values of another time and place. Now the means of enquiry have been established and investigated, we may extend our use of sources and, by immersing ourselves in an historical period, reconstruct its life and use this as a basis for comparison to examine aspects of our own society. We have found it beneficial early in the course to use the 'What is History?' detective work materials for they emphasize certain crucial aspects of history in an interesting way. By working through the 'mysteries' of Mark Pullen, Tollund Man and the Empty Grave the pupils learn much of how the historian works and gain practice at being historians themselves by trying to work out what happened using the source material provided. They learn that the historian has access to fewer sources than they would have thought and this means that the historian's conclusions are necessarily incomplete and tentative. They practise using sources to support lines of argument. In the *Mystery of Tollund Man* they are exposed to the importance of written sources in constructing theories and the necessity for a close reading of such sources. We have adapted the *Mystery of the Empty Grave* so that the pupils engage in a number of structured tasks in small groups until they eventually reach conclusions based on a number of factors. The completion of the *Mystery of the Empty Grave* provides a good lead into an enquiry in depth into Anglo-Saxon England, where the skills of using sources may be extended and concepts of understanding people in the past may be developed. The pupils are beginning to recognize that they are using a number of *types* of sources, they are becoming familiar with the distinction between primary and secondary sources, they are describing what they observe in a source and are being encouraged to use those sources to draw conclusions. They are also becoming used to the vast majority of historical questions having no absolute answer. They are discovering how archaeological finds can help to explain the past but that much of what life was like has to be pieced together by interpreting the sources which survive. Having used a number of sources to investigate the period the pupils are coaxed to apply this research to reconstruct some aspect of life during Anglo-Saxon times. This may take any form which successfully communicates the findings and varies from a play or 'radio interview' to a talk, display or project.

By the beginning of the third year pupils have had the opportunity to develop an awareness of history as a subject, and competence in the skills of using sources which are so crucial in the mode of enquiry. It is beneficial to consolidate the learning which has taken place by presenting the pupils with sources from which they can work out what happened in the past. One very manageable but instructive example is that of the Norman invasion in 1066. Pupils will usually be familiar with the events as a story—but they have learned how historians work, so now they are able to reconstruct the story from the sources and thus find out on what grounds that story was based and whether they agree with the version they had been told. The pupils are surprised to discover how important is the visual Bayeux Tapestry. They are extending their understanding of the limitations of historical enquiry and the difficulties in using and interpreting sources by engaging in historical enquiry themselves. Many of them begin to question accepted hypotheses and begin to formulate alternatives. This becomes stimulating and exciting for the teacher and pupils alike.

Christopher Smallbone

Issues in Modern World History

At some stage during the third year pupils should be introduced to current events and how these have their roots in the past. Clearly one has to be selective, for a whole two-year course could be devoted to modern world history. Nevertheless, some decision should be made, for it is generally accepted by pupils and parents that they should be prepared so they may understand the international events in the world in which they live. We can only lay the foundations for an understanding to develop, but we have chosen the relationship of the superpowers and decolonization as important aspects of international affairs. Choosing Africa as an example, we investigate how it came to be colonized and how nationalism led to decolonization. We then look at the newspapers to record what is happening today, relating the events to what happened in the past. Secondly, we explore how the USA and USSR have dominated world affairs since the Second World War, putting their current relationship in the context of the Cold War and areas of the world where their conflict has surfaced. We hope that the conceptual awareness of these two central issues will be transferred to world affairs generally. This part of the history course also includes the construction of a diary of events relating to an African country or an area where the superpowers are involved in a conflict, making critical use of news items. Pupils record the reports from a variety of media, relate the events to what has happened in the past and attempt to appraise the media sources they have used. Towards the end of their third year many pupils will achieve a sophisticated understanding of complex events and will produce a critical appraisal of their sources. Other pupils will at the very least have their awareness of international events broadened and their awareness of the strengths and weaknesses of the media heightened.

The Reliability of Sources

Some time in the latter part of the course the reliability of sources should be tackled because understanding this is so crucial a skill not only to the historian but to any individual who hopes to participate fully in society. Understanding how to evaluate sources is essential if one is to discriminate critically between the masses of information to which we are subjected in modern industrial society. Reliability of sources is a unifying element in the whole course but it tends to have been explored by those pupils who have successfully understood the lower order skills when using sources. It is such an important contribution to the curriculum that history can make that in our view it should be spotlighted and a section of the scheme of work devoted to it. Pupils will be now have varying degrees of understanding of this type of evaluation and we have found that for most pupils the Schools Council 'What is History?' Richard III materials are too demanding unless the ground is prepared very thoroughly. To this end we have included some home-produced introductory materials based on the controversial goal of the 1966 World Cup. Did the ball cross the line? Interestingly those witnesses most sure of themselves turn out to be those who were in the worst position to see—the pupils search for possible explanations for this. They are encouraged to try to explain inconsistencies and contradictions in the sources (photographs and written statements) and to examine the evidence for *and* against it crossing the line and so to reach a balanced conclusion. This gives the pupils valuable experience by introducing them to the skills they will need when evaluating source material and in seeking a balanced conclusion.

Assessment

Not only has the Schools Council philosophy been applied to the whole history course, but experience built up in the assessment of coursework has shaped our approach to assessment in years 2 and 3. In the Schools Council History Project 13–16 we have worked together to produce criteria by which we assess the assignments which are entered as the coursework part of the examination. Far more are completed than are necessary to fulfil the examination requirements so that a selection is made of those in which the candidate has been most successful. The course unfolds in stages; at the end of each stage an assessment assignment is completed. This strategy has been applied to years 2 and 3.

Assessment, then, is a continuous process, it is an integral part of the scheme of work. The purpose of assessment is to gauge the extent to which a pupil has been able to achieve the objectives of the course. While all written work will normally receive a comment, only the assessed assignments are given a mark, as such. This will reflect how far a pupil has reached the goals of that unit of the scheme of work. These marks and comments then provide the basis for a realistic improvement in the performance of pupils and the basis for grades and comments which will be used to compile reports for parents.

The criteria for assessment have been developed as a result of examining the pupils' performances in meeting the objectives and by standardizing scripts across a whole year group so that the assessment is a reliable discriminator in grading the pupils' achievement in history. Take, for example, the criteria which we have developed to assess the pupils' achievement in *The Mystery of the Empty Grave*. The pupils have completed a number of tasks which help to unravel the mystery: using the finds to suggest what sort of person was connected with the burial; attempting to date the burial to a historical period; attempting to identify the religion of the person.

These tasks will have been completed in small groups, so some assessment of the individual pupils' understanding of the mystery needs to be made. To this end they complete a written assignment in which they should:

    (i)   describe, briefly, the finds made at Sutton Hoo;
    (ii)   use the finds to draw conclusions about the site;
    (iii) use these conclusions to identify possible owners of the hoard;
    (iv) evaluate the sources;
    (v)   construct a coherent synthesis.

The pupils have varying degrees of success in meeting these objectives, and on this basis a numerical mark may be awarded.

Similarly, following extensive group discussion work on Richard III and the missing princes, pupils complete an assignment designed to test to what extent they are able to (a) evaluate sources; and (b) reach a balanced conclusion.

Evaluation

Thus, in conclusion, I have given a number of examples of the issues which I believe, should be considered when constructing a scheme of work. As I said above, content is far too important to be given over to a complete chronological survey of British history. It should be carefully planned to suit the gradual opening out of the subject and to contribute those aspects of the subject which can be fully justified in contributing to the whole education which the pupils will receive. Even as I write, I can see flaws and imperfections in the scheme—large omissions, small errors in mark schemes. But evaluation of such a scheme must be a continual process—schemes of work can only be as good as they stand for the moment and individual components should be adapted and improved as experience reveals their faults. One extremely productive element in our evaluation of the course has been to invite comments from the pupils on the overall impact of the course and the popularity of methods employed in teaching it. All pupils completed a formal questionnaire, the anonymity of which was only exploited by two pupils. The overwhelming spirit was one of constructive criticism in which we were not only encouraged by evidence of widespread satisfaction with most aspects of the course and appreciation of its objectives, but were also directed to increase the amount of small group discussion in the scheme (because of its popularity) and to radically change the format of Richard III and the missing princes (because of its unpopularity). Informal feedback from parents is very supportive, they are very appreciative of the differences between their experience of history and their childrens'. They are delighted when they are reassured that this approach will be continued into years 4 and 5. The problem then is not a general one—we are working along the right lines—but a particular one. We have a constructive philosophy, it is the detailed planning which needs to be worked out. I have outlined our response to applying the Schools Council History Project 13–16 philosophy to our scheme of work. Tinkering with the details is a constructive, continual process. The most elusive aspect of evaluation is in an *overall* appraisal of *objectives and content*—it is very difficult to stand outside one's own work and not only to see omissions but to decide what to axe to make such omissions good. In the words of one of Jerome K. Jerome's *Three Men in a Boat*: 'It's not what you can do with but what you can't do without that matters'.[9]

Notes

1   ELTON, G.R., (1969) *The Practice of History*, Fontana, p. 180.
2   BRUNER, J.S., (1959) *The Process of Education*, Harvard University Press, p. 52.
3   SHEMILT, D., (1980) *History 13–16 Evaluation Study*, Holmes McDougall, p. 77.
4   *Ibid.*, p. 86.
5   DAWSON, I., (1981) 'What shall we do with the third year?', *Teaching History*, February.
6   Objectives (vi)–(x) are reproduced from *HMI Curriculum 11–16 Working Papers*.
7   Schools Council, (1976) *What is History? Teachers Guide*, Holmes McDougall, p. 8.
8   GRAHAME, K., (1971) *The Wind in the Willows*, Methuen, pp. 63–4.
9   MARLAND, M., (1981) 'Drawing up a scheme of work', in MARLAND, M. and HILL, S. *Departmental Management*, Heinemann, pp. 87–115.

9 Some Problems and Principles of Sixth-Form History

Vincent A. Crinnion

Synopsis

History at 'A' level has been slow to respond to the changing educational and societal climate of the last decade. A steady decline in the number of students choosing the subject, general demands for greater social relevance in the 11–18 curriculum and a long-felt dissatisfaction among history teachers with the quality of the current provision for 16–18 year olds are powerful reasons for a radical overhaul of the subject at 'A' level.

This chapter proposes such an overhaul, based firstly upon an estimation of the subject's aims and value in the sixth-form. In particular, it is suggested that the chief characteristics of the subject at this level should be, firstly, syllabuses that take as their point of origin problems, values and ideas that form a salient part of the contemporary world and, secondly, classroom practices that genuinely encourage the acquisition of historical skills and attitudes. The course and assessment work should become *progressively more difficult* and room be accorded to variations in students' individual performance and interest through student-centred assignments and a degree of continuous assessment. The syllabus must be firmly centred on *historical problems* rather than periods of time, *developing outwards* from a single historical happening towards the temporal and spatial context that gives the event its historical meaning. A significantly large space in classroom and examination hall should be found for documents and historiographical debate, in order to provide both a clearer view of the complexity of the subject and also an insight into its fascination.

Five separate but interrelated modules of study are suggested as a framework for the course. *Contrast and progression* are taken to be the overriding principles that should inform such a course, helping to shape both the structure and timing of the modules of study, and also suggesting their content.

A Thing of the Past?

It would be neither original nor wholly controversial nowadays to express deep dissatisfaction with the existing provision for sixth-form history. For more than a decade schools, academics and examination boards have deliberated about 'what is good sixth-form history?'. By and large, their suggestions have been thoughtful, well-intentioned and ignored.[1] More recently a different lobby can be heard posing another question: 'what is sixth-form history good for?'. That these two fundamental questions about the nature and value of the subject at advanced level are linked is obvious. Less clear perhaps is the rapidly changing educational and societal climate that gives to this relationship and the whole desultory debate a new urgency and significance.

The plain fact is that sixth-form history is ailing. For many of its recipients the existing provision is dull, misguided and irrelevant. It is perceived quite simply, and without a trace of irony, to 'be living in the past'.

A recent survey of 200 history students in their lower sixth revealed the extent to which the subject is viewed as a limited option.[2] While many (47 per cent) considered history to be their main subject, only a minority (17 per cent) saw the subject as a possible choice for higher education and less than 5 per cent cited history as part of their thinking about careers when they made their original subject choices for entry into the sixth-form. Interest in the subject at 'O' level accounted for most choices (88 per cent).

More alarming for those who care about the health of a subject that lives in the past is that increasingly fewer students are willing to visit it there. The figures reveal a steady decline in the relative popularity of the subject at school and university. In 1974 7.7 per cent of passes in all 'A' level subjects were history. By 1979 this had fallen steadily to 6.4 per cent. With the ominous exception of Latin, history has been the only subject that is decreasing in the numbers passing at 'A' level. As a percentage of the total number of JMB 'A' level entries, history has fallen every year since 1974 (from 22.8 per cent to 15.8 per cent in 1984). A similar trend is visible at 'O' level and, of course, goes some way towards explaining the decline at 'A' level. (In 1971 applications to study history at university ranked it fourth in popularity. In 1982 it was sixth.[3])

The reasons for this decline in the subject's popularity are undoubtedly varied and complex. What both 'O' level and 'A' level history do share in common, however, is the failure to convince potential clients that history is a subject worthy of pursuit in an age of economic and social change. High levels of youth unemployment, structural changes in the economy and government-assisted educational initiatives (for instance, TVEI, YTS and CPVE) are just a few of the messages heard by pupils selecting options at 13 years, 'A' level at 16 years and higher education courses at 18+. Additionally, the effects of such pressures seem to be disproportionately exacerbated for subjects like history by the organizational and curricular expedients that are invoked by schools to meet these challenges. The back-wash is soon felt in the sixth-form with reduced opportunities to introduce teachers into sixth-form work and the widening of ability in 'A' level teaching groups.

The impact of societal change on the sixth-form curriculum is a difficult area to talk confidently about. An atmosphere of uncertainty has hung over educational discussions for more than a decade. A few points have emerged, however, that may have direct bearing on the future of sixth-form history.

Firstly, vocational relevance is becoming a key consideration in pupils' choices. Exhortations by educationalists about 'balance' and broadly based 'areas of experience' in curricular options, about the need for 'education' rather than 'training' sound melodious; but not to deaf ears. In any case, it has to be readily conceded that 'A' level history is only rarely of direct vocational relevance and certainly not in growth areas of the economy. Even where history at 'A' level purports to provide exemplary intellectual training appropriate to particular professions,[4] it cannot claim anything like an exclusive hold on such skills. In this context it might best serve the interests of history to boast about the unique *combination* of cognitive and communication skills it has to offer.

An increased emphasis is being placed throughout education on courses and subjects that form the basis for directly gaining employment or for proceeding to higher education. The 'A/S' level is but one example of the balance that government may insist upon between 'academic' and 'vocational' studies. Related to this, seemingly irresistible, tendency is the sentiment of 'education for leisure'. Must 'A' level history surrender its academic status and intellectual vigour before it has something to say to the champions of 'relevance'? Indeed, are the issues of employability and self-fulfillment as pertinent at 'A' level as they are deemed to be in the lower school and how are such claims to be balanced against the academic requirements of the universities?

Secondly, a substantial investment is likely to be made in a coherent programme for this age group. A 14–18 scheme is an obvious possibility. Does sixth-form history have a part to play in any such programme? Increased numbers of students are following 16–18 courses but it is clear that not all of these students are of academic quality. Many will only pursue courses for one year or single subjects for two years. What courses or part-courses has history to offer this new breed of sixth-former?[5]

Sixth-form history has been slow to respond to the challenge of social and curricular change. In the light of reduced numbers and new competition from more fashionable subjects and vocational courses, it would seem perilous not to review history's position. It is an historical and not a biological fact that ostriches can become dead ducks.

Perhaps the most valid reason for such a reappraisal, however, lies in the supposed inadequacies of traditional 'A' level syllabuses and methodologies. History in the sixth-form seems firmly rooted in the past. Rarely do the courses, the resulting teaching methods or the textbooks that form the basis of such courses appear to be congruent with current thinking about the place of history in schools or about its wider social value. The viewpoints and methodologies that have been apparent in 11–16 school history for at least fifteen years have an important but, as yet, largely ungranted place in the aims and practices of the subject at 'A' level. Many teachers of history at this level would, I feel, acknowledge the importance of this point. Most pupils have suffered the disappointments and tedium of its consequences.

In the survey of lower sixth history students, while many retained a high level of interest in the subject, 61 per cent deemed the subject to be lacking in intellectual stimulus and challenge. Classroom practice appears to remain didactic. Students from seventeen schools were asked to estimate how much of their total lesson time was taken up by specific teaching devices. The results must be considered to be crude but depressingly predictable. In particular, up to half of lesson time is consumed by the transmission of information in nearly 75 per cent of pupils' experience.

Table 1[6]

Feature	Percentage of lesson time taken up				
	0–25	26–50	51–75	76–100	
(a) Dictated notes	29	49	11	11	
(b) Class discussion	58	36	5	1	
(c) Individual reading and making own notes (excluding essay preparation)	64	27	9	0	Percentage of pupils' response
	0–5	6–10	11–15	16–20	
(d) Slides, TV, Tapes	73	13	9	5	
(e) Primary documents	86	11	2	1	

Perhaps the most damning criticisms of 'A' level history have been delivered by lofty representatives of the academic system it is peculiarly ill-designed to serve. Professor Joel Hurstfield, writing about 'A' level applicants to read history at university, bemoaned their inability to write lucidly or speak knowledgeably about their subject—'they seem to have been brought up on one text-book and one explanation. I find them sometimes well-taught but insufficiently educated'.[7] Sixteen years later Professor Ralph Griffiths has added that 'it is profoundly depressing and increasingly worrying to meet so many university students whose elementary intellectual equipment is seriously deficient'.[8] Clearly not all students share this state of intellectual debility but, nonetheless, the capacity to think and write are traditionally regarded as among the chief virtues of the subject. Failure here surely is a serious condemnation of the way that the discipline is treated in the sixth form.

The deficiencies of much that passes for 'A' level history are well-known and long-recognized. It is perhaps worth summarizing them to (a) remind ourselves that they are not inevitable (still less, venal) sins; and (b) point out how they tend to be self-supporting.

The Past and the Pass

For far too long a probablistic approach to the past has taken second place to the certainties of the pass. 'A' level students spend much time thinking *about* history but are rarely afforded the proper learning situations to think *historically*. To satisfy the requirements of the examination boards the acquisition of information is at a premium, whether that information be regarded as interpretative knowledge or mere factual detail. The temptation for teacher and pupil alike is to absorb both in the same way. If, crudely stated, one primarily learns facts for 'O' level, at 'A' level one primarily learns interpretations.

Of course, a candidate worth his salt would no doubt be able to recognize the difference between two historical statements such as:

A. Lord Abergavenny was fined £70,000 in 1507 for unlawful retaining....

B. Henry's vindictiveness towards the nobility was partly a matter of temperament....[9]

It is less certain, perhaps, whether this same student could (a) properly explain how the latter may derive from the former—the historian's method; (b) understand the varieties of historical meaning in any claim that B is an accurate verdict—the status of historical knowledge; (c) refer knowledgeably to other interpretations that corroborate or challenge B—historiography. It is arguable, however, that unless a history student can satisfy these requirements on at least a minimal level, he lacks true historical understanding. His knowledge of the past, which may indeed be boundless, will necessarily tend to be mechanical and sterile; a mere regurgitation of received, and partially digested, 'truths'.

What, then, are the main causes of these deficiencies?

(i) The traditional history examination is generally conservative and unsatisfactory, disguising as much as it reveals about pupils' historical knowledge and understanding. The rigidities of the system can be seen most obviously in its lack of clearly specified historical objectives, the reliance upon free-response answers as the dominant mode of assessment and the failure to generate sufficiently sensitive grade-criteria for the definition of levels of historical thinking. The selection and organization of relevant information, the development of arguments through the use of appropriate information and the ability to communicate information and ideas persuasively may or may not require significant levels of historical understanding. They can often, however, secure good levels of success in the history examination.

(ii) The traditional syllabuses and examinations tend to inhibit rather than encourage good classroom practice, stifling innovatory or experimental approaches.[10] A relatively narrow range of teaching methods and practices are adequate to achieve examination passes but their authoritarian nature is unlikely to produce the levels of interest, curiosity and independent critical thought that historians value so highly about their discipline.

The Problem of Period

Most history syllabuses at 'A' level, including most of the new 'Common Core' proposals[11], prefer to organize themselves around the principle of periodization rather than historical problems, thus forcing teacher and pupil to work inwards from a chronological periphery, rather than outwards from a problematic centre. The reasons for the survival of such a wrong-headed approach are clear.

(i) Chronological breadth rather than historical depth is a preferred priority. Unfortunately the sheer size of the resulting courses means that treatments of complex historical questions can become didactic, superficial and selective. It is perhaps the supreme irony that history teachers suffer for a want of more time.

(ii) A possibility of choice from the variety of periods on offer at 'A' level is said to exist and is traditionally taken to be one of its greatest strengths. In practice this possibility of real choice is illusory. Firstly, it is teachers and not pupils who select syllabuses and presumably do so according to their own educational background, personal interests and discreet rationalizations about the relative importance of particular periods. Secondly, teachers tend to be extremely conservative in their choices, selecting from a relatively small number of periods (especially sixteenth and seventeenth century Britain, and nineteenth century Britain and Europe). Teachers have also failed to respond to new, innovative alternatives offered by some boards. In 1983 the AEB's pilot scheme at 'A' level only received 6.4 per cent of the Board's total candidature for the subject[12] and in 1984 the JMB's Personal Study Option attracted less than 2 per cent of that Board's history entry.[13] Thirdly, where there is an appearance of real individual choice, (as with special options, individual studies and alternative examination questions) in reality the schemes are prescribed in stifling detail.

The Value of Sixth-Form History

It has been written about the ferment in school history teaching that 'the how is everywhere and the what nowhere; the why never gets discussed...'[14]. Sixth form history does not escape such a criticism easily. Rather like the over-worked and slightly baffled GP who is asked to explain an illness to a patient, the 'A' level teacher might be forgiven for saying that his history syllabus is what it is because 'There is a lot of it about'.

The traditional view of the value of 'A' level history reckons that 'at its best' it provides 'an initiation into true scholarship...while at the lower level of achievement it can at least be a training ground, where earnest minds may learn to acquire and keep some sense of perspective in a rapidly changing world'. Such a view assumes that the attainment of a university place for further academic study is a natural and inevitable part of the educational experience. This view of 'A' level history also demands 'the transformation of the clever schoolboy into a young student capable of independent thought, a balanced judgment and a comprehension of the society in which he will shortly play a part'.[15]

The worthiness and attractiveness of these aims should not be allowed to obscure the fundamental assumptions they make about the nature of the subject at 'A' level and its summative benefits. Any future alterations in the content and methodology of sixth-form history must be made upon the basis of a discussion of this supposed value in the subject. Firstly, it is assumed that the students' work is 'historical' and may be, 'at its best', scholarly. Secondly, it claims certain important cognitive skills result from a study of the past and, thirdly, that sixth-form history provides the student with some form of understanding of his own society. All of these in different ways are problematic.

Clio in the Classroom: Historical History

The most important reason for sixth-formers to study history is to learn about the past. The obviousness of the point should not detract from the significance of its implications. A student cannot be said to know the past without also to some degree knowing how he knows. This is not to say that 'A' level history can or should closely resemble the activities of the academic historian but, more simply, that students should be taught to think historically, and this cannot be done meaningfully without room being made in sixth-form pedagogy and syllabuses for some of the epistemological complexities and fascinations of the subject. History is difficult, perhaps impossible, to understand if it is only *taught* as a series of answers built upon a body of smoothly transmitted and comfortably digested explanations. The problematic and subjective nature of historical enquiry is thus bypassed and the probablistic status of much historical explanation counterfeited.

It does not then follow, however, that the pedagogic emphasis must lie with historical methodology (sources, procedures and verification), or even with historiographical debate. There is a danger that both may be turned into mere teaching fodder and thereby become as sterile as their hapless predecessor. It would be surely more fruitful to look at historical questions and events *substantively* and explore their capacity for contentiousness and contingency from *within*, rather than from without. Beginning with single, and relatively simple, accounts of an event (perhaps in narrative form at first) and then, by a process of question-framing about cause, course and consequence, widen the historical significance of the event (for instance, the Pilgrimage of Grace) until the fullest context that is possible is drawn out (for instance, the reign of Henry VIII, the tradition of social obedience, religious dissent, etc.) Along the way discussion of such matters as causation and motivation, change and continuity, periodisation and historiographical debate would grow naturally out of *the study of events*, not be grafted onto it before/after.

The conventional arguments against such approaches concentrate on the supposed intellectual limitations of many 'A' level students and the unhistorical (i.e. non-academic) pedagogic techniques used to develop such thinking in students. It would certainly be foolish to try to underestimate the intellectual and personal maturity required for true historical scholarship. On the other hand, an *imperfect* historical understanding is still worth having. It is helpful to be reminded by Professor Elton, a formidable opponent of the approach to 'A' level suggested here and later, that an 'inability to know all the truth is not the same thing as total inability to know the truth'.[16] Empirical research during the last decade, however fragmentary, suggests that schoolchildren's ability to think historically has been underestimated and that levels of historical understanding, however rudimentary initially, can be *developed* significantly. Besides, is not this issue of maturation as pertinent to the professional historian as it is to the 'A' level student grappling with some modest historical problem— 'whenever (the historian) finds certain historical matters unintelligible, he has discovered a limitation of his own mind; he has discovered that there are certain ways in which he is not, or no longer, or not yet, able to think'.[17]

Sixth-form history inevitably deals in generalizations, second-hand interpretations, limited contextual knowledge and so forth. Whatever reforms take place cannot completely escape such things. The main issue here, however, is not whether such deficiences invalidate the worthiness of the course but whether the syllabus and pedagogy encourage students to learn to work with and beyond such imperfect beginnings. Existing syllabuses, with rare exceptions, can hardly be said to do this.

The Practical Past: Criteria of Relevance

It has always been something of a commonplace to suggest that history, and the educational process of which it forms a part, should be socially relevant. Further, it seems obvious that this claim has of late achieved the status of a talisman and sixth-form history must also fall under its spell. Less clear perhaps are the varieties of meaning that may be attached to this notion of relevance: that the study of history helps students understand their present world, that it increases self-understanding, that it provides a useful intellectual training. The problem of relevance for sixth-form history is (a) clarifying the proper relationship between social relevance and historical contemporaneity; and (b) ensuring that the syllabus and classroom practice actually facilitate rather than obstruct the realization of the three types of relevance mentioned above.

Recent opinions about the value of history for providing social understanding[18] tend to underestimate the complexities in linking a study of the past with a comprehension of the present, and tend to overestimate the ability of 'contemporary history' to provide such understanding.[19] Any study at sixth-form level is bound to be partial and incomplete, will tend to be subjective in its selection of content and alternative interpretations and thus must be self-supporting in its explanation of the present (where the selection began from). Even a perfect understanding of an historical topic, if such a thing is possible, will not of necessity provide an understanding of *other* present-day topics and events.

In practice, most modern sixth-form syllabuses terminate in the 1970s before current 'A' level students had reached their own 'age of reason'! It is difficult therefore to see how such courses satisfy the educational requirements of contemporaneity since they are probably as remote to students as those courses ending in 1945 or even 1918. Ending the course in the present day would also be problematic. Most seriously there is the danger that students, present-minded as they are, will anachronistically view the past merely as a potential answer to present questions. 'It is the mistaken idea that the proper way to do history is to prune away the dead branches of the past, and to preserve the green buds and twigs which have grown into the dark distorted forest of our contemporary world'.[20] The past is thus distorted and pupils' conception of the value of historical inquiry falsified. Historical judgments in such 'A' level syllabuses are likely to be laden with modern values that are perhaps impossible for an adolescent either to appraise objectively and use, or set aside. Perspective and distance, such fundamental components of historical understanding, are thus sacrificed. The teacher is burdened with the problem of discovering and selecting from a mountain of evidential sources (unassisted by the professional 'text-book'), relating to a constantly shifting contemporary scene. It is impossible in 'A' level history to provide explanations for events until it is known *what* has happened and it is difficult to know the answer to this until events have run their full course.

If contemporary history is to find a place in 'A' level syllabuses, it should be a minor one and with greatest value to be derived from its capacity to display, negatively, the problematic nature and evidential procedures of the discipline.

There is, of course, nothing improper in the use of current social issues and educational needs for determining the shape and substance of the 'A' level history curriculum. The study of the past may be an inadequate way of understanding the present but it is nonetheless a necessary part of the process. An historical understanding of the present, however, surely comes less from the accumulation of knowledge about particular contemporary events than from the learning of general historical skills and predispositions towards those events. The social relevance of the subject at 'A' level is best judged by this capacity to equip a student with those intellectual skills and attitudes appropriate to an understanding of self and society.

Which of these are most salient for a reformed syllabus? The following list is clearly neither taxonomic nor exhaustive. It does claim to provide a list of *attributes* of key social relevance and it does, of course, subsume other important intellectual skills, concepts and attitudes. Some of these, like those of communication, cannot be considered to be exclusively historical skills. Nonetheless, they are characteristic of the true relationship that is here thought to exist between school history and the wider needs of education and society.

(i)   The skills of communication:
   (a)   an ability to write fluently and concisely, organize ideas and information in an ordered and logical manner, marshall evidence in support of cogently constructed argumentation;
   (b)   a willingness and facility for oral discussion and debate, to listen and to persuade.
(ii)   The attributes of rational enquiry:
   (a)   a willingness to always view information in an open-minded and critical way;
   (b)   a capacity not to be imprisoned in familiar ideas or viewpoints or to accept habitually statements of authority (personal, political or scholarly);
   (c)   an ability to expand upon what is given, to attain new levels

of thought, more subtle or profound, which go beyond first impressions and instincts; acquiring different ways and techniques of looking at a question, idea or event;

    (d) a tolerance of ambivalence, uncertainty and contingency.

(iii) The ability to appraise and use evidence:

    (a) an acquaintance with the importance and nature of the relationship between explanation and the concept of proof (especially, but not only, in the sense of empirical evidence and inductive thinking);

    (b) a discriminatory attitude towards the concept of 'facts' and types of opinion or degrees of bias;

    (c) a familiarity with basic statistical ideas and quantitative methods whenever such discrimination as to data is significant.

(iv) The awareness of important aspects of social change:

    (a) some understanding of man's capacity for improvement and decline, together with an appreciation of the contemporary values (democracy, scientific rationalism, materialism, etc.) that help shape such viewpoints;

    (b) an insight into the logical and methodological problems involved in discussions of causation (primary and secondary, necessary and sufficient, long and short term, etc.);

    (c) an acceptance of the co-existence of social elements of continuity and discontinuity in those periods usually characterized in terms of one or the other.

'A' level history's value, like all educational experience, 'is not only to provide persons with techniques but, more importantly, to provide techniques with critical, informed and humane persons'. Its relevance lies in its unique ability 'to help form a society in which its ideals of free inquiry and rationality shall themselves become chief touchstones of relevance'.[21]

Perhaps the ultimate justification of all historical study is that 'it enhances our self consciousness, enables us to see ourselves in perspective, and helps us towards that greater freedom which comes from self-knowledge'.[22] In particular history provides an insight into man's variety and potentially. In the sixth-form a history student can be exposed to contrasts of a political, economic and cultural kind; should develop a disciplined tolerance of other viewpoints and beliefs; must focus his attention on what man has been and is becoming. The possibility of only partial achievement of this 'self-consciousness' and 'greater freedom' at 'A' level does not seriously detract from its importance or its social relevance.

If current syllabuses and classroom practices fall short of such lofty aims then the teacher cannot primarily be blamed. After all, when one is struggling to keep a professional head above water the issue of historical navigation assumes little importance.

A New 'A' Level Syllabus

Principles and Priorities

What implications does all this, our critique of traditional syllabuses and estimations of the true value of the subject, hold for the construction of a new syllabus?

(1)   'A' level syllabuses should take as their point of origin problems, values and ideas that form part of the contemporary world. This view implies neither that this origin should lie with contemporary happenings nor that the mode of presentation be a 'tunnel' of development. It is surely possible to provide such insights into the present as may be afforded by a study of history by means of *contrasts* in the past. This at once preserves the separateness in space and time that is such an important part of developing an historical attitude and also remains *overtly relevant* to the contemporary needs and preoccupations of the sixth-form student.[23] It helps syllabus constructors out of the paradox that all historical study begins in present day experiences, values and knowledge but must minimize these influences if the past is to be understood. The philosophical complexities of this issue are well known. It is sufficient to recognize here the peculiar difficulties an 'A' level student has learning from his own experiences and yet being distant from them when necessary.

Syllabus content may be chosen in order to inform contemporary issues that are deemed to be not morally *right* but *salient*. The dangers here of anachronism, whether in the form of historical determination or moral indoctrination, are obvious. Lessons may be learnt by sixth-formers from the past but only insofar as their personal-social consciousness and critical faculties are heightened, not because some immutable and universal truth has been discovered lurking in the past.

Such a list of topics might include the development of individual liberty and equality, man's mastery of nature (science, industry and technology), the triumph of rationality, the origins of war, and so forth.

It may be objected at this point that criteria of importance such as these do not necessarily help us to select content. If rationality, for instance, is deemed important to sixth formers' understanding of the world, then so might 'revolution' be, or 'democracy', or 'urbanization'. Nor can such a criterion necessarily select which content best serves the understanding of, for instance, 'democracy' or even serves the needs of teaching methodology. Does one choose the whole story of the development of democracy or only key periods, individuals and case studies? If the latter, by what criteria are selections to be made and how much more of the history of the period does one include apart from the supposed 'democratic' elements? Does one, in fact, best teach such criteria by 'opposites' and contrasts—democracy by a study of the suppression of radical ideas during the Interregnum, or rationality by a study of the witchcraze of the sixteenth and seventeenth centuries?

Perhaps the most serious objection to a criterion of educational importance is that the syllabuses may be unhistorical insofar as they select and arbitrate for present-minded ends. It is difficult to see, however, how such selectivity is less historical than currently employed criteria used to periodize and thematize 'A' level syllabuses. The preoccupations with national development (especially and compulsorily Britain) and with the emergence of liberal traditions (for example, 'The Age of the Chartists' AEB or 'The French Revolution to 1802' and 'The English Revolution' LUB, AEB, JMB, to name only a few), are clear examples of this apparent consensus. More fundamentally, the very act of teaching the subject/syllabus must overcome both the enormous quantity of knowledge that exists and the variety of historical interpretations about this knowledge by a process of teacher-selection. This is presumably informed by some sort of criteria even if it only be that of expediency and desperation!

It is more important to recognize in discussions about the selection of content that the real issue 'has nothing to do with the point of origin of historical studies, but with the mode of treatment of historical problems'.[24] Content permits desired themes and ideas to be pursued and allows students to confront and *interact* with such ideas and values *for* contemporary relevance *in* a historically legitimate way. There is no necessary conflict here, simply an admission and definition of educational principle and priority.

It is in the best interests of all individuals in a liberal society, and not merely those individuals who are educated thus, that sixth formers be introduced to at least some of the values that underpin their society and several of the ideas that help explain it. As a discipline history is particularly well-suited to this task since its very methodology and chief objectives do embody many such values and ideas—the appeal to rational argument, the insistence upon free and open enquiry, the search for deep understanding and acceptance of others. More substantively, the subject continuously demands complex understandings of concepts such as social change, causation and man's control over his own actions and circumstances. These experiences do not guarantee social understanding but they are a necessary part of such an achievement.

(2)   Students pursue a course that encourages the possibility of acquiring genuinely historical skills and attitudes as *a direct consequence* of
the structure, pedagogy and methods of assessment of the syllabus.
Only in this sense can history be considered as a valuable aid to
understanding the present, for only by trying to see the past 'as it
actually was' can we gain a valid *contrast* with the present 'as it is'.

The idea of identifying specific objectives in terms of historical
skills, attitudes and concepts is as well-known as it is problematic[25],
particularly when it is invoked as a way of selecting content. It is
difficult to see how a truly skills-based study of the past can be
anything other than sterile and bogus at 'A' level. It certainly will
tend to give precedence to 'simple but observable attainments' over
'perhaps fragmentary and incomplete learning of complex forms of
understanding'.[26]

Secondly, it obscures the point that 'it is only by considering a
thing deeply and for its own sake...that one can properly begin to
enjoy and understand it'.[27]

For 'A' level the answer to this dilemma lies less in the drafting
of 'advanced' taxonomies than in the adoption of a different *syllabus
structure*, informed by precise historical considerations and also by
proper concern about the intellectual development of the students
over two years. 'From the point of view of learning, the priorities
that the structure of explanation provides are not relevant...the
only possible procedure for an educationalist is to find out empirically what parts of a subject are the easiest to learn'.[28] Two consequences for the 'A' level syllabus seem to follow on from the
acceptance of this view:

(a)   the syllabus and assessment work must become progressively
more difficult, for example, (i) begin with a single event that
later gains complexity through a widening temporal and spatial
context, itself produced by increasingly more sophisticated
questions and inquiries; (ii) begin with those facts and concepts (if such exist) that must be known if further progress is
to be made, for example, facts and narrative of people's actions
in the past;

(b)   that room be accorded to variations in students' individual
performance and interest through student-centred assignments
and a measure of continuous assessment.

If this irreducible minimum of ideas was to be acquired while *first* studying the Pilgrimage of Grace, for example, then the following points would
surely need to be grasped, on at least a minimal level:

(i)   History is a discipline of enquiry into and reconstruction of past
events:

(a)   the presentation of an accurate account of people's past actions
by the evidential use of a variety of records of that past;

Figure 1

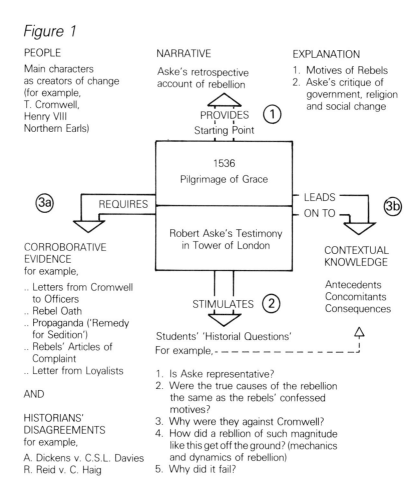

PEOPLE

Main characters
as creators of change
(for example,
T. Cromwell,
Henry VIII
Northern Earls)

NARRATIVE

Aske's retrospective
account of rebellion

PROVIDES ①
Starting Point

EXPLANATION

1. Motives of Rebels
2. Aske's critique of
   government, religion
   and social change

1536
Pilgrimage of Grace

Robert Aske's Testimony
in Tower of London

③a REQUIRES

LEADS
ON TO ③b

CORROBORATIVE
EVIDENCE
for example,

.. Letters from Cromwell
   to Officers
.. Rebel Oath
.. Propaganda ('Remedy
   for Sedition')
.. Rebels' Articles of
   Complaint
.. Letter from Loyalists

AND

HISTORIANS'
DISAGREEMENTS
for example,

A. Dickens v. C.S.L. Davies
R. Reid v. C. Haig

STIMULATES ②

Students' 'Historial Questions'
For example, - - - - - - - - - - - - - -

1. Is Aske representative?
2. Were the true causes of the rebellion
   the same as the rebels' confessed
   motives?
3. Why were they against Cromwell?
4. How did a rebllion of such magnitude
   like this get off the ground? (mechanics
   and dynamics of rebellion)
5. Why did it fail?

CONTEXTUAL
KNOWLEDGE

Antecedents
Concomitants
Consequences

the mode of presentation being a combination of narration, description and analysis, the records being the substance of a critical and interpretative apparatus of discovering and comparing the sources, ordering, selecting and interpolating them;

(b) the notions of contemporary sources and secondary interpretation of 'fact' and 'judgment'; the fundamental idea that 'most formative history is the outcome of a more or less continuous interchange among historians, past and present, over the meaning of the evidence.'[29]

(ii) History is a discipline of explanation but its accumulated knowledge often only enjoys a probablistic status and its methodology is problematic:

(a) problems with the explained: people as complex phenomenon; gaps and ambiguities in the surviving evidence;

(b) problems with the explaining: inferential analysis and generalization, causation and motivation, contingency and accident.

(c) problems with the explainer: personal competence of historians' intellectual ability and his opinions, bias and values.

This is, of course, not meant to suggest a model of historical practice but, more simply, provide an example of teaching practice and a principle for syllabus construction. Students' understanding of both period and historical knowledge would hopefully mature as the course developed progressively out of this simple beginning. This idea is discussed in more detail later at pages 173–7.

(iii) 'A' level syllabuses should be firmly centred on historical problems rather than encapsulated periods of time, developing outwards from a single happening towards the context that gives the event its historical meaning. Historical thought is surely best understood by trying to think historically about problems in the past:

(a) 'What caused the failure of the Pilgrimage of Grace?' rather than 'The Reign of Henry VIII' or even, more narrowly, 'Tudor Government and Religion'.

(b) 'Why did Stalin undertake the Great Purge, 1936–39?' rather than 'Russia in the 1930s' or 'The Stalinist Regime'.

(c) 'How important was the Californian gold rush to the settlement of the American West?' rather than 'The USA in the Nineteenth Century' or 'The American Frontier'.

If historical understanding is largely the product of the debate between different historians about the meaning of their evidence, and it is this which invests past events with their coherence and significance, it seems right that students should be presented with examples of historians' agreements and disagreements.

A clearer view of the complexity of historical problems should thus be provided and also an insight into their fascination. The flavour of the passion and vigour of historical debate tends to be cooked out of the traditional 'A' level stew. The historiographical dimension has a further advantage in that it naturally 'brings into sharp focus the nature of historical sources and historical methodology and shows the basic agreed criteria upon which the historian operates'[30]—problems of question-framing, of factual significance and verification, and of historical explanation and argumentation.

The obvious danger here for 'A' level students is that they will be taught historiography and not history, or that their historical thinking will extend no further than choosing one historical interpretation above another without real understanding of its merits. Historiography should be used only as a starting point for student investigation. As such it is better that historiographical points occur naturally and at intervals rather than in a separate module or unit.

During students' investigations of, for instance, the social origins of the English civil wars, the celebrated 'Gentry Debate' could be used to illustrate certain historiographical issues which ultimately were central to that debate: the development of reliable statistical techniques; the problems of historical language; the pervasive importance of historians' values and social theories.

(iv) The syllabus must allow students to pursue their investigation in sufficient depth to grasp 'the surrounding circumstances of (the historian's) problem, antecedents and consequences, concomitants and contrasts which affect the solution of the specific details of the problem itself. That is what one means by an understanding of history...'[31] The issues chosen for study should lend themselves to narrative presentation and should have sufficient dramatic force and complexity to intrigue sixth formers. Interest and motivation at 'A' level have to be created and sustained, not merely assumed. There must always be an element of subjectivity in judgments about interest-value, though a far greater consensus probably exists among the students themselves: the achievements and failures of Henry VIII rather than Henry VII; the downfall of the Stuart monarchy before 1660 rather than the restoration of that same dynasty after 1660; the Bolshevik revolution rather than the unification of Germany. Further, it is through the mastery of detail that the student can best exercise his imaginative faculties. Real achievements in historical empathy (whether mere imaginings, supposal, or genuine insights) are produced by building on *existing* levels of knowledge and understanding, deepening and expanding upon what is given and known.[32] The contrasts that exist between local and national developments and between individual and collective responsibility for events could more naturally be made. Finally, in-depth studies permit the use of historical sources in a limited but coherent manner.

(v) Documents and sources should form a significant part of any 'A' level syllabus. This approach would be as valuable for its insights into the concept of rationality and intellectual freedom as for its *introductions into the evidential bases of the discipline of history*. Greater emphasis is to be placed on documents in the new 'common core' 'A' level courses, but it remains to be seen how significantly and imaginatively the sources are embodied into the actual classroom practice. Most current syllabuses treat sources as mere illustrative stimuli or as historical evidence which is divorced from an understanding of the content to which it relates.

Clearly any advocacy of a fuller use of documents at 'A' level needs to be cautious. Pretensions to historical validity are dubious. Material would have to be pre-selected and delimited in scope for teaching purposes and by students' widely varying abilities. In addition, any new 'A' level syllabus would need to be quite precise about its concept of 'evidence' and its consequent usage in the classroom.

The issue for the new 'A' level syllabus is not 'sources *for* courses' or 'courses *from* sources', for that kind of dichotomy is surely misconceived and misleading (the former being trivial, the latter being impossibly difficult), but how to construct syllabuses, course materials and assessment regimes that permit content *and* sources to be married together to produce historically legitimate offspring. Again, particular problems approached through case-studies appear as one possible alternative—perhaps with students being first given a general context (secondary sources and teacher guidance) and then provided with a selected body of primary sources to analyze the historical correctness of a given statement or discover the solution to a particular problem. This case-study approach seems to lend itself, for instance, to questions about the role and motives of the individual in history.

.. 'Who was most responsible for the downfall of the Earl of Essex in 1601?'

.. 'General Haig's command of the campaign at Passchendaele in 1917, was ill-conceived, irresponsible and stubborn.'

.. 'Who killed J.F. Kennedy in 1963?'

(vi) A final priority of any new 'A' level syllabus must be the achievement of a sense of distance and difference in time and space. Ideas of change and continuity are best grasped when studied in developments occurring over centuries, not decades. Similarly a parallel study of a geographically and culturally distant topic (for example, Japan at the time of the English Revolution; The American Western Frontier at the time of the Industrial Revolution) would help to create an impression of continuity in periods of change and also suggest something of the rich variety of human experience. The historical imagination cannot be expected to develop fully without stimulus from the unfamiliar.

How then might these principles and priorities take shape in an 'A' level syllabus?

Modules As Spotlights on the Past

A framework of separate but interrelated modules of study would best serve our purposes in that they overcome some of the most serious deficiencies of conventional surveys and provide flexible and economic vehicles for the principles that should underpin an 'A' level syllabus.

(i)   Modules encourage a clearer definition of curricular objectives for teacher *and* student. This in turn should assist the generating of precise assessment criteria and various modes of assessment.

(ii) Different resources (commercial and home-produced) and teaching strategies can be adopted for particular units. This may especially help students' explorations of the meaning of historical explanation. Does one always begin with only primary sources? with opposed historians' viewpoints? with a summary of the whole topic or issue? with a series of key questions?

(iii) The gradual, progressive nature of units and their essential coherence mean that the exact sequence of modules can be 'repeated' or studied simultaneously to suit the particular learning needs or interests of classes of students. In this way knowledge and understanding can be reinforced and deepened by increasing students' exposure to more detailed information and ideas of greater complexity. In addition, the intensive nature of the units and variety of approach should help sustain student motivation.

(iv) Variations in subject matter or resources could be made according to regional preferences. A choice of units in the foreign study, for instance, could be provided from which individual centres select one. Alternatively, schools could be allowed to create their own units after consultation with the appropriate board. This flexibility would be more economical than a Mode III arrangement and less constraining than individual student 'projects' or 'study options'.

(v)   A syllabus based on modules also lends itself to adaptation to the needs of non-specialist history students—one-year sixth-formers, 'A/S' level, vocational courses—and inter-disciplinary approaches to sixth-form study. It would certainly help to fulfil the claim that 'history should be able to fit better into future transformation of the structure of the sixth-form than almost any other subject'.[33] Indeed, history could provide an important general study for all sixth-form subjects through historical case studies which reveal the characteristic structure and methodology of particular subjects—Faraday's 'discovery' of electricity for Physics—or provide a contextual knowledge for a proper study of a topic—Molière's plays or Eliot's poetry.

Together the units would provide strong spotlights on past people and problems, not weak floodlights on whole periods. Of course, large areas of the past will be unilluminated and therefore not viewed by the student. This selectivity does not seem a serious disadvantage—so long as students understand that what *is* viewed by spotlight is only one part of a greater whole, not yet visible but nonetheless there, perhaps influencing the visible action.

> Great history is not necessarily that on the largest scale, but that which in bringing the past to life, makes the largest number of factors intelligible.[34]

A temporal nexus would provide the matrix for such a syllabus with vertical (depth study) and horizontal (development study) axes for the same period. The separate units of study would be coherent insofar as they relate to one another historically. The course would begin with a particular event, simply told, and then gradually move outwards to wider and more complex contexts in time and space.

Possible examples of such an inter-relationship are:

1 (a) The Sarejevo Assassination → (b) The Great War → (c) Exploration, Expansion and Imperialism
2 (a) The Reign of Terror → (b) The French Revolution → (c) Monarchy, Popular Unrest and Radical Thought

It is therefore hoped that a *progressive* deepening of knowledge would be permitted and the kind of interconnections and perspectives that help make up an historical understanding of period would be encouraged.

Although flexibility in the choice of module-content and assessment-assignment could be permitted the inclusion of all the modules should be considered to be mandatory and the order in which they are studied prescribed. Some movement, backward and forward in time and from unit to unit, would be possible, however, and could be used to reinforce earlier ideas as well as stimulate new lines of enquiry and debate. This element of compulsion is dictated by (i) the fact that each module is meant to fulfil specific historical requirements (see below) and, together, the units are therefore intended to be interdependent; (ii) the desire to create a *progressively* more complex course in which students' knowledge and understanding is deepened as the study unfolds.

Overall, it is hoped that the structure should be better placed than existing provisions to fulfil the recommendation that 'disciplines of learning and modes of thinking are best developed by memorable experience rather than memorizing'.[35]

The only major modular course for history is the Schools Council 13–16 Project which has continued to enjoy increasing acceptance since its inception. Personal experience of teaching this course suggests a number of important criticisms which bear on our own discussions.

(a) The essentially discontinuous nature of the course often fails to provide pupils with the depth of knowledge which forms the basis of

Figure 2: Schematic Representation of Modular Syllabus

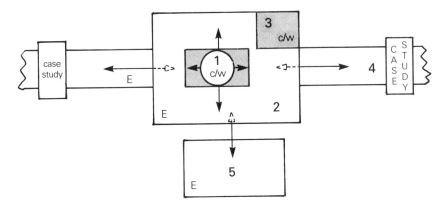

any true historical understanding. Furthermore, the required trans-ference of thinking skills from one unit to another about causation, for example, is not easily made without resort to quirky and artificial teaching strategies. A greater interdependence and coherence of units is required at 'A' level.

(b) Imaginative changes in syllabus structure do not of themselves pro-duce desirable alterations in classroom practice. The eradication of exclusively didactic methods requires careful attention at 'A' level. This is discussed more fully on pages 176–8.

MODULE 1: The Role of the Individual in an Historical Event
A simple narrative account of sufficiently compelling form and substance to intrigue as well as inform.

(a) Provides focus for some of the main characters and ideas to be developed in a depth study.

(b) Provides a starting point for students' understanding of historical explanation and historiographical debate.
   (i) idea of facts, explanation and historical sources.
   (ii) alternative historical interpretations based on same facts and sources.
   Two historians' opposed viewpoints can be introduced and 'unravel-led' as the course develops.

Students' questions about the event (for example the Pilgrimage of Grace, 1536, in 'the Henrician Reformation'; the Trial and Execution of Charles I, 1649, in 'the English Revolution'; the General Strike, 1926, in 'the Great Depression') and about historical method should be stimulated and left largely unanswered. Lines of enquiry are meant to be *opened up* at this stage.

At the centre of this introductory module is a biographical study to which pupils can return as the course develops and their understanding matures. Ideas of personal choice and intention should be set against the circumstances and constraints within which such decisions are made. Individuals are to be discovered as agents of historical action as much as victims.

MODULE 2: *A Depth Study*

A detailed study of a particular historical event that encourages students' historical thinking to develop and also possesses some measure of contemporary relevance (for example, rationalism, democracy, liberty, materialism). In particular a study of causation and personal motivation (of which the biographical study forms an important part). Ideas of multiple and various causes, of contingency and necessity, of primary and secondary causes, and of possibility and probability should all be explored through the subject matter. The various threads that may make up a historical event (political, social, economic, intellectual, and so forth) can be considered separately and in combination. Examples of depth studies might include: the Henrician Reformation, The Chartists, Hitler's Germany 1933–45, America in the 1920s.

MODULE 3: *A Local Study*

An opportunity for students to deepen their knowledge of a historical event through a detailed study of local variations in national developments (for example, the lake counties during the Pilgrimage of Grace of the 1530s; Cheshire during the English Revolution of the 1640s and 1650s; London during the 1930s). Not a local study in the sense of comprehensive 'coverage' but a problematic view of historical generalizations (for example, 'how successful was the Henrician Reformation outside London?'; 'was Cheshire really a Royalist county in the 1640s?'; 'what impact did economic depression have on the City of London in the 1930s?').

Provides an opportunity for local variations and initiatives by teachers and students in terms of both the content and precise form of the module. Documents can be used here in a major way. Students may be required to do some simple historical reconstruction and interpolation from a range of selected sources.

MODULE 4: *A Study in Development*

An appreciation that change and difference are the chief characteristics of the past through a broad survey of a theme pertaining to and helping to inform the depth study (for example, Religious Dissent from The Henrician Reformation; Parliamentary Growth out of the English Revolution; Men, Machines and Money out of The Great Depression).

A study of change which reveals the fundamental importance of the idea of continuity:

(i)   that in times of greatest apparent change much remains the same (i.e. *degrees* of change)

(ii) all historical ideas and events have antecedents which influence and constrain.

There is the opportunity to pursue these ideas through two or more case studies, as short features in the longer account of a development, which highlight the historical conceptualization by focussing sharply on particular moments in time—either points of change or the appearance of significant factors of change. Such case studies have additional advantages.

Firstly, they pointedly raise the issue of periodization by concentrating on a supposed turning-point in the past. Secondly, they permit important opportunities for depth during the development study. 'Vertical' sections through essentially 'horizontal' threads. The contrast then between, on the one hand, the somewhat superficial survey of broad periods of time and, on the other, the immersion into detailed study of particular moments in time would introduce an interesting variety in the module and would also serve to remind students of the gradations of depth and understanding that are possible in the discipline.

MODULE 5: A Foreign Parallel

A study of a non-European society contemporaneous with the depth study (1 and 2). To promote the idea of difference and variety in human experience, reinforce students' ideas of change/continuity and stimulate their historical imagination through sharp contrasts and comparisons (for example, 'Japan under the Shoguns' with the English Revolution or 'The British Raj' with The Great Depression).

Methodology and Assessment

There is not space here to develop proposals in detail but a number of characteristics seem to follow naturally from what has been said about curricular principles and the suggested syllabus structure.

(i)   The concept of evidence must figure strongly in classroom and examination hall. Thus primary and secondary sources should be employed in a variety of historically substantive and methodological ways, both in isolation and as 'clusters' of sources for comparison, contrast and reconstruction. They should figure in all modules but most especially in the depth study where the development of a detailed context allows both for a proper understanding of their meaning and an estimation of their value. See (iii) (b), below for a brief example of this.

(a) Sources should be introduced carefully and progressively according to their inherent difficulty and the extent to which they inform students' understanding of the historian's mode of explanation

for example, Module 1: ...variety of sources at his disposal
...selection and ordering
...Narrative, Description and Analysis

Modules 2 and 3: ...Fact and explanation

(b) Historiography should be used carefully to provide a flavour of the passion and vigour of debate and an insight into the nature of particular problems, not to teach particular historians' views.

(ii) Coursework provides an important aspect of the syllabus since it is thought here to better motivate students, introduce variety into classroom practice and, at its best, more subtly discriminate levels of historical thinking (practical problems of cost and marking reliability are not to be underestimated but are far from being insurmountable).

(a) Assignments should always be *propositional*—a specific question or problem is to be resolved within carefully defined parameters and upon a given body of historical evidence (primary and/or secondary).

(b) Work should be assessed as a *process of enquiry*, with stages, perhaps, rather than a mere outcome or 'finished' product. Rewards given to skills considered appropriate at each stage, for example, Stage 1: Question Framing;

Stage 2: Data-Collection and Proposition Testing;

Stage 3: Report.

(c) Work must follow on from a detailed *contextual knowledge* (i.e. Modules 1–3) if students' thinking is to be genuine and intelligible. This also should be rewarded.

(d) An *oral component* should be employed in final assessment to fully test and classify students' understanding of specific historical ideas and to explore the stages of their thinking and enquiry.

(i) Structured discussion or (ii) formal presentation and defence of coursework.

(iii) Examinations form a crucial part of the assessment influencing, as they do, classroom practice. A greater variety needs to be introduced and a more innovative and imaginative approach adopted. It is assumed that the ubiquitous essay will remain as a stalwart but some possible ways forward (all well-known but none well-accepted) are:

(a) *Objective testing* of understanding rather than mere knowledge (different forms are possible) to:
  (i) increase coverage of the syllabus
  (ii) specify particular historical objectives
  (iii) more carefully discriminate between levels of thinking.

(b) *Case-studies*, using a variety of stimuli and focussing on a single problem may be a more imaginative way of assessing pupils' understanding of a topic than the general essay. All the necessary primary and secondary information could be provided and task(s) structured or left open-ended to test understanding of a topic or event. The *general context* would be familiar to the student but the details of the *individual case* to be studied would not. Students must therefore bring to the question posed in the case-study (i) contextual understanding, (ii) an appraisal of the sources provided, in terms of their authenticity, usefulness and reliability.

Table 2

	Context	Case-Study	Question
1	Witch craze of the sixteenth and seventeenth centuries	The trial of Edmond Robinson in 1633: a 10 year-old boy accused of witchcraft	Why were the boy, and his father, found guilty of witchcraft?
2	America's entry into the First World War.	The Zimmerman Telegram: its purpose and decoding.	Why did the USA not enter the war until details of this telegram were revealed?

(iv) Classroom practice is the ultimate test of the virtues of any syllabus and most 'A' level teachers require *assistance*, especially in terms of:
  (a) Resources—texts, source-packs, audio visual materials are all required. Like the final examinations they must fully incorporate the historical principles of the syllabus and not merely pay lipservice to it: translate curricular aims into recognizable and valid classroom objectives and practices.
  (b) Pedagogy—very specific advice is required about producing coursework assignments and constructing appropriate classroom exercises. 'Models' need to be provided and a variety of approaches suggested (for example, simulation, problem-solving, oral discussion and debate, fieldwork, etc.).
  (c) Feedback from examination boards and genuine opportunities to enter into dialogue with them.

THREE EXAMPLES OF CONTENT

A. THE ENGLISH REVOLUTION

MODULE 1: The Trial and Execution of the King, 1649.
Biographical Study: Oliver Cromwell.
MODULE 2: The origins of Civil War and Radical Revolution.
MODULE 3: Cheshire: A Royalist Stronghold?
MODULE 4: Parliament and Monarch: Power and Privilege.
MODULE 5: Japan under the Shoguns.

B. THE GREAT DEPRESSION

MODULE 1: General Strike, 1926.
Biographical Study: Ramsay Macdonald.
MODULE 2: Boom and Slump in Britain.
MODULE 3: The City: Trade during the Depression.
MODULE 4: Men and Machines: Technology and Trade.
MODULE 5: The British Raj in India.

C. THE GREAT WAR

MODULE 1: The Assassination in Sarajevo
Biographical Study: Wilhelm II or Douglas Haig
MODULE 2: Great War 1914–18
MODULE 3: A Village/Town
Newspaper's Reaction to The War
MODULE 4: Exploration, Expansion and Imperialism
MODULE 5: China: Manchu versus Nationalist.

Notes

1 See, for instance, ROBERTS, M. (1969) 'Contemporary problems of sixth-form history', *History*, 54; HURSTFIELD, J. (1969) 'History in the sixth form and in higher education' in *The Undergraduate Historian* (Historical Association pamphlet, 1969); ELTON, G.R. (1970) 'What sort of history should we teach?' in BALLARD, M. *New Movements in the Study and Teaching of History* and (1967) *The Practice of History*, especially at pp. 145–60; JONES, J.A.P. (1975) 'Specially approved 'A' level history syllabuses at Huddersfield New College', *Teaching History*; BROWN, R. and DANIELS, C. (1976) 'Sixth-form history—an assessment', *Teaching History*, 15.

   Despite the cautious claim in 1975 that 'recent developments in lower school history teaching and examining...would seem to indicate that a re-examination of 'A' level objectives and techniques may now be required' (JONES, J.A.P. (1975) *op. cit.*, p. 13) little of substance has materialized in the intervening decade. Limited experiments have been undertaken by the JMB (Personal Study Option), AEB and Cambridge Board (method paper and personal project). Only since September 1985, however, has a major attempt been made to provide a radical new direction for 'A' level History. Sailing with the flag of the Schools Council Project, and under the auspices of the Cambridge Board, it resembles several of the ideas contained in this essay. Unfortunately, news of this welcome venture arrived too late for me to include detailed references to it.

2   The survey was conducted in July 1985 and consisted of a sample of 200 lower sixth history students from seventeen schools of different kinds within Cheshire and the Liverpool area. No pretence is made at scientific exactitude but some clear conclusions emerged: (a) teaching methods remain predominantly authoritarian; (b) few students wish to go any further with the subject; (c) documents have made appearances on examination papers but have not had a significant impact on classroom practice; (d) students' interest in history has survived all these former points.
My thanks are due to Mr. S.M. HARRISON for helping to conduct the survey.

3   Statistics of Education (HMSO) 1979 edn., 'School Leavers' table 32; JMB. Annual Report 1980–81, p. 81 and 1983–84, p. 81. The decline in the number of history entries at 'O' level for this Board is from 25.7 per cent of the total numbers in 1974 to 17.2 per cent in 1984. It is not intended to suggest here that history is the only subject waning in popularity but relative to most others it is faring far worse. In 1974 history was the third most popular 'A' level at the JMB (after English literature and physics—excluding General Studies). In 1983 it had fallen to sixth, having been overtaken by pure/applied mathematics, chemistry and biology. Furthermore, the competition for students has been increased by the arrival of new, sometimes fashionable, subjects. The JMB for instance, offered forty-seven subjects at 'A' level in 1984, ten more than a decade before.
At 'O' level history has fallen from third place in 1974 (behind English literature and geography—excluding mathematics and English language) to seventh place in 1984 (overtaken by physics, chemistry, biology and art). A similar decline was noted in Wales. See JONES G.E., (1984) 'History: A future?', *The Welsh Historian*, 2, pp. 4–8. In all this it is the *trend* that is significant and it is incontrovertibly downward.
History at 'A' level is not in danger—yet. Such figures contrast oddly with the view that 'the time for this kind of defensiveness is past. Of course people should learn history, and of course it should be taught in schools...' DICKINSON, A.K., LEE, P.J. and ROGERS, P.J. (1984) *Learning History*, Heinemann, p. x.
Even at university level the danger has been noted. In May 1983, for instance, the 'History at the Universities Defence Group' was set up to promote the value of historical study.

4   A survey of the destinations of history graduates in 1983–84 revealed that more of them (18.4 per cent) entered financial work than teaching (16.6 per cent). In fact, only one in nine historians failed to find employment, which is no worse than the average. BECK, P. (1986) 'Going up in history', *Times Educational Supplement*, 21 February, p. 24. More worrying for the future of the subject in school is that the route into history teaching has been greatly narrowed. Between 1974 and 1984 the number of PGCE history students was reduced from 1000 to 300.

5   In 1983 in Cheshire, for example, only half of its sixth-forms offered one-year history courses for 16–18 year olds and 85 per cent of these were for 're-sit' purposes. Report on Joint LEA/HMS Conference for Teachers of History, (1983) Cheshire Education Committee, p. 8.

6   Such experiences come as an even greater shock to those students who have been used to the more interactive and problem-directed methodology of the Schools Council History Project at 'O' level. A real mismatch exists and serious problems of adjustment occur for such students in over 800 schools currently following the Project.

7   HURSTFIELD, J. (1969) *The Undergraduate Historian*, Historical Association, p. 5.

8   GRIFFITHS, R. (1985) 'The teacher and the lecturer', *The Welsh Historian*, 3, p. 16.

9   DAVIES, C.S.L. (1977) *Peace, Print and Protestantism*, Paladin, pp. 107 and 108.
10 The important relationship between syllabus and assessment is a vexed question and one of daunting complexity. Simplistic talk about 'the tail wagging the dog' makes examiners see red and history teachers dream of Manx cats. Examiners prefer, it seems, to dwell on the complexity of change; history teachers on the speed of change. Neither of these attitudes does much to balance the proportions of validity and reliability; yet a major overhaul at 'A' level requires that it be done. Cf. HURSTFIELD'S fear 'that the 'A' level examination is too often treated as the voice of God speaking to the universities', *op. cit.*, p. 6.
11 At the time of writing the nine examination boards have achieved a striking commonality in their suggested reforms of syllabuses. Caution and conservatism are the keynotes: two papers with eight essay style questions of three hours' duration; a combination of an outline study and a special paper. Documents are given increased status but are usually limited to one paper and are 'unseen' single documents, rather than clusters. Only two or three Boards will provide for extended essays or regional history and none (except, perhaps, WJEC) take on board multiple-choice questions, case studies or structured questions. The issue of grade-related criteria has been left in abeyance.
12 AEB. Annual Report (1982–83), p. 56.
13 JMB Annual Report (1983–84), p. 69.
14 ELTON, G.R. (1978) 'Putting the past before us', *Times Literary Supplement*, 8 September, p. 993.
15 IAAM, (1965) *The Teaching of History in Secondary Schools*, 3rd edn., p. 84. It is a commonplace attitude that the subject is supposed to provide a 'special intellectual training...at any level'. ELTON, G.R. (1967) *Practice of History*, p. 149.
16 ELTON, G.R. (1967) op. cit., p. 51; Cf. 'A wanton underestimation of children's ability must not be allowed to serve as an excuse for practices that put history in danger only by failing to teach history at all.' DICKINSON, A.K., LEE, P.J. and ROGERS, P.J. (1984) *op. cit.*, p. x.
17 COLLINGWOOD, R.G. (1946) *The Idea of History*, quoted in DICKINSON, A.K., LEE, P.J. and ROGERS, P.J. *ibid*, p. 44.
18 '...we believe that history and related disciplines provide a necessary perspective which assists the young in understanding the context within which their lives are to be lived...' in THWAITES, B. and WYSOCK-WRIGHT, C. (Eds.) (1980) *Education 2000* CUP, p. 41; Also see PARTINGTON, G. (1980) *The Idea of an Historical Education*, NFER Publishing Company, p. 114.
19 Cf. ELTON's verdict: 'It should be said with regret that there is no proof that a knowledge of history, recent or distant...succeeds in giving a man much under-standing of his time'. ELTON, G.R. (1967), *Practice of History*, p. 148. For a forthright but unacceptable contribution to this question see CONNEL-SMITH, G. and LLOYD, H.A. (1972) *The Relevance of History*, Heinemann. It is logically and historically suspect to treat historical scholarship and educational relevance as separate and opposed concerns (i) much of the educational value of the better school history derives from the standards and concerns of the professional discipline; (ii) all the content is provided by the scholar; (iii) the equation of relevance and contemporaneity is misconceived and falsifies the links between the present and the past. It might be more accurate to suggest that the *universities* have tended to have a stultifying effect upon the development of sixth-form history.
20 FISCHER, F. (1971) *Historians' Fallacies: Toward a Logic of Historical Thought*, Harper and Row, p. 135.
21 SCHEFFLER, I. (1973) 'Reflections on education relevance' in PETERS, R.S. (Ed.) *The Philosophy of Education*, OUP, p. 84.
22 THOMAS, K. quoted in MARWICK, A. (1973) *The Nature of History* Macmillan,

p. 246. Cf. 'the point of teaching history well exemplifies the point of education itself. From his encounter with (carefully chosen) experiences the child inductively elaborates the whole conceptual system within which he can conceive of the world in an educated way'. ROGERS, P.J. (1984) in DICKINSON, A.K., LEE, P.J. and ROGERS, P.J. (1984), p. 30.

23 Much of genuine psycho-social relevance is undermined in schools because insufficient attention is paid to (a) drawing out for pupils the underlying purposes and social values of units of work (b) building stages of reinforcement of such purposes into schemes of work (c) permitting negotiable elements into the curriculum: both in decisions about subject-matter and opportunities for collaborative work between students. The social value of sixth-form history should be *obvious* to student, parent and employer. The subject's survival may depend upon it.

24 HEXTER, J.H. (1961) *Reappraisals in History*, Longmans, p. 8.

25 GILES, P. and NEAL, G. (1973) 'History teaching analyzed', *Trends in Education*, 32, pp. 16–25; GARD, A. and LEE, P.J. (1978) 'Educational objectives for the study of history' reconsidered, in DICKINSON, A.K. and LEE, P.J. *History Teaching and Historical Understanding*, Heinemann, pp. 21–38. The arguments apply to sixth-form history also:

   (i)   many objectives like 'analysis' and 'evaluation' are not peculiarly historical skills;

   (ii)   it is difficult to isolate and evaluate such objectives in a behaviourally precise manner without debasing and, possibly, damaging the historical context in which objectives are identified and 'taught';

   (iii) skills are acquired by doing history rather than the other way around.

26 GARD, A. and LEE, P.J. (1978) *op. cit.*, p. 28.

27 WARNOCK, M. (1973) 'Towards a definition of quality in education', in PETERS, R.S. (Ed.) *op. cit.*, p. 118.

28 HAMLYN, D. (1973) 'The logical and psychological aspects of learning', in PETERS, R.S. *op. cit.* p. 220.

29 LEFF, G. (1969) *History and Social Theory*, Merlin, p. 15.

30 MARWICK, A. (1973) *op. cit.*, p. 213.

31 ELTON, G.R. (1967) *op. cit.*, p. 149.

32 For a stimulating discussion of this fundamental aspect of the subject see SHEMILT, D. (1984) 'Beauty and the philosopher: Empathy in history and classroom' in DICKINSON, A.K., LEE, P.J. and ROGERS, P.J., *op. cit.*, pp. 39–84. Although her definition of the concept of imagination is different, MARY WARNOCK makes the point 'that it is only if the imagination is alive and active that the pupil will be able to *go on* with a subject, beyond the point at which the teaching stops...We ought, therefore, to give serious thought to the precise question what makes a person believe that there is an infinity of things to do, an infinity of questions to be asked and answers to be sought'. PETERS, R.S. (1973) *op. cit.*, p. 115 and 118.

33 DAWSON, K. in HURSTFIELD, J. (1969) *The Undergraduate Historian*, p. 14. 'What we need is far more co-operation and cross-reference between the disciplines, without the indeterminate mush which so often follows attempts at integration.'

34 LEFF, G. (1969) *op. cit.*, p. 77.

35 THWAITES, B. and WYSOCK-WRIGHT, C. (1983) *op. cit.*, p. 63.

10   Testing Skills in History

Henry G. Macintosh

Synopsis

Curriculum development and curriculum change in secondary schools in Britain has always had to come to terms at some point with public examinations. This has created particular problems for those responsible for national curriculum projects and the resulting relationship between project teams and the examining system has been a tense one often without much in the way of creative outcomes. It has been rare in consequence for projects to try and use GCE and CSE examinations as an integral part of their development programme and of their summative evaluation.

A notable exception to this has been the Schools Council History 13–16 Project and this chapter describes one aspect of an extremely fruitful relationship between the project and the national CSE examination administered by the Southern Regional Examinations Board (SREB). The aspect chosen is the development of a model for assessing within a CSE examination the use of skills in relation to historical source material.

The chapter starts by setting down the rationale for the model used—a closed set written paper—and highlights its strengths and weaknesses. It then goes on to describe the methods developed for setting, marking and weighting questions which will enable the objectives of the project in this area to be validly and reliably assessed. The overall methodology and in particular the establishment through the creation of paper level scales of descriptions of what has actually been assessed in a particular examination has significant implications for the new General Certificate of Secondary Education (GCSE) and for the development of grade criteria. It has also greatly enhanced the opportunities open to teachers to make diagnostic use of assessment which has not previously been possible in public examinations.

The chapter concludes by stressing that the methods described do not constitute the only approach to the testing of skills in history. The information available however from ten years of experience suggests that the examinations have been successful in evaluating and furthering the project's objectives and in stimulating the interest and enjoyment of the youngsters taking them. As such they provide a sound basis for further work in the future.

Introduction

The relatively small amount of research undertaken in the late 1960s and early 1970s into children's capacity to reason and exercise judgements in history has not been particularly helpful to those wishing to change the teaching of history in schools. Very strongly influenced by the work of Jean Piaget and E A Peel'[1] (the latter specifically in the context of history) it led to the general conclusion that children could only do particular things when they reached particular ages. It also suggested that whilst children at around the ages of 13–16 were capable of thinking logically about presented information even the ablest amongst them would find the utmost difficulty in understanding situations involving a large number of variables and almost certainly could not generalize or formulate and test hypotheses.

Such work did not preclude the possibility that the level of historical thinking could be improved by different approaches in the classroom. It did, however, serve to confirm the view of many in universities and teacher training institutions who agreed with G R Elton[2] that real history could not be undertaken by pupils in any worthwhile sense below university or even doctoral level. The legacy of that belief causes many history teachers today to undervalue the capacities of their own students and helps to ensure that their own teaching methods make it a self-fulfilling prophecy.

Not all, however, have accepted these views and in particular in Britain they have been challenged over the past fourteen years by the work of the Schools Council History 13–16 Project established in 1972. The project team from its inception took the view that pupils of age 13–16 (its principal target area and hence its name) should have history presented to them not as a body of information but as an approach to knowledge. History should therefore be seen as a formal discipline which had developed its own characteristic ways of exploring and making sense of past experience. This involved first of all the reconstruction of events using the surviving sources, whatever form these might take, and then their explanation in terms of the three crucial concepts of change, causation, and motivation. More significantly perhaps this view of history was to be presented to all pupils and not only to the most able. When translated into a curriculum prescription as it was by the project team and then implemented by teachers, this approach requires a radical review of the pupils' capacity to think. Such a view of history will require them *inter alia* to distinguish between information and evidence, to make inferences from given information, to suggest causes and consequences for actions and events, to form hypotheses, to test these hypotheses by using a range of procedural tools including empathy and then to amend or reject them as starting points for further investigations and to use organizing themes and ideas (behavioural, causal, temporal). In summary the 13–16 course requires those taking it to reason at a far more sophisticated level than had previously been thought possible. In such circumstances 'History 13–16' has become more than a curriculum development project. It has also become a research project designed to investigate the nature of adolescent ideas about history as a discipline and to see whether these ideas can be enhanced by teaching and assessing the subject as a distinct way of knowing rather than as a body of information.[3]

In order to provide examinations as economically as possible for such projects the GCE boards which examine nationally have devised arrangements whereby one of them develops a special examination based upon the particular project's philsophy and objectives on behalf of all the other boards which are able to borrow it for use by schools who wish to enter candidates. The regionally-based CSE boards do not, however, have a similar arrangement and each of the fourteen individual boards develop examinations based upon national projects if they deem it appropriate. Very often schools have been forced to devise their own examinations under mode 3 arrangements. This situation is far from satisfactory and serves to reinforce the love/hate relationship that exists between secondary school curriculum developers and examining boards—a relationship that has all too often led to the development of examinations which fail to match project philosophy and in consequence prevents them from being used as an integral part of summative evaluation.

This position seemed likely to obtain initially with History 13–16. The first Project Director, David Sylvester, then based at the University of Leeds, was able to negotiate a national CSE examination with the Southern Regional Examinations Board (SREB) which assumed responsibility for the two written papers, coursework remaining the concern of the regional boards. Since 1972 the SREB has worked in the closest partnership with the Project Team under four successive directors. The aim of this partnership has been to translate the aims, objectives and philosophy of the Project into an assessment pattern which on the one hand could meet the requirements of a national public examination and on the other form a part of the Project's evaluation programme. It has I believe been extremely successful in this endeavour and the national CSE examination has not only pioneered a range of techniques not previously used in public examinations, some of which will be referred to later in this article but also a much more open approach to the dissemination of information about the examination. It has in consequence played an important and integral part in both curriculum development and in-service training. It would obviously have made sense for the CSE national examination to have worked in close cooperation with the parallel GCE O-level examination particularly in view of the move towards a single system of examining at 16+ and the creation of GCSE in 1988 but this unfortunately proved impossible. The Project's philosophy and the assessment methodology developed for the CSE examination has however exercised a very considerable influence upon the determination of the national criteria for history upon which the GCSE examination will be based after 1988 and the potentially damaging effects of this lack of cooperation have therefore been limited. For those interested in studying the two-year syllabus upon which the CSE and GCE 'O' level examinations are currently based the aims, assessment objectives, assessment pattern and syllabus content are set out in outline in appendix A to this chapter. For the GCSE, this pattern will remain virtually unaltered. Two new topics have, however, been added. 'Energy Through Time' as an alternative to Medicine, and Japan as an additional Modern World Study. Others will follow.

It is hoped that this introduction will have provided the reader with sufficient information to set the discussion which follows upon testing skills in history in context. It is obviously not possible to deal with all the skills which the Project intends that students should develop and attention will therefore be concentrated upon the skills relating to the use of sources, whose development is designed to enable students to make the crucial distinction between information and evidence. In the assessment pattern developed for the CSE and GCE 'O' level examinations these are assessed primarily although not exclusively within paper 2, sometimes called the method paper. Substantial use of sources also takes place within coursework and forms therefore part of the assessment of that component. The remainder of this chapter will therefore consider the rationale behind this particular paper, the questioning and marking techniques and the system of *post-hoc* weighting which has been applied. In so doing it will endeavour to justify what has been done not as the only approach to assessment but as one approach which has appeared to work validly and reliably in relation to certain skills in history. Readers interested in obtaining further information about the Project and its assessment should contact either the author, or Denis Shemilt, formerly the Project's third Director and only Evaluator, who is currently Principal Lecturer in charge of In-Service Training at Trinity and All Saints College, Leeds.

The Use of a Written Paper—Rationale and Format

The use of an end-of-course (terminal) examination as a major element in the assessment of skills relating to the study and use of historical source material is, of course, open to significant objections, some of which stem from the structure of the Project itself whilst others are of a more general nature. The existence of four distinct elements within the syllabus (see appendix A) which can be taken in any order must mean that different schools will be teaching different elements at different times over a two-year period. Terminal assessment at the end of this period is likely, therefore, to place some students at an advantage and others at a disadvantage. Since, however, the study of relevant sources is central to the philosophy of the Project and hence permeates every aspect of the course it was felt reasonable to assume an increase in mastery over the course as a whole. In such circumstances end of course assessment was thought to be justified.

At the general level the main criticism is that of artificiality. No student of history would normally study a particular period or a particular problem and the information relating to it under conditions which severely restricted the time at his or her disposal, which selected the sources which had to be studied, and which denied access to other sources and other people. These are all restrictions which written papers if they are to be manageable are obliged to impose. The justification for using such an approach and indeed the justification for any attempt to test the use and study of sources under examination conditions must lie in the extent to which performance in the examination reflects student ability to use the skills being tested in more natural situations outside the examination hall. In other words is the mastery transferable? Indirect assessment of this kind of course not only measures student performance but can also monitor teacher effectiveness throughout a course, although the possibilities of this latter role are not normally exploited constructively within public examinations.

Having taken the decision to use a written paper, despite its disadvantages, it was necessary for those setting the examination to develop an appropriate format and to work through the implications of that format in practice. To date the CSE paper 2 has used a 'closed-set'. The key features of this model are that the answers to all the questions should be found by reference to the material provided within the paper itself and that all questions are compulsory. A rather more flexible interpretation of the words 'by reference' had led to some changes in relation to the first of these two points but the second remains unaltered. The main advantages arising from the use of a 'closed-set' are that it provides a relatively stable base for comparison between students and it enables use to be made of topics which do not form part of the specific course content. This last permits teachers to concentrate upon developing the relevant skills through the use of those sources which are appropriate to whatever topic is being studied and thus frees them from the need to try and 'spot' the examiner's choice of topic. Amongst the subjects chosen for the CSE paper 2 to date have been the following: John—King of England 1199–1216 (1976), Propaganda (1979), What Happened to the Romanov Family? (1980), Cromwell in Ireland

(1981), Arthur—Legend or History? (1983), and Sweeney Todd—Demon Barber of Fleet Street? (1985).[4] This range simply serves to underline the impossibility and hence the uselessness of trying to read the examiner's mind. What needs to be done is to teach and develop the skills and leave the examination to test them.

No approach to assessment however is without disadvantages. Because those answering the questions in a closed-set do not need to use information additional to that provided it is not easy to ensure that the sources are used in their historical context. This tends to encourage questions which do little more than test comprehension—usually reading comprehension. When describing papers like the History 13–16 paper 2 the term 'content free' is often used. This is extremely misleading unless it is intended to mean no more than 'syllabus content free'. No examination using historical sources can ever be 'subject content free'. Comprehension will therefore always have a subject dimension and those students who understand the basic vocabulary of a subject will rightly have an advantage over those who do not. The line between technical and basic vocabulary in a subject such as history is not always easy to draw but it is one which needs to be borne carefully in mind when selecting topics for an examination of this type.

It will, it is hoped, be clear from what has been said so far that the choice of topic and the type of questions set upon that topic—and the two are of course closely related—are crucial to the success of the closed-set model as indeed they are to any written examination. Before exploring the ways in which the 13–16 paper 2 has tackled these issues it is necessary first of all to outline the skills which the paper aims to test.

The four assessment objectives for paper 2 as set out in the Project's Information Brochure are as follows:

1. Understanding sources (for example, comprehension);
2. Evaluating sources (for example, for bias, gaps etc);
3. Making Inferences;
4. Synthesis.

These objectives appear straightforward and simple even limited by comparison with say the full range of objectives set out in the Coltham and Fines elaboration for History of the Bloom taxonomy.[5] This apparent simplicity was reflected to a substantial degree in the types of question used in the first two paper 2s in 1976 and 1977. The 1976 King John paper, for example, contained questions such as (a) 'Which of John's brothers is the speaker quoted by Roger of Howden in extract H? Show how you have arrived at your answer,'; and (b) 'Which two extracts contradict each other the most?'. These were both quite deliberately intended to elicit answers which ranged along a single skill dimension as for example comprehension or evaluation, and were only saved from the criticism that they could be answered by students who had neither studied the course nor studied history by the inclusion of a requirement to justify or to give reasons. This was, of course, overt in the first question but only implied in the second. The balance of marks awarded as between the answer and the reason is of course crucial here in determining where the emphasis will lie.

A number of things occurred, however, which raised major questions about the design of paper 2 and led to significant changes. First, when specifically given the opportunity to justify their answers, students provided a range of perfectly respectable reasons which often went well beyond those anticipated by those who set the questions. Secondly, analysis and observation of tasks designed to develop particular skills suggested that student responses to these tasks fell into a series of levels which were hierarchical in the sense that progress through the levels increased the range and potential of the answers but not in the sense that success at the lower levels was a prerequisite to success at the higher.[6] One example of such a task is as follows. If students are given two or more historical sources and are asked questions about them which require comparisons to be made with the intention of trying to develop the distinction between evidence and information, their answers will fall almost inevitably into the following six categories:

(i)   Random Usage—Here the students either pick one source and ignore others or answer the same question again and again for different sources.

(ii) Collates Sources—Here the student shows that he or she can use the sources systematically and sequentially and is able to add information from 'y' to information from 'x'.

(iii) Conflates Sources—Here the student systematically mixes or overlaps information from 'y' with that from 'x' but never questions the legitimacy of doing this.

(iv) Cross References—by looking for points of positive correspondence. Here the student checks compatibility of the reference. For the first time the sources are being used as evidence not information.

(v)   Correlates Sources—Here the student looks for negative as well as positive correspondence. (Closed-set correlation)

(vi) Correlates Sources—Here the student looks for null correspondence. (Open set correlation)

The sources used can, of course, be made more or less complex as can the questions both in what is asked and how it is asked but whatever the degree of difficulty and the age or ability of the students the same pattern of answers emerges in terms of what is actually being done by the student.

Exercises such as these—and there was extensive trialling of materials and observation of classroom practice throughout the period 1972–76 led those concerned with the setting of paper 2 to undertake a number of interrelated steps which were to transform the whole nature of the paper.

First the notion was abandoned that it was possible to set questions which beyond a peradventure could test specific skills in isolation. These were replaced by problematic or dilemmatic questions which had a number of broadly-based targets in mind and encouraged the students to exercise those skills which they deemed most appropriate to the resolution of the problem posed. The one major exception to this was the retention of one or two straightforward comprehension questions usually at the beginning of the paper which were designed to provide data upon the general comprehensibility of the sources used. Secondly, a model was designed for constructing questions which were based upon consideration of what makes a particular question difficult. Thirdly, it was recognized that the conceptual/skill dimensions proposed for the paper needed unpacking. This resulted in a more complex model whose component elements overlapped considerably. Fourthly, a much closer look was taken at the format and orientation of the chosen topic for paper 2 in order to provide the maximum interaction between material and question. Finally, and to some extent most crucial of all, a marking methodology was developed including question weightings which could accommodate the range of student answers likely to arise from changes in the format of the questions, and operate reliably for substantial numbers within the constraints of a public examination.

Since those involved were dealing with a live examination, upon which results of significance to the students were being issued, and not with a research project, it was necessary to proceed with care and hence at a relatively slow pace. It was therefore not until 1980 when the paper 2 topic was 'What Happened to the Romanov Family?' that these changes were fully implemented. Work since then has been largely concerned with refining the model with particular reference to *post hoc* question weighting and marking procedures. The progress made does not of course eliminate the criticisms of the model itself to which reference was made at the start of this chapter. These five steps will now be looked at in turn and their overall effect on the paper illustrated.

Written Questions

The decision to use more dilemmatic and problematic questions led to a re-examination of the notion of structure within written questions. If one chooses to use as a basis for classifying questions the room for manoeuvre which they provide for those trying to answer then one obtains a continuum which runs from closed (Paris is the capital of France. True/False.) to open (History is Bunk. Discuss.) One needs to remember however that the ways in which the latter question is marked may close the opportunities open to those answering it very significantly.

Classification of questions in this way raises a number of points which are significant both for those trying to answer them and for those trying to construct them. The first of these is the question of 'supply' and 'select' and the balance between the two. As one moves from the open to the closed end of the continuum, the respondents have to move from a situation in which they are required to select from given information into one in which they are asked to supply their own information. For those constructing the questions the demands shift from setting problems at the closed end i.e. is there a correct answer and if so what, or more relevantly what makes this answer better or worse or as good as that answer? The shift along the continuum also changes some of the underpinning demands made by questions upon those answering them. Closed questions place much more emphasis upon reading or interpretation of visual material whilst open questions emphasize writing skills and the capacity to marshall thoughts into a logical and coherent explanation or argument. Inability to meet these demands may well turn out to be the principal reason for 'failure' rather than inability to meet the requirements that the setter had in mind. The position of a question along the continuum also has implications for content coverage. In general a larger number of questions can be answered in a given time at the closed/select end although this will depend upon the amount of material used, its complexity and the length of answer that is necessary to do justice to a given question. As a consequence of this 'select' questions can usually provide a more comprehensive content coverage in a shorter space of time than can 'supply' questions.

In the past the tendency has been to use the two ends of the continuum and to neglect the middle. Teachers in the classroom have always made substantial use of short answer (essentially closed) quiz questions whilst public examinations in history have concentrated upon open-ended essay questions although as has already been indicated these are often marked in a fairly closed fashion. Public examinations in the United Kingdom then went through a phase in the early and mid-1970s of using questions from both ends within a single examination. This might consist of a section of multiple-choice objective items or short answer questions often in association with so called stimulus material and a section of essay questions. This trend is now on the wane although it is not completely over as reference to a number of current GCE 'O' levels will show, but the current major effort is now directed towards setting questions which fall somewhere in the middle. Such questions are often referred to not very originally or informatively as structured questions. Over the past three or four years the forms of structuring used have become increasingly sophisticated with the aim of tapping a wide range of skills and concepts and encouraging a wide range of responses. The resulting questions thus involve those answering them in both selection and supply and in both reading and writing, and they impose considerable demands in terms of both setting and marking.

The first thrust towards the use of 'structured questions' arose from a desire to unpack the format of traditional essay questions in order to make them more comprehensible to the less able. Thus for example 'Describe and account for the success and failures of the Irish Home Rule Movement in the period 1912–1921' would be turned into the following three-part question:

(i)   Describe the efforts to gain Home Rule in Ireland 1912–1921.
(ii)   Why were the Irish Nationalists more successful in 1921 than before?
(iii) In what ways was their success marred?

(This incidentally is not a very well worded question. How much before is 'before' in part (ii) and does it matter? How many students would be put off by the word 'marred' in part (iii)?)

It soon became apparent from using questions of this type that making a question easier to comprehend did not of itself make it any easier to answer (it had been rather facilely assumed that it would). Indeed unpacking questions in this way might well make them more difficult because additional questions were now being asked of whose existence the respondents might have been blissfully unaware and would have remained so had the questions been left in their original form.

It was also considered that structuring could ease the problems of the less able by limiting the field from which an answer could be drawn. For example, instead of reading 'Discuss the role played by Arab physicians in the history of medicine' the question might read instead

Source A (iii)—An illustration showing Hippocrates examining the urine of one of his patients.
Hippocrates was an Ancient Greek physician but in Source A (iii) he is not shown wearing Greek clothes.

What does this suggest about the ways in which medieval doctors came to learn about the ideas of Hippocrates?

This revised question raises a number of significant issues. First its length by comparison with the original. One of the problems of structuring is that it is almost impossible to achieve without lengthening the questions. This may well result in additional reading demands and hence inhibit access to the question. Second, the extent to which profitable use is or is not made in the matter of the illustration. It is all too easy for such material to become mere window dressing. Thirdly, there is the problem of whether limiting the focus of the question from Arab physicians and the history of medicine to the links between Hippocrates and the medieval period makes it an easier or more difficult question to answer. Does it not simply impose a different range of demands which some may find easier and others more difficult? Finally, there is the way in which the problem is posed in the form of a paradox rather than asking for description or discussion. This has important implications for both teaching and for the evaluation of student responses.

If it is one's primary aim in structuring questions to assist the student then it is necessary to take note of what goes on in the classroom and in particular to take note of the kinds of questions teachers ask of their students and those which students ask of themselves and their fellows in order to develop particular skills and concepts. Part of the material in the one-term 13–16 'What is History?' unit designed for students around the ages of 13 and 14 relates to the incident in the 1913 Derby when a suffragette, Emily Davidson, threw herself under the King's horse and was killed. The sources made available consist of a photograph of the incident and a written account and questions are asked which encourage comparisons to be made between these to elicit differences and similarities between them, and to account for these. It is clear from classroom observation of this material in use that those students who come most quickly to terms with the issues raised by the questions are those who ask themselves at an early stage 'I wonder where the photographer was standing when he took the photograph?' Consideration of this question whose correct answer is impossible to determine is absolutely crucial to an understanding of how Emily Davidson managed to do what she did. A number of students never ask themselves this question—neither incidentally do some teachers—whilst others arrive at it only after considerable help.

It is possible indeed desirable to build in questions such as this as part of the overall questioning process with the aim of drawing attention to issues which might be ignored or neglected and hence making it more likely that more respondents will get to grips with the main question and give themselves a greater chance of success. In the jargon these preliminary questions have come to be called 'feeder' as contrasted with 'pay-dirt' questions. Feeders are questions which are primarily designed to help students whilst pay-dirt questions are primarily designed to help examiners. Another facet of this kind of structuring is to make use of students misconceptions as part of the scaffolding for a question. For example, photographs are seen by many students of 13–16 as inherently more reliable than other sources because they are scientific. Similarly, primary sources are thought to be more reliable than secondary sources because they are primary. One needs deliberately to challenge these assumptions as part of the questioning process itself. A topic like propaganda would provide a good framework for doing this and was indeed used for the 1979 CSE History 13–16 paper 2. Another illustration of a question designed to exploit possible misconceptions was the following used in the 1985 CSE History paper 2 which had as its theme Sweeney Todd, Demon Barber of Fleet Street?

> There is no legal record of any Sweeney Todd having been tried or convicted. Does this mean the story is untrue? Explain your answer.

Despite some misgivings arising from trialling this question worked well in the actual examination and produced a range of extremely interesting and thoughtful responses. Another question on similar lines appeared in the 1980 CSE History paper 2 and read as follows:

> Historians generally regard eye-witness evidence as reliable. Do you agree or disagree with this statement? Give reasons for your answer.

A Possible Model for Structuring Questions

Work over the past five years in relation to written questions had led to the development of a model for structuring questions which takes account of the various ways in which questions can be made more or less difficult for those answering them. Difficulty can be introduced into a question along one or more of four dimensions as illustrated in the following diagram.

These four dimensions are orthogonal, that is to say every one of them can be altered independently of the others; thus the ease or difficulty of any question can be altered in a variety of different ways. For example, some sources are harder to make sense of than others. Inference may be harder than comprehension, objective items make different demands from essay questions and so on. Ideally, one ought to contain the principal difficulty of any question within the conceptual/skill dimension and avoid

Figure 1

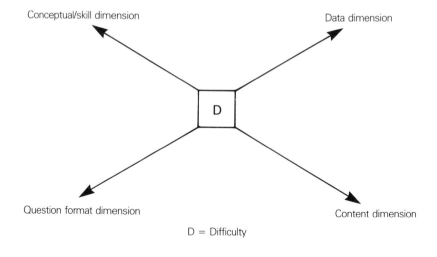

D = Difficulty

making the other dimensions gratuitously difficult but this is inevitably a council of perfection since the source, the content, the skills, the concepts and the format all need to be knitted tightly into a unified whole.

What kinds of question result from this approach to question setting? This can best be answered by providing an example.

Study the sources below:

SOURCE A *Weekly budget of a farm labourer from Lavenham, Suffolk, in 1843*

Name	Age	Earnings		Expenditure		
		s	d		s	d
Robert Crick	42	9	0	Bread	9	0
Wife	40		9	Potatoes	1	0
Boy	12	2	0	Rent	1	2
Boy	11	1	0	Tea		2
Boy	8	1	0	Sugar		3½
Girl	6		—	Soap		3
Boy	4		—	Blue		½
				Thread etc.		2
Total earnings		13	9	Candles		3
				Salt		½
				Coal and wood		9
				Butter		4½
				Cheese		3
				Total	13	9

SOURCE B *Weekly expenditure of a semi-skilled town worker with three children in 1841*

	s	d
Bread	3	6½
Meat	2	1
Beer	1	2
Coals		9½
Potatoes	1	4
Tea and sugar	1	6
Butter		9
Soap and candles		6½
Rent	2	6
Schooling		4
Sundries		5½
Total	15	0

(N.B. 1s 0d = 5 new pence; 15s 0d = £0.75)

Now answer these questions:

(i)   What differences do these sources show in the diets of the two families?

(ii) How might the children of Robert Crick have earned their money?

(iii) Why was it likely that children like those in Source A would have to work in the mid-nineteenth century?

(iv) What is there in these sources to suggest that one family was better off than the other?

(v)   What further information would you need to have about the families to decide whether one family was better off than the other?

In the actual examination this question appeared in a question/answer booklet which indicated through the use of numbers of lines the length of answer expected. This whole issue of how best to help candidates in an examination to use their time most profitably is one which has not yet been satisfactorily resolved and the Project is currently looking at the implications of starring questions as a means of indicating the length of answer required.

This question taken from paper 1 (Britain 1815–1851) unlike those in paper 2 assumes study of the topic and hence requires those answering it to make use of knowledge that it is hoped they will have acquired. This requirement however is more specific in some parts of the question than in others as for example part (iii). The effect of structuring on the questions in paper 2 is rather less obvious because they all relate to a common set of sources but it leads to the use of questions such as the following. (This was Question 11 out of a total of 14 in the 1980 paper 2 What Happened to the Romanovs?):

> Sokolov claimed that the diagram (Source 8) shows the position of the Imperial Family, their four servants and the guards in the room in Ipatiev House at the time of the shooting.
>
> Does this diagram make the story that the entire Romanov family and all their servants were killed easier to believe or not? Explain how you arrive at your conclusions.

The material provided for the candidates taking this paper consisted of eight sources divided into an introduction and four sections. The Introduction set the scene very briefly. The first section (Sources 1 and 2) provided background information about the groups involved in the Russian Civil War and some key dates between May 1918 and 14 July 1919. The remaining three sections (Sources 3 to 8) provided information regarding three investigations undertaken into the death of the Imperial Family by Judge Sergeyev, Sir Charles Eliot and Judge Sokolov.

Another and rather different example taken this time from the 1982 paper 2 'Cromwell in Ireland' where it was the last question of ten reads as follows:

> Which is the most important task for the historian—to show how actions like those described in this paper were brutal and wrong; or to show the reasons why people did them? Explain your choice.

Since substantial reference will be made both to the design and marking of the 1982 paper it is reproduced in its entirety in appendix B to this chapter. The reader might care to try and answer the question above and see how his or her answer is or is not accommodated by the mark scheme which is provided later in the chapter. As presented to the candidates the paper is a combined question and answer booklet which provides a rough indication of the length of response required. To save space the question only and the overall timing have been printed here together with the sources which would be issued on a separate sheet in the examination.

The Assessment Objectives for Paper 2

Work on these questions, and in particular the requirement that paper 2 should have as its central concern candidate response within the conceptual/skill dimension, made it necessary to rethink the appropriateness of the hierarchy of objectives set down for it. This produced a set of objectives which with one exception appeared very similar to the original set namely

    I   Comprehension—extraction of what is relevant
    II Evaluation—appropriate judgment
    III Inference—going beyond what is directly given
    IV Employment—consideration of issues outside the immediate context.

The exception is, of course, the last of the four 'employment'. The reader may recall an earlier reference in this article to the problem created by the closed-set model for setting questions which enabled the material to be used in its historical context. The employment category helps with the resolution of this issue. Put simply such questions take advantage of the general orientation of a particular paper 2 and its associated source materials to ask questions which require the candidates to generalize within an historical context. Cromwell in Ireland, for example, describes a particularly brutal incident, 'The Massacre at Drogheda' hence the question on the role of the historian already referred to. Three of the sources used are extracts from letters. This permits the following question to be asked: 'Three of these sources are letters. What advantages and disadvantages do letters have as evidence for historians?' The 1984 paper 2 (topic: The Peasants Revolt of 1381) contained the following question 'We judge historians by looking at the evidence they use. Why then do we need historians at all—why do we not just rely on the evidence?' whilst the 1985 paper (topic: Sweeney Todd, Demon Barber of Fleet Street?) included as its last question 'Is it more important for historians to tell us about major events like wars and elections or to tell us the things people thought about in their everyday life like stories they read? Give reasons for your answer.'

This rethink also highlighted the point that the range of skills actually required of and employed by candidates in the examination were a great deal more complicated and sophisticated than these four words suggested. There were three main reasons for this:

    (i)   because the candidates were presented not with a single source but with an array;

(ii) because of the crucial distinction between sources as information and sources as evidence;

(iii) because of the degree of interlocking and overlapping between the component parts of the hierarchy.

Thus, for example, I Comprehension, could produce

Figure 2

Comprehension (sources seen as information): extract from single source → extract from more than one source → cross-refer in terms of positive → negative → null correspondence

Comprehension (sources seen as evidence): advance proposition from single source → advance proposition from more than one source → cross-refer in terms of propositions advanced to show positive → negative → null correspondence

---

At the final stage, cross-reference in terms of propositions advanced to show null correspondence, it is clear that

(i) the candidate has reached a very high level of source comprehension;

(ii) in order to reach this level the candidate must possess the capacity to exercise skills other than comprehension, for example, inference.

The implications of this degree of overlap for question weighting in a situation where candidates are being set problematic questions designed to exploit such issues as the information/evidence distinction are far reaching and will be referred to later in the article. The rigidity of the I to IV hierarchy is also exposed as are its limitations as a basis for setting questions.

Overall Format for Paper 2

Paper 2 is unlikely, however, to achieve its potential as a vehicle for encouraging students to use a wide range of skills if the topic, the sources and the questions do not constitute a unified whole. Achieving this requires a much closer look to be given to the relationship of topic, format and orientation and the necessary degree of integration was not satisfactorily achieved until the 1980 paper. One important factor in realizing this was the abandonment of the original arrangement whereby the chief examiner acted primarily as the compiler of the examination making use of questions set by a number of people (including the chief examiner). Despite the burden placed upon a single individual it was found to be much more satisfactory for the entire paper including all the questions to be set by one person. The change was accompanied by the introduction of a much more comprehensive and systematic pretesting programme which trialled the mark scheme as well as the questions.

The result of all this work can best be illustrated by reference to a single paper 2, that of 1982, when the topic was Cromwell in Ireland. It is not necessarily the best paper but it is the one that has been most used for in-service training purposes and a wealth of illustrative material exists particularly in relation to candidates' answers.

The format of the paper consisted of an array of primary and secondary sources together with background detail meant for use as contextual information. The sources sought to explore in particular problems of reliability and the nature of the historian's task. The complete paper is as already mentioned reproduced as appendix B and it is hoped that its study will illuminate the general points made in this chapter.

Marking Procedures

The last and most crucial change lay in the marking. It is of no use whatsoever setting an interesting paper which encourages a wide range of answers if the approach to marking adopted cannot reward these. The crucial importance of devising an appropriate mark scheme was recognized very early in the life of the examination but it wasn't until the 1978 paper (Education) that a mark scheme based upon allocation of marks for criteria was used. Initially tentative hierarchies of criteria based upon progressive levels of abstraction were developed for each question prior to the examination as a result of discussion and informal trialling. These were constructed by identifying what was to count as a baseline answer and then working upwards. An example of such a hierarchy which it must be stressed is only applicable to a single specific question is as follows:

Level 1 Ability to relate conclusions to sources supplied
Level 2 Ability to ask specific questions of sources
Level 3 Ability to make simple generalizations on the basis of evidence
Level 4 Ability to extend an account by cross-referencing between sources
. . . .
Level N Ability to consider what is to count as sufficiency of evidence

The gap between Level 4 and Level N which is considered to be the ultimate criterion in this set applicable to 14–16-year-olds indicates that there are other levels which could be measured. Subsequent investigation in fact suggested another three.

The process of developing the mark scheme which is actually used takes time and trouble. The initial tentative levels or marking criteria are trialled along with the question paper upon a sample of some 500 and are then adjusted, some levels being collapsed and others added. The issue of manageability for marking which in this case means identifying criteria in students' written work needs also to be borne in mind. How many levels can a marker actually hold in his or her mind at once? This needs to be balanced against the question of how fine a distinction the examination needs to make between students and hence between levels.

Exercises are then developed out of the material used in the trials in order to give further experience to the examiners prior to the actual marking. These exercises are also used to train potential new examiners and for pre- and in- service training workshops for teachers and students.[7] As a final check the chief examiner selects immediately following the examination a random sample of some 300 paper 2s in order to see whether the actual examination answers appear to be following the evidence of the trial and hence that the marking criteria are appropriate.

Each examiner is asked to mark a maximum of 200 paper 2s and these are randomly allocated. The coordination meeting takes the form of a residential weekend during which a wide range of answers selected by the chief examiner from his sample of 300 are discussed and as necessary the criteria are finely tuned. The examiners, instead of being required to assign a mark, are asked to identify the highest order criterion or level achieved by each answer. Originally no marks were used at all but subsequently a notional mark of ten was assigned to every question and a small band of marks was allocated to each level. The reason for this was two-fold, first because examiners find it difficult not to use marks and secondly to permit distinctions in quality to be made within a single criterion or level. Thus the award of marks although governed by the criterial level of the responses is flexible enough to accommodate a personal appraisal of quality by the examiner.

This rather bare description can best be provided with bones by looking at the scheme actually used for marking one of the questions illustrated earlier in the chapter namely question 10 from the 1982 Cromwell in Ireland paper which reads:

> Which is the most important task for the historian; to show how actions like those described in the paper were brutal and wrong or to show the reasons why people did them? Explain your choice.

Mark Scheme Answers which make assertions unsupported by reasons are below the baseline level and should receive no credit.

Mark Bands

Level 1 Asserts that historians should do both and offers   1
valid reasons.

Beyond this level candidates should be rewarded for a balanced argument but they must as the question requires 'come off the fence'.

Level 2 Either but produce reasons which are not central   2–3
to the historian's task. For example, sees history
as a moral tale or in order to ensure that we learn

from past experience. An alternative possibility for Level 2 is an undeveloped reason for example because that's what history is all about.

Level 3 Argument based on a clear grasp of the nature of   4–6
the historical task; history as a rational activity or
a process of enquiry.

Level 4 Considers the question of how moral purposes   7–8
might impede the real historical truth.

Level 5 Grasps idea of period. Understands that a term   9–10
like 'brutal' and therefore attitudes to it must be
related to the point of view of the age under
consideration.

Another and rather simpler example taken from the same paper is question 2 for which the mark scheme used was as follows. This particular question incidentally has been used by the writer as a workshop exercise all over the world with groups ranging from upper primary (11–12 year olds) to university history departments. To date I have not been given an answer which does not fall into the suggested four levels, although of course the answers have varied greatly in their knowledge, language and ingenuity. In the actual examination question 2 is linked with question 1 which acts as a feeder to it (not always good examination practice) but for the purpose of the workshop exercise it is taken on its own and is reworded as follows.

Which of the two sources A and D is most likely to be correct about the total number of defenders killed at Drogheda? Explain your answer.

Mark Scheme
The fact that Source D is reported testimony may create problems. Those candidates who confuse the author with the participant are unlikely to get beyond Level 1.
NB: Reward balanced argument at all levels.

		Mark Bands
Level 1 Focusses on		
writers—Cromwell present at Drogheda, Anthony Wood not; date—A written at the time, D later		1–2

Such answers confuse accuracy and reliability.

Level 2 There are three possibilities here.		3–6

1 Conclusions based on the position of the participants. Which of Cromwell/Thomas Wood was in a better position to give correct figures?
for example, Cromwell because he was a

general and had the overall picture. Thomas Wood because he was closer to the action.

Position can mean both position in terms of job or rank (who was he?) and in terms of geography (where was he?).

It is not sufficient to say Wood was there, Cromwell was not.

2 Conclusions which point to the degree of certainty or uncertainty in the two sources, for example

Source A   'I think'
Source D   'At least'

3 Conclusions based on assessing plausibility through information available in any of the sources and the background information. Cross-referencing.

Level 3	Evaluation in terms of interests/motives of the writers and/or participants.	7–8
Level 4	Evaluation in terms of interests/perspectives of the recipients i.e. Parliament or Anthony Wood. To reach this level an answer must do more than say	9–10

A = official document
B = conversation with his brother.

It is hoped that enough will now have been said to ensure understanding by the reader of the principles behind the mark scheme and how it is operated in practice. One way of testing whether or not this is the case would be for the reader to construct a mark scheme for other questions which have been illustrated in the paper as for example question 11 from the 1980 Romanov paper or any of the remaining eight questions from Cromwell in Ireland which appear in appendix B.

Post Hoc Weighting

One final point about paper 2 needs consideration and that is the weighting of the questions. Clearly the setting and marking procedures used make it impossible to provide any specific advance indication to the candidates of relative weighting. The use of lines which vary from question to question in the CSE paper 2 answer booklet are primarily guidance to the candidates on how to use their time and do not necessarily relate to weighting at all. Clearly therefore a mark scheme based upon anticipated rather than actual responses is likely to fail to accommodate the range of answers generated by the kinds of questions being asked in paper 2. Pre-testing makes it possible to narrow the gap between anticipated and actual level of performance but it still remains (perhaps too frequently for comfort) and the capacity for correction and adjustment within the mark scheme remains essential.

The solution devised for this problem has been called *post hoc* weighting. As has already been incidated the marks used by the examiners are simply a convenience and do not at the marking stage indicate the final weighting which any one question will carry. This is achieved by:

(i)   establishing those question levels which are in practice reached by a significant number of candidates in the actual examination;
(ii) constructing a paper level scale;
(iii) relating question levels to equivalent paper levels.

(Author's Note: The points made in the remainder of this section all relate to the Cromwell in Ireland paper which is set out in full as appendix B.)

Actual Question Levels

For logistical reasons identification of the range of question levels actually achieved is based on a sample of approximately 7 per cent of the entry. This detail is supplied by a number of the senior examiners. The actual base level must have at least 10 per cent of the sample using it (i.e. if the proportion of the sample failing to score $\geq$ 10 per cent then level 0 constitutes the base level; if the proportion failing to score <10 per cent and the proportion hitting level 0 plus level 1 $\geq$ 10 per cent, then level 1 constitutes the base level). Similarly the actual top level must have at least 10 per cent of the sample using it or using it in combination with a higher level. For example, in question 10 the top level 5 was not reached by a sufficient number of candidates and level 4 was taken to be the actual top level. In question 2, however, the top level 4 was reached and was therefore used.

Paper Level Scale

Crucial to the construction of the paper level scale is the notion of difficulty as it applies to the demands made of candidates. As has already been indicated in the section on written questions difficulty in relation to paper 2 questions can be introduced along one or more of four dimensions. Concept/Skill, Data, Question Format, and Content. These four dimensions cannot however offer a sufficient basis for allocating differentiated weightings unless purely arbitrary decisions are made, for example, that questions relating to source material are of themselves more or less difficult than those demanding factual recall. More legitimately it is the manner in which each of these dimensions is unpacked into a hierarchy of difficulty which will form such a basis. Inevitably any hierarchy will reflect:

(i)   the available empirical evidence, for example, how candidates have performed now or previously;

(ii) certain philosophic assumptions, for example, about the nature of historical explanation.

Whilst therefore it is probably the case that a hierarchy within one given dimension will meet with wider approval than within another it is most unlikely that any would be free from contention. Paper 2 is centrally concerned with candidate response within the conceptual skill dimension i.e. the dimension which relates to the assessment objectives. The marking scheme as already indicated in the section on marking procedures establishes hierarchies for each question—the paper level scale attempts to subsume these within a hierarchy for the paper as a whole.

The point has already been made earlier in this chapter in the section on assessment objectives for paper 2 that the pattern which emerged from unpacking an apparently simple four-stage hierarchy of assessment objectives was an extremely complex one and that an expansion of any one of the four not only identified a very wide range of skills but showed also that these skills could not be uniquely allocated to any one stage. There was in consequence very substantial overlapping and interlocking. This range and the degree of overlap both ought to be reflected in the paper level scale.

Given that this is the case it is necessary in deriving the paper level scale and allocating a weighting to the various levels to move outside the rigidity which an analysis of the kind shown in the four stage model would inevitably impose. It is thus untenable to advance a form of weighting such as

1.   Comprehension (level 1, 2, 3, etc) = weighting 1–10,
2.   Evaluation (level 1, 2, 3 etc) = weighting 11–20,

and so on. Instead judgments have to be made about the points at which levels within one concept/skill area key into those within a different area. Then the more likely pattern of weighting is

Table 1

Weighting	Comprehension	Evaluation	Inference
1	Level 1		
2	Level 2		
3	Level 3	Level 1	
4	Level 4	Level 2	
5	Level 5	Level 3	Level 1
6	Level 6	Level 4	Level 2
↓	↓	↓	↓

Theoretically, at least, it appears feasible to derive a paper level scale, allocate a weighting and devise appropriate questions, bypassing the need for *post hoc* weighting altogether. In reality, however, this is not so. One major reason for this is that it is difficult (if not impossible) to isolate the conceptual/skill dimension in which we are interested, from the other dimensions such as data or content in which we are not interested. Whilst the closed-set nature of the paper may exclude the content dimension, it is by no means inconceivable that a low weighted question may be rendered significantly more difficult (or less accessible) than one which is weighted more highly, because of difficulties within the data or question format; dimensions which had not been foreseen. Broadly speaking, increasing the data or format difficulty of a question will depress the concept/skill level of the responses elicited. In consequence, it is impossible to determine the concept/skill threshold of any question other than by an empirical analysis of candidate responses. Our inability to control data and format difficulty may mean that candidates, although they have mastered high level concept/ skills, are, in practice prevented from displaying that mastery on a given occasion.

Finally, in establishing the paper level score it may be necessary:

(i)   to reinterpret and redefine certain question levels. This is permissible since question levels are initially defined so as to facilitate ease of marking;

(ii) to collapse question levels in cases where the distinctions made are too fine or too subtle to apply to a paper level scale.

In practice, only a minority of question levels were transformed in either of these ways.

Awarding mark bands to paper levels sufficiently wide to attempt to 'wash out' the effects of question level mark bands, the paper level scale employed in 1982 was as follows:

Paper Level Scale—1982

Level			Mark
I	*Effect Source Comprehension*		
	(a)	Extract information from single source	3
	(b)	Paraphrase information from one or more sources	4
	(c)	Extract specific related information from more than one source	5
II	*Classify evidence by type of origin of source*		8
III	*Effect Source Interpretation*		
	(a)	Comment on quantity/clarity/type of information presented	11
	(b)	Comment on plausibility of information presented by employing 'everyday empathy'	12

	(c)	Summarize general impression created by source	14
IV	*Extrapolate Information*		
		Grasp that source may evidence propositions not directly given or shown (thoughts, feelings, view-poings, etc.)	17
V	*Cross-refer*		
	(a)	Relate information given in sources in terms of positive correspondence	20
	(b)	Relate information given in sources in terms of negative correspondence	21
VI	*Effect Source Evaluation*		
	(a)	On basis of what is given about writer/participant	23
	(b)	On basis of cross-reference with other sources	24
	(c)	On basis of what may be inferred about writer/participant	25
VII	*Grasp nature of historian's task*		28
VIII	*Operate within a model of what is necessary for adequate history to be written*		30

Relating Question Levels/Paper Levels

For the purpose of calculating weighting, the key relationship is that between the top *actual* level for a question and its equivalent paper level. Thus, for example, the top actual level for question 2 was level 3, and its paper level equivalent was determined at VI(b). Since paper level VI(b) carried 24 marks, and question level 3 for question 2 carried a maximum of 8 marks, $\frac{24}{8}$ gives a weighting function of 3.00. The weighting functions for each question are set out in table 2 below.

In order to arrive at a mark out of 30 for each candidate, one further calculation is needed, i.e.:

$$\frac{\text{Candidate's total score adjusted according to weighting}}{\text{Maximum possible paper score}} \times \frac{30}{1}$$

It is thus mathematically possible for a candidate to exceed a score of 30/30 but, when this happens the mark will be rounded down to 30.

Readers wishing to obtain further details about the mark scheme and the procedures for *post hoc* weighting are invited to contact the writer. These procedures have now been used satisfactorily since 1978 although through-out this period they have been continuously refined. They raise a number of significant issues not least in relation to the legitimacy of using a marking/weighting system within a national public examination which is

Table 2

Question Number	Top actual Question Level	Maximum Mark	Paper level equivalent	Mark	Weighting Function	Maximum possible mark adjusted according to weighting
1	3	10	I (c)	5	0.50	5.00
2	3	8	VI (b)	24	3.00	24.00
3	2	2	I (c)	5	2.50	5.00
4	5	10	VII	28	2.80	28.00
5(a)	3	10	III (c)	14	1.40	14.00
(b)	4	10	VIII	30	3.00	30.00
(c)	3	10	VIII	30	3.00	30.00
6	3	9	VI (a)	23	2.55	22.95
7 (i)	3	8	V (a)	20	2.50	20.00
(ii)	3	8	V (a)	20	2.50	20.00
(iii)	3	8	V (a)	20	2.50	20.00
8	3	10	VIII	30	3.00	30.00
9	4	10	VIII	30	3.00	30.00
10	4	8	VIII	30	3.75	30.00

Maximum possible paper score = *308.95*

influenced by the actual candidate entry in a given year and does not in consequence reflect the notion of absolute standards over time. The whole concept of a paper level scale is also highly relevant to the possible introduction in the early 1990s within the new GCSE in England and Wales of grade-related criteria although at present the paper level scale is unique to a given year and is therefore unstable over time. To date these issues have not been adequately explored and it is the writer's hope that what has been written in this chapter may stimulate discussion on these and related issues.

Conclusion

The arrangements described in this chapter describe one approach to the testing of skills in history through the use of a written paper. The model has its deficiencies not least in the range of skills with which it is concerned and the limitations that it places upon their usage in context. The range of skills listed by John Fines in his pamphlet on *Source Based Questions at GCE A-level*[8] which he divides up into three sections: handling sources, evaluation of sources and application, show clearly the limitations of the Paper 2 model and the need in particular to use wider ranging-assignments over which the students can take much more time than the one hour thirty minutes allocated to the CSE paper 2 examination. It needs however to be remembered that those taking this paper are aged 14–16 and are not amongst the most able within that age group. There is moreover enough evidence to suggest that the paper 2 model has been successful in developing the skills which constitute its assessment objectives, that performances in the examination do substantially reflect teachers informal assessment of their pupils' competence upon the same skills, and that candidates taking the examination both enjoy it and have been encouraged by the format to take risks which has enabled them to show the examiner that they can think. The approach would thus seem to provide a solid platform upon which to base at least the initial assessment of such skills for pupils of this age range. It is essential, however, to ensure that this whole question of testing skills in history is kept under constant review and that the paper 2 model or any other model for that matter doesn't ossify, and in public examinations nothing ossifies faster than a good idea. The purpose of this chapter is to stimulate criticism and prevent stagnation and the writer would welcome comments and requests for further information.

Appendix A—Schools Council History 13–16 Project Joint GCE/CSE Syllabus

Introduction

The two-year examination course has four elements: a study in development, an enquiry in depth, a study in modern world history and a study of the history around us. Sections 1 and 2 below set out the aims and assessment objectives of the examination in relation to these four elements. Section 4 sets out the current syllabus content.

1 Aims
A course based on this syllabus should enable the following to be achieved:

Aim	*Course Element*
(a) the stimulation of interest in and enthusiasm for the study of the past	All
(b) the acquisition of knowledge and understanding of human activity in the past, linking it, as appropriate, with the present	All, but particularly the study in modern world history and the enquiry in depth
(c) the rooting of a candidates' knowledge in an understanding of the nature and use of historical evidence	All
(d) the development of an understanding of cause and consequence, continuity and change, similarity and difference	All, but particularly the study in development
(e) the development of essential study skills such as the ability to locate and extract information from	All

sources, to analyse and organize this information and to construct a logical argument

(f) the provision of a sound basis for further study and the pursuit of personal interest

All, but particularly the study of history around us

2   Assessment Objectives

The examination will assess a candidate's ability to:

Objectives	*Course Element*
(a) understand and use the concepts of change, development, continuity, cause, progress	Study in Development (Examination Paper 1 Section A)
(b) —analyze causation and motivation; —make empathetic reconstruction of the ways of thinking and feeling of people of a different time and place; —analyze the role of individuals in relation to their historical context	Enquiry in Depth (Examination Paper 1 Section B)
(c) —interpret the current situation in the context of past events; —relate a current regional study to its wider global setting	Modern World Study (Coursework)
(d) —investigate a historical site personally; —relate a site to its historical setting; —relate site evidence to other forms of evidence	History Around Us (Coursework)
(e) —comprehend, interpret and evaluate sources; —distinguish between fact, opinion and judgment; —detect bias or other deficiencies in sources as historical evidence; —make inferences from evidence; —recall and select relevant information; —organize and present historical ideas logically and clearly	All Elements

3   Assessment Pattern

A   *Two written papers* will be set, each worth 30 per cent of the total marks.

Henry G. Macintosh

Paper 1 (2 hours)
Section A (Study in Development) (20 per cent of the total marks)
Candidates will be required to answer either two or three questions.
Any or all of these may be based on a variety of sources. One of them
will require an answer in the form of extended writing. For this
question a choice will be given.
Section B (Study in Depth) (10 per cent of the total marks)
Candidates will be required to answer two questions. Either of these
may be based on a variety of sources. One of them will require an
answer in the form of extended writing. For this question a choice will
be given.
Paper 2 (1 hour 30 minutes)
Questions will be based on a variety of historical sources concerned
with one or more topics which do not form part of the prescribed
syllabus. All questions will be compulsory. The purpose of this paper
is to measure candidates' ability to comprehend and evaluate historical
sources, to make inferences and judgments based upon them and to
select and synthesize information from them, without at the same time
measuring the recall of specific knowledge related to a specific
historical period.
Please see specimen papers 1 and 2—appendix B.
Coursework—40 per cent of the total marks.
The coursework assignments submitted for moderation, must between
them fulfil all of the eight objectives listed below. An assignment is any
piece of work which has a unity of theme or objective (see below), and
the table shows the three units within which assignments are to be set
with the requirements for each unit. It is assumed that the coursework
will be marked out of 100, although its ultimate contribution to the
examination as a whole is 40 per cent of the overall marks. Below the
table is a list of the objectives, five of which (numbers iv–viii) are
related to particular units.

Unit	Number of Assignments	Maximum Length	Mark Allocation
Modern World Study	2 or 3	2500 words	40
History Around Us	2 or 3	2500 words	40
Enquiry in Depth	1 or 2	1500 words	20
Total	Between 5 and 8	6500 words	100 (= 40%)

(a) *General Objectives* (which may be satisfied by work related to any
of the three units mentioned in the table).
  (i) Evaluation and Interpretation of Sources.

210

(ii) Empathetic Reconstruction of the ways of thinking and feeling of a people of a different time or place.

(iii) Analysis of Causation and Motivation.

(b) *Objectives Specifically Related to Particular Units*

(iv) Interpretation of the Current Situation in the context of past events (Modern World Study).

(v) Relation of the Modern World Study to its wider global setting (Modern World Study).

(vi) Personal investigation of a site which relates it to other forms of evidence (History Around Us).

(vii) Relation of a Site to its Historical Context (History Around Us).

(viii) Analysis of the Role of the Individual in History (Enquiry in Depth).

4 Syllabus Content

A *Study in Development—Medicine Through Time*

The development of medical knowledge and techniques from the earliest times to the present

—Early man and Medicine

—Greek and Roman Medicine

—The Middle Ages

—The medical Renaissance

—The battle against infectious diseases in the nineteenth and twentieth centuries

—The revolution in surgery in the nineteenth and twentieth centuries

—The development of public health in the nineteenth and twentieth centuries.

Teachers should note that this part of the syllabus is a Study in Development: candidates will be expected to be able to support their answers with accurate evidence, but the purpose of the examination will be to measure their understanding of change and development in medicine, not their recall of detail from its history.

B *Enquiry in Depth—ONE of the following*

(a) *Elizabethan England, 1558–1603*

Topics: How was England governed?

Catholics and puritans

Trade and discovery

Shakespeare's theatre

The poor

Case Studies: The Earl of Essex's Rebellion 1601

The Execution of Mary, Queen of Scots

(b) *The American West, 1840–1890*

Topics: Plains Indians

Cowboys and cattlemen

                        Homesteaders
                        The fate of the Indians
                        Law and order
            Case Studies: The Mormons
                        The battles of the Little Big Horn and Wounded
                        Knee
    (c) *Britain, 1815–1851*
            Topics: Railways
                        The poor
                        The Church and social reform
                        Broadsheets and ballads
                        The vote
            Case Studies: Emigration
                        The Sunderland by-election, 1841
C   *Study in Modern World History—ONE of the following*
    (a) The Irish Question
    (b) The Rise of Communist China
    (c) The Move to European Unity
    (d) The Arab-Israeli Conflict
    In each case the focus of the study is the problem current at the time of
    study. Historical material from any period which is relevant to that
    problem may be included. Please see the coursework objectives above
    (pp. 210–1).
D   *History Around Us*
    The syllabus content is chosen by the teacher. It might combine
    elements from different options, or deal with one aspect only of an
    option, according to the particular site.
    There are nine options:
    (a) Prehistoric Britain
    (b) Church Buildings and Furnishings
    (c) Roman Britain
    (d) Castles and Fortified Manor Houses
    (e) Country Houses
    (f) Town Development and Domestic Architecture
    (g) The Making of the Rural Landscape
    (h) Industrial Archaeology
    (i) Aspects of the History of the Locality.
EXAMPLE History Around Us (Country Houses)
(1) Study of one country house. c.1200 words.
    This must include a time-chart, site-plan including the park, des-
    cription or drawings of stylistic features, discussion on source material
    including the guide-book, explanation of why the house was built and
    kept up.
(2) Study of a second country house. c.1200 words.
    This must include a time-chart, site-plan including the park, descrip-

tion or drawings of stylistic features, explanation of why the house was
built and kept up, and a piece of writing reconstructing life there at a
chosen date in the past.

(3) Short essay. c.500 words.
    'Why should we maintain country houses in the later 20th century?'

APPENDIX B – SCHOOLS COUNCIL PROJECT
HISTORY 13–16

Administered by

SOUTHERN REGIONAL EXAMINATIONS BOARD

for the

CERTIFICATE OF SECONDARY EDUCATION

1982

PAPER 2

WEDNESDAY, 28 APRIL 1982 – Afternoon   TIME: 1½ hours

CROMWELL IN IRELAND

QUESTIONS

Answer ALL the questions.
1. How do the sources disagree about the total number of defenders killed at Drogheda?
2. Which of these is most likely to be correct? Explain your answer.
3. Which sources say that women and children were killed?
4. In view of the fact that the other sources say nothing about this, do you think that it happened? Explain your answer.
5. Read **Sources B, C** and **E** again. These say that soldiers were killed after they had surrendered and been disarmed. How reliable do you think each one of these sources is likely to be on this point? Give reasons for your decision in each case.
   (*a*) **Source B:**
   (*b*) **Source C:**
   (*c*) **Source E:**
6. Now take into account the Background Information as well as *all* the evidence. Do you think that soldiers were killed after they had surrendered? Explain your answer.
7. In **Source A** Cromwell gives several reasons why the killings took place. Select *three* of these reasons, and explain each *in your own words*, using the Background Information where it helps to make the explanation clear.

   First reason: . . . .

   Second reason: . . . .

   Third reason: . . . .

8. Look at the Background Information again. Can you suggest other reasons for the killings which Cromwell does not mention?
9. Three of these sources are letters. What advantages and disadvantages do letters have as evidence for historians?
10. Which is the more important task for the historian—to show that actions like those described in this paper were brutal and wrong; or to show the reasons why people did them? Explain your choice.

SCHOOLS COUNCIL PROJECT
HISTORY 13–16
PAPER 2–1982
CROMWELL IN IRELAND
SOURCES

Study the Background Information, the map and all the sources carefully. You are advised to spend at least ten minutes doing this.

Then answer ALL the questions in the question booklet provided.

Background Information

In the seventeenth century Ireland was ruled by England, and many English and Scottish settlers went to live there.

In *1641* the Irish rebelled against this, and many English and Scottish settlers were killed. The English accused the Irish rebels of brutality and wanted to punish them, but in *1642* a Civil War broke out in England, so this was impossible.

In *1648* the English army and Oliver Cromwell, its leader, won the Civil War and were in complete control of England.

In *1649* Cromwell and the English Parliament had King Charles I executed, and declared that England was now a Republic, with no king.

Most countries in Europe in the seventeenth century were ruled by kings, and thought that the execution of a king was a dreadful deed of wickedness. Many English people thought this, including the English people in Ireland, and so did most of the Irish. Many thought that Charles I's son was now the rightful King Charles II. He was in France collecting soldiers, weapons and ships.

In *July 1649* the Marquis of Ormond sent 2871 of his best soldiers, led by Sir Arthur Aston, to hold the fortified town of Drogheda, north of Dublin.

On *15 August, 1649* Cromwell landed in Ireland with an army of 12 000 men.

On *3 September* he marched to Drogheda and began to attack it.

On *10 September* Cromwell's army captured Drogheda.

Fighting continued in Ireland until 1653. By then the last of the Irish towns which supported Charles II had been captured, and Cromwell's army was in complete control of Ireland.

Two rules of war were generally accepted by European armies in the seventeenth century—

(i) To attack a town cannon were first used to knock a hole or 'breach' in the wall, through which the attacking soldiers then charged. If a breach had been made big enough for a successful charge, and the defenders still refused to surrender, then they were to blame for the extra bloodshed. They could all be put to death by the winning side as a punishment.

(ii) You could agree to give 'quarter' to an enemy. This meant that they surrendered and gave up their weapons. After that had happened, it was against the rules to kill them, or to let anyone else kill them.

Source A *Letter from Cromwell to the Speaker of the House of Commons* Dublin 17th September 1649

Sir,
Your army came before the town of Drogheda upon 3rd September and upon Monday 9th. the battering guns began to play. I sent Sir Arthur Aston, the Governor, a summons to deliver the town.

Receiving no satisfactory answer, the guns, after some two or three hundred shot, beat down the corner tower, and opened two reasonable good breaches in the east and south wall.

Upon Tuesday the 10th. about five o'clock in the evening, we began the storm and after some hot fighting we entered, about seven or eight hundred men, the enemy disputing it very stiffly with us.

Several of the enemy retreated into the Mill Mount, a place very strong and difficult to attack. The Governor, Sir Arthur Aston, being there, our men getting up to them were ordered by me to put all to the sword. And indeed, being in the heat of action, I forbade them to spare any people who carried weapons in the town. In the great church called St. Peter's near 1000 of them were put to the sword, fleeing there for safety. I think that night they put to the sword in all about 2000 men. This is a righteous judgement of God upon these barbarous wretches who have dipped their hands in so much innocent blood. It will tend to prevent bloodshed for the future.

I do not think we lost 100 men, though many be wounded.
Your most obedient servant,
Oliver Cromwell

Source B *From a letter from Drogheda printed in a London news-sheet, 1649 (writer unknown)*
The Mill Mount was very strong, and manned with 250 of their men, Sir Arthur Aston being in it, who was Governor of the town. Lieutenant-Colonel Axtell, with some twelve of his men went up to the top of the mount and demanded the surrender of it. The Governor was very

stubborn, but at length was persuaded to go into the windmill on the top of the mount, and as many more of them as it would contain, where they were disarmed and afterwards slain.

Source C *From a letter from the Marquis of Ormond written on 29 September 1649*
All Cromwell's officers and soldiers promised to spare the lives of any who would lay down their arms, and kept the promise as long as any place held out, which encouraged others to yield. But when they had once all in their power, the word 'No quarter' went round.

Source D *From a book of biographies published in 1674 by Anthony Wood. Wood's brother, Thomas, was a soldier in Cromwell's army, and he was said by Anthony to have told him:*
That at least 3000, besides women and children, were put to the sword on September 11 and 12, 1649.

Source E *From a History written by Edward Hyde, a close friend of the Marquis of Ormond. Hyde was chief adviser to Charles II in France in 1649. He wrote this part of his History in 1668–70.*

Although the Governor retired into a fort, where they hoped to have made conditions for surrendering, panic fear possessed the soldiers so that they threw down their arms on a general offer of quarter. So the enemy entered the works without resistance and put every man to the sword. They executed all manner of cruelty and put every soldier to the sword and all the citizens who were Irish, man, woman and child.

Acknowledgements

A modified version of this chapter was originally published in January 1986 in the German book *Schülergerechte Diagnose* and the author would like to thank the editor, Dr Hanns Petillon and the publishers Beltz Verlag for permission to reproduce it here.

The author would like to record his indebtedness to Denis Shemilt, formerly Evaluator and Director of the History 13–16 Project and John Hamer HMI, without whose ideas and hard work much of what has been described in this article would never have taken place.

Notes

1. PEEL, E.A., (1967) 'Some problems in the psychology of history teaching', in BURSTON, W.H. and THOMPSON, D. (Eds), *Studies in the Nature and Teaching of History*, Routledge and Kegan Paul, p. 1
2. ELTON, G.R., (1970) 'What sort of history should we teach?', in BALLARD, M. (Ed.) *New Movements in the Study and Teaching of History*, Temple Smith, p. 1
3. Schools Council History 13–16 Project (1976) *A New Look at History*, Holmes McDougall, p. 2
4. (1976–1985) *Examiners Reports: Written Papers*, Southern Regional Examinations Board, p. 6
5. COLTHAM, J. and FINES, J., (1971) *Educational Objectives for the Study of History*, The Historical Association Teaching of History Series No. 35, p. 7
6. SHEMILT, D., (1980) *History 13–16: Evaluation Studies*, Holmes McDougall, p. 8
7. 1981 (updates 1982 and 1984) *Explorations: History 13–16 Project*, Southern Regional Examinations Board, p. 24
8. FINES, J., (1984) *Source Based Questions at GCE 'A' level*, The Historical Association Teaching of History Series No. 54, p. 36

11 Computing, History Teaching and the Curriculum

Jon Nichol with Jonathan Briggs and Jackie Dean

Synopsis

The introduction of computing in the history curriculum is seen as being subject to the conditions that influence all educational innovation.

New developments now enable simple computers to undertake logical reasoning and allow pupils to write their own programmes or to analyze information—even to conduct a dialogue with the computer.

The applications of computing to four central areas of history teaching are considered with attention to the requirements of equipment and organization and with detailed discussion of some appropriate programmes.

Information technology (IT), artificial intelligence (AI) and computer-assisted learning (CAL) are buzz words impinging on the consciousness of history teachers. To many computing is a swarm of hornets in the history beehive, itself an element within 'the secret garden' of the curriculum. In general, history teachers and teacher trainees see the computer as a potential threat. Teacher and student concern can be phobic. A consistent refrain at in-service courses we have run in Britain, Australia, New Zealand and Norway has been suspicion of the claim that the computer can play a major role in the teaching of humanities subjects, suspicion which can spill over into hostility and anger. Where does this negative concept of computing come from, the removal of which is essential for the development of computing as a natural element within the teaching of history to all age and ability ranges?

Mental models of computer programming and CAL are based on direct experience of programming and computer awareness courses, hearsay, casual contact with micro-computers of limited memory and power, and the use and evaluation of existing closed CAL packages. Programming and awareness courses are usually in BASIC, or rely upon programs written in it. Most history teachers who have learned BASIC see little relationship between it and their teaching needs. Despite the massive efforts of the MEP (Microelectronics in Education Programme), in Devon and Cornwall we know of only one teacher who has managed to write history software for his classroom; a pattern which is reflected nationally (Wilkes, 1985).

The roles of hearsay and casual contact are important in forming teachers' mental models of computing. Actual experience within history teaching is very limited. A survey of Devon secondary schools showed that only 1–5 per cent had purchased *any* history software (Beard, 1985). Even the use of existing authoring programs, which enable teachers to enter their own data direct into the computer without having to learn a computer language, can cause problems. Such programs can be inflexible and of limited application. The teacher coordinating the introduction of QUEST into pilot Avon schools said that its complexity and inflexibility had caused serious problems for teachers. Despite this, the relatively popular role of QUEST and micro-QUERY as authoring programs suggests that they represent a major step forward from CAL packages on set topics.

Before more history teachers can accept computing in teaching their curriculums they will need to change their views of it. History computing will have to satisfy a variety of criteria essential for successful educational innovation and the sustaining of change. These criteria all relate to a key factor, the conceptualization which the teacher has of computing within his teaching environment. Instead of a swarm of hornets we need teachers to see computing as a swarm of benign bees, who will be a source of educational honey. The development of computing within the history curriculum should be seen as part of a more general pattern of introducing innovation. The findings of Bolam (1976) and Skilbeck (see Prescott, 1976) stress the need to relate innovation to the immediate needs and circumstances of the classroom teacher. MacDonald and Walker's analysis (1976) of the Geography for the Young School Leaver Project produced a model for innovatory success linked to the teachers' conceptualization of the Project as being directly related to their teaching requirements. In their Open University unit they noted that innovation is essentially a 'social process' (Walker and MacDonald, 1976). Havelock's (1982) revised model of innovation also stresses the social context within which it occurs.

For computing to become an element within the history curriculum a conscious decision requires to be taken in each school history department concerned, bearing in mind the decentralized and autonomous nature of the English educational system. Such decisions depend upon the decision-making hierarchy within the school, as it involves the allocation of resources and overall school policy. The argument we develop below is that external circumstances have now changed to provide a milieu in which school history departments will be able to accept and support computing in their subject. Skilbeck provides a paradigm which can be used for relating computing in the history curriculum to a changing teacher's conceptualization of it (Prescott, 1976).

The Skilbeck model for curriculum development is based upon a situational analysis, and begins with a review of the external factors which produce the context within which computing in the history curriculum must occur. This is analogous to the appropriate siting of a beehive, and the development of an environment within which the bees can flourish.

Table 1: Situational analysis

Review of the change situation		Analysis of factors which constitute the situation
(a) external	(i)	Cultural and social changes and expectations including parental expectations, employer requirements, community assumptions and values, changing relationships (for example, between adults and children) and ideology.
	(ii)	Educational-system requirements and challenges, for example, policy statements, examinations, local authority expectations or demands or pressures, curriculum projects, educational research.
	(iii)	The changing nature of the subject-matter to be taught.
	(iv)	The potential contribution of teacher-support systems, for example, teacher training colleges, research institutions, etc.
	(v)	Flow of resources into the school.

How can computing in the history curriculum relate to point (i), *cultural and social changes and expectations?* The existing teacher view of computing in history teaching analysed on page 220, is at variance with the ideas which teachers, pupils and parents have of computing and information technology in society at large. The spread of home computing means that many pupils are already acquainted with computers, even if only at the level of computer games. Within society generally computing impinges on the consciousness, whether it be in the use of PRESTEL facilities, a computer terminal for the booking of rail or air tickets, library use, word processing, computer design or computerized accounts and mailing. Media coverage of IT developments is extensive and continuous. These developments can be summarized as:

(i)   video-disc interfacing, using the computer as an information retrieval device;

(ii)   adventure gaming;

(iii)   simulation;

(iv)   data processing;

(v)   viewdata;

(vi)   information processing;

(vii)   intelligent knowledge based-systems, which can explain their reasoning to the user;

(viii)   expert systems, with computer containing the knowledge of an expert with which the user can interact;

(ix)   reference systems, for use in libraries;

(x)   word processing;

(xi)   large memory micros, with an almost infinite capacity to absorb information;

(xii)   portable micros, battery powered.

Such applications of the computer are linked to the provision of a user friendly interface for ease of use, and the development of authoring programs, for the use of which the user needs little or no knowledge of computer programming.

The changing *expectations of society* are reflected in the government's increased emphasis on information technology. This can be seen in the establishment of a national chain of ITEC (Information Technology Education Centres), the launching of the TVEI (Technical and Vocational Education Initiative) and the key role of IT within the CPVE schemes (Certificate of Prevocational Education). Within schools the growing importance of computing is seen in the explosion of entries for computing examinations, (Burghes, 1984).

For a hive to succeed there must be demand for its honey. Skilbeck's second element, 'educational requirements and challenges', is directly pertinent to computing's role in the history curriculum. Indeed, if history does not rise to the computing challenge, its failure to do so could be a factor in its being a subject at risk within the curriculum. The major government report of September 1982 into advanced information technology, the Alvey Report, has outlined the general framework within which the debate on computing in the curriculum should take place. Alvey was a direct response to a Japanese initiative concerning the direction of computing in the 1980s and 1990s: the MITI Fifth Generation Computing Project. Alvey stated in stark terms the threat to Britain as an advanced industrial society. Alvey said Britain would be reduced to client status in a world where economic power lay in the hands of industrial societies which controlled 'Fifth Generation' computing, should Britain fail to participate fully in the development of new approaches to computing in the 1980s and 1990s. The Alvey Report made a series of recommendations for Britain to meet the 'Fifth Generation' challenge, most of which the government accepted in 1983. The Report led to the establishment of a national research programme which is a major collaborative effort between industry and research organizations, heavily government-funded.

The Alvey Report has serious implications for both industrial training and more general educational provision. In relation to schools Alvey was magisterially dismissive of current practice. In its one paragraph on this subject, the Report commented:

> Action must start in the schools. We support the moves which are now putting computing on the curriculum. But it is no good just providing schools with micro-computers. This will merely produce a

generation of poor BASIC programmers. Universities in fact are having to give remedial education to entrants with 'A' level computer science. Teachers must be properly trained, and the languages chosen with an eye to the future. Uncorrected, the explosion in home computing with its 1950s and 1960s programming style will make this problem even worse.

Subsequent reports have more fully mapped out the higher educational ground briefly covered in by Alvey. The ESRC Sage and Smith Report (1983) into computing in education recommended a programme of action research, based upon developments in artificial intelligence. Sage and Smith envisaged a marriage between the worlds of education, AI and computer science research, which would develop approaches to computing based upon an understanding of pupils' cognitive structures and mental processes. The Sage and Smith initiative led to the ESRC in 1985 establish its 'Information Technology in Education Programme—An Inquiry into Artificial Intelligence'. Its remit indicates government thinking on the potential future of educational computing, a model only loosely related to that which history teachers at present have of computing within the classroom:

> ... it is hoped that appropriate AI methodologies can be used in the next generation of educational software ...
>
> In considering desirable learning activities, opportunities provided by it should support pupil centred learning and creativity. Human communication between learners and teachers is an essential element of such learning activities. This carries implications for the role of teachers. (Lewis, 1985)

The emergence of the Alvey, Sage and Smith and ESRC programs relate to earlier government attempts to promote computer awareness and literacy through the Microelectronics Education Programme.

Skilbeck's third reference point, *'the changing nature of the subject-matter to be taught'*, reflects the preoccupations of Alvey, Sage and Smith and the ESRC, and suggests that there is a realistic marriage between AI, computer science research and history pedagogy. The 'new history' accepts that history is a separate domain of knowledge with its own procedural and propositional knowledge, (Rogers, 1979). Pupils' learning arises from them actively working on the record of the past, that is, historical evidence. Central to the development of historical understanding is the asking of questions, and refining and reformulating them on the basis of answers and additional information. The exploration and processing of evidence and the identification of patterns within the historical record enables the mental recreation of historical situations, and an insight into the minds of those who peopled them. The use of historical imagination to recreate the past can lead to an understanding—that is, an explanation of why things have happened in the past. The emergence of the 'new history's' pedagogy since the late 1960s has provided a fertile milieu for the application of educational computing based on an understanding of the mental processes involved in historical thinking, and pupil activities such as gaming, simulation and resource-based enquiry work.

In terms of classroom activities the 'new history' and computing are natural allies. Individual or pair/small group work, involving pupils in the historical process (under teacher supervision) is a perfect foundation for pupils to write their own computer programs. Their program writing is the central focus of our approach to educational computing.

A successful beehive needs the care, attention and expertise of a bee-keeper. *The potential contribution of teacher-support systems*, Skilbeck's fourth heading, is crucial for the application of Fifth Generation Computing in the history classroom. The in-service structure is already available through a national network of LEA computer advisers and advisory teachers, coordinated through NACE (National Advisors for Computer Education) and through the MEP (Microelectronics Education Programme). Colleges of education and university departments also have a role to play in supporting innovation. A key element is liaison between history and humanities advisers and their computing colleagues, and the coordination of activities through user-groups of teachers. The model of diffusion we favour is that of local groups with central and LEA in-servicing and support, (Nichol, 1985). For a support service to succeed it will need to provide computing which meets the needs and demands of teachers.

Current teacher conceptualization of computing outlined on page 220 sees educational computing as an extension of *arithmetical computation*. The computer science and AI research community has now provided us with an alternative view of computing which has greater appeal to teachers. Computing can now provide a powerful tool to carry out *logical reasoning* within an existing curricular pattern. The new generation of 16, 24 and 32 bit micros, with their extensive memories, and the new generation of computer languages like LOGO and PROLOG give teachers the resources for a different approach to computing. As significant as the emergence of large memory micros is the portable, battery powered micro. Potentially, there can be a micro in every school bag, in the same way as there is a pocket calculator.

Work in LOGO has already been extensively developed. LOGO's beauty is that it allows pupils to write their own computer programs; it thus gives children the initiative and the opportunity to control their own learning (Papert, 1981). LOGO's main use has been in turtle geometry, predominantly within mathematical domain. We will concern ourselves with PROLOG, a complementary language to LOGO, suited to the teaching of humanities subjects. PROLOG—PROgramming of LOGic— has been adopted as the starting point for Fifth Generation Computing projects in Britain, Japan and Europe.

PROLOG is based upon a radical departure from traditional approaches to computing, for it can be used in a *declarative* as well as a *procedural* way. A *declarative* program consists of discrete blocks of information. Such information can be used to describe a 'state of the world'. PROLOG's power comes from the application of logical rules to separate blocks of data. Rules can be infinite in number and complexity, and can be inter-linked and recursive.

PROLOG can be applied to data in any form, and can search within blocks of data for separate items. Thus it can be used not only to handle information about historical evidence in a unitary sense, but can process data which appears in the form of consistently structured lists. Rules can sort, order and correlate elements in the lists. When it has produced an answer to a question, PROLOG can tell the user the steps which it has taken to arrive at its answer. Rules give the computer a capacity to *reason logically*. PROLOG also has a query-the-user facility, which involves the computer asking questions and building up a database from the user's answers. In turn, the computer can explain its steps in producing an answer to a user's questions (Sergot, 1984). Thus PROLOG has an interactive capacity, which enables it and its user to carry on a dialogue.

PROLOG's potential derives from its harnessing of the computer's ability to process infinite amounts of information. Its major application is in the area of *logical reasoning*, a small subset of the complex and mysterious process of historical thinking and understanding. PROLOG provides pupils with an alternative intelligently based source of information—as one of our pupils commented on his first acquaintance with it, 'It's a brain, Sir'. How can it be applied to the historical domain of knowledge?

For a swarm of bees to be productive it needs a hive in which to live, and a source of pollen from which to make honey. The final element in Skilbeck's situational analysis of external factors *the flow of resources into the school*, represents both the hive and the presence of pollen. The history teacher can now apply computing to four central areas of his teaching, and two others concerning the initiation and resolution of pupil work. The four main areas of application are:

(i)   historical enquiry, involving the questioning of historical evidence;
(ii) the mental recreation of historical situations, and an empathetic awareness of people in them;
(iii) an examination of causation in historical situations and their subsequent development;
(iv) the tapping of expert knowledge on historical topics.

The two subsidiary areas are reference retrieval and word processing.

Reference retrieval facilitates pupil work through speeding up and making feasible access to a range of resources in both libraries and record offices. Word processing is valuable in pupils' resolution work.

How will this vision of computing operate in the history classroom? A minimum requirement will be a single micro, and two large VDUs (visual display units). A printer would be an excellent additional facility. This equipment enables the pattern of learning laid out below to occur, although ideally we would like far more micros to be available within the history classroom. Computing across the curriculum means computers across the curriculum! Computers are the hive without which the bees cannot function.

Although pupil work with existing closed programs is a central feature in computing in history (at present the predominant one), we consider the key feature in the future is the development of opportunities for pupils to write their own computer programs. For pupils to program they must be introduced to programming in an accessible, user-friendly form. We have therefore developed the concept of 'toolkit' programs, written in PRO-LOG. Each toolkit or authoring program allows pupils to write their own programs without any formal knowledge of computing. All they have to do is pose an historical question, research the historical topic the question relates to, and organize and structure their information into an appropriate form for entering into the computer. The programming is the *pupil's*

Figure 1

Users	Programs		Programming		Word Processing/ Study Aids	
	school	home	school	home	school	home
Teachers (own work)	√	√	√	√	√	√
Pupils (independent work) —single/pairs	√	√	√	√	√	√
—group	√		√			
—class	√		√			
Pupil/ Teachers (cooperative work) —pair	√		√		√	
—group	√		√			
—class	√		√			

representation of his historical knowledge. The pupil program can then enable him to use the information now in the computer to deepen his understanding of the subject he is investigating, for example, the pattern of Saxon settlement based on place-name analysis. Such program writing

---

Figure 2

AREA	*AUTHORING PROGRAM*	
Historical enquiry	DETECT	For handling discrete blocks of text, accessed through key subject words. DETECT allows the discovery, questioning and processing of evidence, the framing of new questions and the formulation and testing of hypotheses.
		Example programs GREENDIE—a murder mystery based on Collingwood's John Doe investigation (Collingwood, 1946). BOGBOD—an investigation into an Iron-age body found in a peat-bog, based on the School's Council History 13–16 Project Tollund Man investigation (Schools Council, 1976). MOUNDING—an archaelogical dig into a Viking burial mound on the Isle of Man.
	PLACES	For processing information which appears in the form of coherently structured lists of data; in this case place-name information.
		Example program CREDPLAC—an investigation into local place-names around our project school.
Mental recreation	THE PLAN	An adventure-writing toolkit. It allows pupils to create their own imaginary world or recreate an historical reality, inside the micro which they can then explore. Note that DETECT and SIMPLAY also encourage mental recreation.
Causation	SIMPLAY	For writing simulations or other programs involving decision-making and a branching structure of enquiry; for example, the classification of information as in the identification of types of historical evidence
		Example program SEADOG—the re-creation of an Elizabethan privateering voyage to the Spanish Main.
Expert systems	APES	This program enables us to write programs which contain the knowledge of an expert. Such programs can interrogate the user, and respond to the user's questions. The user can add information to the program, and thus establish a dialogue with it. APES is a commercially available expert system available only on a 16-bit micro. At present we are developing EXPRESS, an expert system for educational use.

---

engages pupils fully in the historical process. What do 'toolkit' authoring programs, the educational pollen, involve in history teaching?

For each of the four main areas of history teaching (see page 226), we have written an authoring program. They are tools for the pupil to use. Each toolkit reflects the logical structure of a learning or enquiry strategy needed to explore a particular type of historical question or problem. What form do our 'toolkits' take? (see Figure 2)

Within our teaching we have used all five authoring programs, and although our work is at an early experimental stage, the signs are encouraging. We have tested several different procedures for introducing pupils to programming, from sitting them down cold in front of the computer with an instruction booklet to extensive explanation of structures, provision of models and long pen-and-paper planning sessions. The pattern we favour is the latter, usually introduced through working with the pupils through an existing program. Such programs pass through the stages of questioning, researching data, structuring it in the form of a structure diagram and organizing it under headings for entry into the computer.

For DETECT they have as an example a diagram showing the links between the different blocks of information in the GREENDIE program (figure 3) Each block of information is stored in the computer under its keyword, for example: information about the dead man's body is contained under the heading *body*. Figure 4 is a typical pupil's diagram for sorting out the story of the death of William Rufus. The diagram links together the separate pieces of information, and serves as the basis for writing a program on Rufus' killing. Once the diagram and the information linked to the keywords are completed, the program is typed straight into the computer, using the pattern laid down in the authoring program.

The same procedure is followed for using THE PLAN. Here the pupil aims to re-create within the computer an historical situation based upon researching it. THE PLAN requires the drawing of a plan of the world within which the adventure occurs, such as figure 5. In the micro world the pupil can link areas, introduce objects into them, and develop actions involving people. For example, an adventure in a castle could entail researching an actual siege, an what happened in medieval siege warfare. Such adventures are potentially most exciting, as the worlds which the pupils create will reflect their analysis of the historical record and historical evidence. As such, they enable them to bring the past to life, and in a very real sense develop an 'active' understanding of the nature of historical re-creation. The analogies between adventuring and historical fiction are very close. For example, an adventure set in a monastery can echo historical processes involved in writing a novel like Umberto Eco's *The Name of the Rose*. There is also potential in adventuring for the user to explore the meaning of historical terminology and concepts like feudalism, revolution and industrialization. Adventure games can be written indepen-

Figure 3: Greendie: Plan Showing Links Between Subject Keywords

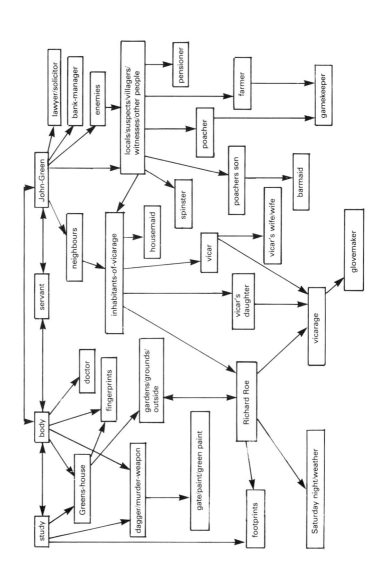

Figure 4: Murder of William Rufus Thursday 18 October 1984: home-work for half-term

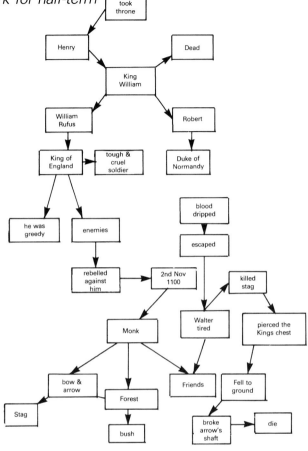

dently by single pupils or as cooperative ventures involving other pupils and/or the teacher.

In our project school we have gained considerable experience of the pupils researching a database using information which appears in a consistently structured form. The resulting program enables the pupils to build up an understanding of the nature of past societies and the relationships between its members. Programs have been written based upon Roman tombstones; the economic supply and demand network of a medieval village and nineteenth-century trade directories. At a one-week residential course the potential of authoring packages in this area was shown through the use of PLACES for pupils to produce their own program of local place-names. The students had to research the subject through the use of ordnance survey maps, place-names volumes, place-name dictionaries and local history books. They entered the data in a standard form.

SIMPLAY work is in an early stage, although two 14-year-old pupils we have introduced it to grasped its essential structure with ease. Again they have to research a topic and then organize the data in diagrammatic form (see figure 6). The diagram enables them to see causal links between events, choice and outcomes; and how events at one point in time can have consequences much later. Although this is a simple model of causation, it is capable of being used in a simulation of fiendish complexity and subtlety.

Computer programming using toolkits is motivating for all pupils we have encountered. While programming they are on task 100 per cent of the time, usually about one hour.

Already we have begun to translate our vision of the future of computing in the history curriculum into practice in our project school. The proposed teaching program below is based on our experiences over the past two years. It relates to the teaching of a Saxon module to a second year form for a one-hour period per week:

Week	Session	Potential computer use
1	Introduction	Reference retrieval for finding out about sources for Saxon history, and how they can be obtained
2	Saxon invasion	Simulation on choice of families, equipment, animals, to undertake voyage from Saxony
3	Saxon settlement	Simulation on settlement of a Saxon village
4	Settlement work	—
5	King Arthur	Detective work, historical mystery
6	Religious settlement	—
7	Local history	Place-name enquiry
8	Sutton Hoo	An archaeological dig
9	King Alfred	—
10	King Alfred	Expert system
11	Alfred and the Vikings	Simulation

Computing can now play a substantial role in the history curriculum 5–18. The teaching of a future GCSE class on the enclosure movement might take the following form:

> After explaining the purposes and mechanism of enclosure, and its effects on field patterns, with the aid of a videodisc which draws upon archival and contemporary resource material to produce relevant

Figure 5: Example Plan for an Adventure World

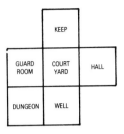

In the example above the links might be marked as follows:

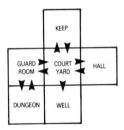

visual evidence, the teacher indicates the range of computer programs available to the pupils. They are working in pairs with their portable 16 bit micros which have over 500k of RAM available. Pupils in their pairs are set the task of carrying out the enclosure commissioners' work in redrawing the field boundaries, and producing a report which justifies their decisions. They plan the work out in rough on paper, but use a mouse to draw in their boundaries of fields, and to place icons of different features on the outline map. The computer calculates the different proportions of land allocated between the various freeholders, and the relative quality of their new holdings. The different solutions give rise to useful class discussion about what the commissioners were supposed to do and how they actually went about it. Finally, the teacher puts on to the screen the commissioners' actual plan. The pupils are set homework on analyzing the factors which underlay the commissioners' action. To help them they have in their computer a map of the actual enclosure awards, and an expert system which interrogates them about the various decisions which commissioners took, and the reasons for them. The expert system will deal with both their own solution to the enclosure problem, and the one which actually occurred.

Figure 6: Diagram showing how earlier actions can affect later events

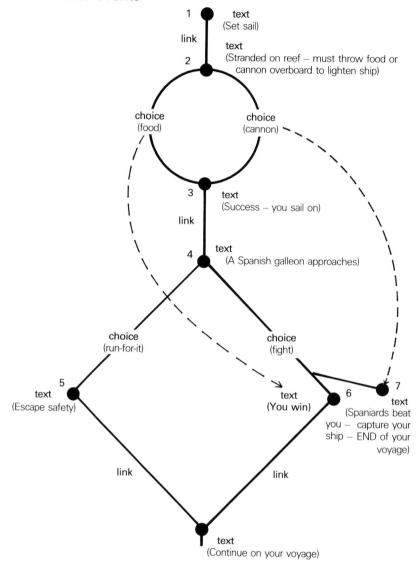

If you were an Elizabethan sea-captain, and your ship lodged on a reef, what would you throw overboard to lighten your ship to free it – cannon or food? The *immediate* consequence of either choice is that you escape the reef. Later, however, when attacked by a Spanish galleon or becalmed in the doldrums that early choice will matter. So, the decision to *fight* the galleon can have two possible outcomes, depending upon what was jettisoned earlier.

Next day in class the teacher sets an essay on the spread of enclosures over England. She mentions, as well as the standard text-book, that the computer data directory has some useful information listed under enclosure awards.

Roger reads in his text-book that 'most of south-east England had been enclosed by 1820'. Living in Sussex, he wonders whether his county counts as south-east in this generalization. He switches on the computer, consults the data directory and connects the computer to the appropriate computer data bank by pressing a few keys. He feeds in his question. Almost at once, he obtains on the TV screen attached to the computer the number of known enclosure awards in Sussex before and after 1820—and finds that Sussex does not fit the generalization. This leads him to wonder what the text-book means by 'most'; so he gets similar information for other south-eastern counties and discovers that, whilst the writer's generalization is not untrue, it hides the fact that 'most' means no more than 65 per cent and that this percentage was unevenly distributed between counties. At the touch of a key, the computer printer gives him a printed record of the figures he wants.

Roger uses the word-processor for the writing of his essay. The computer screen is divided up into windows, so when he requires information on various headings in his essays he can call up the relevant piece of data to add to his essay. The essay takes half an hour to write, and is printed at the central printing terminal. (Dean J. *et al*, 1985).

Such use of the computer reflects a skills and process-based approach to history teaching. Because our 'toolkits' rely on an understanding of the philosophical nature of both history and logic programming, it has led to a marriage which places the teaching of history at the frontiers of information technology. History, along with other arts subjects, can now be seen as responding fully to the information technology challenge of the 1980s and 1990s. The view that history teachers have held of computing can now be replaced with an idea of computing which sees it as a natural tool for historical learning. As such, computing is ready to take a place in the teaching environment alongside other aids such as the OHP, the video and the textbook.

References

ALVEY, J. (1982) *Advanced Information Technology*, HMSO.
BEARD, D. (1985) *The Use of Micro-Computers/Information Technology In Devon Schools, no. 2 Software and Teacher Learning Situations*, School of Education, University of Exeter.

BOLAM, R. (1976) 'Innovation at the local level' in *Supporting Curriculum Development—E 203—Unit 26*, Open University.

BURGHES, D. (1984) 'Computer assisted learning in schools', in RAMSDEN M., (Ed.) *Microcomputers in Education 2*, Ellis Horwood.

DEAN, J., NICHOL, J., and SPEDDING, R., (1985). *The Computer in the Teaching of History Trainer Pack*, Microelectronic Education Programme.

HAVELOCK, R.G. (1982) 'The utilisation of educational research and development' in HORTON, T. and RAGGATT, P. (Eds). *Challenge and Change in the Curriculum*, Hodder and Stoughton.

LEWIS, R. (1985) *Spring Seminars Report, Occasional Paper ITE/3/85*, Department of Psychology, University of Lancaster.

MACDONALD, B. and WALKER, R. (1976) *Changing the Curriculum*, Open Books.

NICHOL, J. (1985) 'Classroom based curriculum development, artificial intelligence and history teaching', *Journal of Curriculum Studies*, 17, 2, pp. 211–4.

PAPERT, S. (1981) *Mindstorms*, Harvester.

PRESCOTT, W. (1976) 'Curriculum design and development' in *Supporting Curriculum Development—E 203—Unit 26*, Open University, pp. 96–7.

ROGERS, P.J. (1979) *The New History: Theory into Practice*, Historical Association.

SAGE, M. and SMITH, D.J. (1983) *Microcomputers in Education*, Social Sciences Research Council.

Schools Council, (1976) *Schools Council History 13–16 Project*, Holmes MacDougall.

SERGOT, M. (1984) 'A query the user facility for logic programming' in YAZDANI, M. (Ed.) *New Horizons in Educational Computing*, Ellis Horwood.

WALKER, R. and MACDONALD, B. (1976) 'Innovation, the school and the teacher—Curriculum innovation at school level' in *Supporting Curriculum Development—E 203—Unit 26*, Open University.

WILKES, J. (1985) *Exploring History with Micro-computers*, CET.

Bibliography

ALVEY, J. (1982) *Advanced Information Technology*, HMSO.

BALLARD, M. (1970) *New Movements in the Study and Teaching of History*, Temple Smith.

BAMFORD, S. (1893) *Passages in the Life of a Radical*, Fisher and Unwin.

BARNES, D., BRITTON, J. and ROSEN, H. (Eds) (1969) *Language the Learner and the School*, Penguin.

BEARD, D. (1985) *The Use of Microcomputers/Information Technology in Devon Schools, no. 2 Software and Teacher Learning Situations*, School of Education, University of Exeter.

BECK, P. (1986) 'Going up in history', *Times Educational Supplement*, 21 February, p. 24.

BOLAM, R. (1976) 'Innovation at the local level', in *Supporting Curriculum Development—E 203—Unit 26*, The Open University.

BOOTH, M.B. (1980a) 'A modern world history course and the thinking of adolescent pupils', *Educational Review* 32, 3, pp. 245–257.

BOOTH, M.B. (1980b) 'History teaching in the U.K., past, present and future', *Australian History Teacher* 7.

BOOTH, M.B. (1980c) 'A recent research project into children's historical thinking and its implications for history teaching', in DANCY, J.C. (1980).

BOOTH, M.B. (1983a) 'Inductive teaching in history', in FINES, J. (1983).

BOOTH, M.B. (1983b) 'Skills, concepts and attitudes: The development of adolescent children's historical thinking', *History and Theory*, 22.

BROWN, R. and DANIELS, C. (1976) 'Sixth-form history—an Assessment', *Teaching History*, 15.

BRUNER, J.S. (1960) *The Process of Education*, Harvard University Press.

BURGHES, D. (1984) 'Computer assisted learning in schools', in RAMSDEN, M. (Ed.) *Microcomputers in Education 2*, Ellis Horwood.

COBBETT, W. (1853) *Rural Rides*, Dent.

COLLINGWOOD, R.G. (1946) *The Idea of History*, Oxford University Press.

COLTHAM, J.G. and FINES, J. (1971) *Educational Objectives the Study of History*, Historical Association.

CONNEL-SMITH, G. and LLOYD, H.A. (1972) *The Relevance of History*, Heinemann.

DANTO, A.C. (1965) *Analytical Philosophy of History*, Cambridge University Press.

DANCY, J.C. (Ed.) (1980) *Developments in History Teaching: Perspectives 4*, School of Education, University of Exeter.

DAVIES, C.S.L. (1977) *Peace, Print and Protestantism*, Paladin.

DAWSON, I. (1981) 'What shall we do with the third year?' *Teaching History*, February.

DEAN, J., NICHOL, J. and SPEDDING, R. (1985) *The Computer in the Teaching of History Trainer Pack*, Microelectronic Education Programme.

DICKINSON, A.K., GARD, A. and LEE, P.J. (1978) 'Evidence in history and in the classroom', in DICKENSON, A.K. and LEE, P.J. (1978a).

DICKINSON, A.K. and LEE, P.J. (Eds) (1978a) *History Teaching and Historical Understanding*, Heinemann.

DICKINSON, A.K. and LEE, P.J. (1978b) 'Understanding and research', in DICKINSON, A.K. and LEE, P.J. (1978a).

DICKINSON, A.K. and LEE, P.J. (1984) 'Making sense of history', in DICKINSON, A.K., LEE, P.J. and ROGERS, P.J. (1984).

DICKINSON, A.K., LEE, P.J. and ROGERS, P.J. (Eds) (1984) *Learning History*, Heinemann.

DONALDSON, M. (1978) *Children's Minds*, Fontana.

DRIVER, R. (1978) 'When is a stage not a stage?' *Educational Research*, 21, pp. 54–61.

DUNLOP, F. (1984) *The Education of Feelings and Emotion*, Allen and Unwin.

EDWARDS, A.D. (1978) 'The language of history', in DICKINSON, A.K. and LEE, P.J. (1978a).

EGAN, K. (1983) *Education and Psychology*, Methuen.

EISNER, E. (1982) *Cognition and Curriculum*, Longman.

ELTON, G.R. (1967) *The Practice of History*, Fontana.

ELTON, G.R. (1970) 'What sort of history should we teach?' in BALLARD, M. (1970).

ELTON, G.R. (1978) 'Putting the past before us', *Times Literary Supplement*, 8 September, p. 993.

FINES, J. (1981) 'Towards some criteria for establishing the history curriculum', *Teaching History*, 31, October.

FINES, J. (Ed.) (1983a) *Teaching History*. Holmes McDougall.

FINES, J. (1983b) 'Is there no respect of place, person or time in you?', in FINES, J. (1983a)

FINES, J. (1984) *Source Based Questions at GCE A-level*, Historical Association.

FISCHER, F. (1971) *Historians' Fallacies: Toward a Logic of Historical Thought*, Harper and Row.

GARD, A. and LEE, P.J. (1978) 'Educational Objectives for the study of history reconsidered', in DICKINSON, A.K. and LEE, P.J. (1978a).

GILES, P. and NEAL, G. (1973) 'History teaching analyzed', *Trends in Education*, 32, pp. 16–25.

GRAHAME, K. (1971) *The Wind in the Willows*, Methuen.

GREENFIELD, P.M. (1966) 'On culture and conservation', in BRUNER, J.S., OLVER. R.R. and GREENFIELD, P.M. *Studies in Cognitive Growth*, Wiley, chapter 11.

GRIFFITHS, R. (1985) 'The teacher and lecturer', *The Welsh Historian*, 3.

HALLAM, R.N. (1966) *An Investigation into Some Aspects of the Historical Thinking of Children and Adolescents*, M. Ed. thesis, University of Leeds.

HALLAM, R.N. (1967) 'Logical thinking in history', *Educational Review* 19.

HALLAM, R.N. (1970) 'Piaget and thinking in history', in BALLARD, M. (1970).

HALLAM, R.N. (1972) 'Thinking and learning in history', *Teaching History* 2, 8, pp. 337–350.

HALLAM, R.N. (1975) 'Study of the effect of teaching method on the growth of logical thought with special reference to the teaching of History'. PhD thesis, University of Leeds.

HAMLYN, D. (1973) 'The logical and psychological aspects of learning', in PETERS, R.S. (1973).

HAVELOCK, R.G. (1982) 'The utilization of educational research and development', in HORTON, T. and RAGGATT, P. (Eds) *Challenge and Change in the Curriculum*, Hodder and Stoughton.

HEXTEN, J.H. (1961) *Reappraisals in History*, Longman.

HEXTER, J.H. (1971) *The History Primer*, Basic Books.

HURSTFIELD, J. (1969) *The Undergraduate Historian*, Historical Association.

Incorporated Association of Assistant Masters (IAAM) (1965) *The Teaching of History in Secondary Schools*, 3rd. edition.

INHELDER, B. and PIAGET, J. (1958) *The Growth of Logical Thinking from Childhood to Adolescence*, Routledge and Kegan Paul.

JONES, J.A.P. (1975) 'Specially approved A level history syllabuses at Huddersfield New College, *Teaching History*, 13, pp. 13–17.

KITSON CLARK, G. (1967) *The Critical Historian*, Heinemann.

LALLY, J. and WEST, J. (1981) *The Child's Awareness of the Past—Teacher's Guide*, Hereford and Worcester County History Advisory Committee.

LEE, P.J. (1978) 'Explanation and understanding in history', in DICKINSON, A.K. and LEE, P.J. (Eds) (1978a).

LEE, P.J. (1984) 'Historical imagination', in DICKINSON, A.K., LEE, P.J. and ROGERS, P.J. (Eds) (1984).

LEFF, G. (1969) *History and Social Theory*, Merlin.

LEON-PORTILLA, M. (1962) *The Broken Spears*, Constable.

LE ROY LADURIE, E. (1978) *Montaillou*, Scholar Press.

LEWIS, R. (1985) *Spring Seminars Report, Occasional Paper ITE/3/85*, Department of Psychology, University of Lancaster.

LIGHT, P. (1983) 'Social interaction and cognitive development: A review of post-Piagetian research', in MEADOWS, S. (Ed.) *Developing Thinking*, Methuen.

LITTLE, V. (1983) 'What is historical imagination?', *Teaching History* 36, pp. 27–32.

MACDONALD, B. and WALKER, R. (1976) *Changing the Curriculum*, Open Books.

MARLAND, M. (1981) 'Drawing up a scheme of work', in MARLAND, M. and HILL, S. *Departmental Management*, Heinemann, pp. 87–115.

MARWICK, A. (1973) *The Nature of History*, Macmillan.

MOORE, R. (1982) 'History abandoned', *Teaching History*, 32, February, pp. 26–28.

NATALE, S. (1972) *An Experiment in Empathy*, NFER.

NICHOL, J. (1985) 'Classroom based curriculum development, artificial intelligence and history teaching', *Journal of Curriculum Studies*, 17, 2, pp. 211–4.

NOVE, A. (1972) *An Economic History of the USSR*, Penguin.

OAKESHOTT, M. (1962) *Rationalism in Politics*. Methuen.

PAPERT, S. (1981) *Mindstorms*, Harvester.

PARTINGTON, G. (1980) *The Idea of an Historical Education*, NFER.

PEEL, E.A. (1967) 'Some problems in the psychology of history teaching', in BURSTON, W.H. and THOMPSON, D. (Eds) *Studies in the Nature and Teaching of History*, Routledge and Kegan Paul.

PAUL, E.A. (1971) *The Nature of Adolescent Judgement*, Staples.

PETERS, R.S. (Ed.) (1973) *The Philosophy of Education*, Oxford University Press.

PIAGET, J. (1932) *The Moral Judgement of the Child*, Routledge and Kegan Paul.

POPPER, K.R. (1959) *The Logic of Scientific Discovery*, Hutchinson.

PORTAL, C. (1983) 'Empathy as an aim for curriculum: Lessons from history', *Journal of Curriculum Studies*, 15, 3.

PRESCOTT, W. (1976) 'Curriculum design and development', in *Supporting Curriculum Development—E 203—Unit 26*, Open University.

Bibliography

ROBERTS, M. (1969) 'Contemporary problems of sixth form history', *History*, 54.

ROBERTS, M. (1973) 'History', in DIXON, K. (Ed.) *Philosophy of Education and the Curriculum*, Pergamon, pp. 75–134.

ROGERS, P.J. (1979a) *The New History: Theory into Practice*, Historical Association.

ROGERS, P.J. (1979b) 'History and political education', *Teaching Politics*, 8, 2, pp. 153–69.

ROGERS, P.J. (1982) 'Epistemology and history in the teaching of school science', *European Journal of Science Education*, 4, 1, pp. 1–10.

ROGERS, P.J. (1984a) and (1984b) 'Why teach history?', and 'The power of visual presentation', in DICKINSON, A.K., LEE, P.J. and ROGERS, R.J. (Eds) (1984).

SAGE, M. and SMITH, D.J. (1983) *Microcomputers in Education*, Social Sciences Research Council.

SANSOM, C.J. (1985) *The History Syllabus—A Survey of Recent Research and Its Implications for the Teacher*, Derbyshire County Council Education Committee.

SCHEFFLER, I. (1973) 'Reflections on educational relevance', in PETERS, R.S. (1973).

SERGOT, M. (1984) 'A query the user facility for logic programming', in YAZDANI, M. (Ed.) *New Horizons in Educational Computing*, Ellis Horwood.

SHEMILT, D. (1980) *History 13–16 Evaluation Study*, Holmes McDougall.

SHEMILT, D. (1983a) 'The devil's locomotive', *History and Theory*, 22.

SHEMILT, D. (1983b) 'Formal operational thought in history', in FINES, J. (1983).

SHEMILT, D. (1984) 'Beauty and the philosopher: Empathy in history and classroom', in DICKINSON, A.K., LEE, P.J. and ROGERS, P.J. (1984).

Schools Council (1976) *History 13–16* (including *What is History?—Teachers' Guide* and *A New Look at History*), Holmes McDougall.

Secondary Education Council (1985) *Draft Grade Criteria*.

SLATER, J. (1984) Speech to Historical Association, *The Historian*, 2.

SOUTHERN, R.W. (1963) *St. Anselm and his Biographer*, Cambridge University Press.

Southern Regional Examinations Board. (1976–85) *Examiners' Reports: Written Papers*, SREB.

Southern Regional Examinations Board (1981–4) *Explorations: History 13–16*, SREB.

Southern Regional Examinations Board (1986) *Empathy in history: from Definition to Assessment*, SREB.

STEELE, P. (1982) *Medicine Through Time—A Pupil Handbook*, County of Avon Resources for Learning Development Unit.

THOMPSON, D. (1984) 'Understanding the past', in DICKINSON, A.K., LEE, P.J. and ROGERS, P.J. (1984).

THWAITES, B. and WYSOCK-WRIGHT, C. (Eds) (1983) *Education 2000*, Cambridge University Press.

WALKER, R. and MACDONALD, B. (1976) 'Innovation, the school and the teacher—curriculum innovation at school level', in *Supporting Curriculum Development—E 203—Unit 26*, The Open University.

WALSH, W.H. (1967) *An Introduction to the Philosophy of History*, Hutchinson.

WARNOCK, M. (1973) 'Towards a definition of quality in education', in PETERS, R.S. (1973).

WASON, P.C. (1977) 'The theory of formal operations—A critique', in GEBER, B.A. (Ed.) *Piaget and Knowing*, Routledge and Kegan Paul.

WATTS, D.G. (1972) *The Learning of History*, Routledge and Kegan Paul.

WEST, J. (1981) *History 7–13*, Dudley Teachers' Centre.

WILKES, J. (1985) *Exploring History with Microcomputers*, Council for Educational Technology.

YOUNG, G.M. (1936) *Victorian England: Portrait of an Age*, Oxford University Press.

Notes on Contributors

Rosalyn Ashby teaches history at the Bramston School, Witham, Essex.

Martin Booth is a Senior Lecturer in Education at the University of Cambridge.

Jonathan Briggs is a Senior Lecturer in Information Technology, Kingston College of Higher Education, Surrey.

Vincent A. Crinnion is Head of the Faculty of Humanities, Leftwich High School, Northwich, Cheshire.

Jackie Dean was a Research Assistant at the School of Education, University of Exeter.

John Fines is Head of the Department of History at the West Sussex Institute of Higher Education.

Peter Lee is a Lecturer in Education with special reference to the teaching of history at the University of London Institute of Education.

Henry G. Macintosh was formerly Secretary to the Southern Regional Examinations Board.

Jon Nichol is Director of the Exeter Project into Logical Programming and History Teaching, University of Exeter.

Christopher Portal was formerly a Lecturer in Education at the University of Manchester.

Peter Rogers is a Senior Lecturer in Education at the Queen's University, Belfast.

Chris Sansom is Head of the Faculty of Humanities, Southlands School, New Romney, Kent.

Denis Shemilt is currently Head of the Department of Education at Trinity and All Saints Colleges, Leeds and was formerly Director of the Schools Council Project History 13–16.

Christopher Smallbone is Head of the Department of History at Hartford High School, Northwich, Cheshire.

Index